Modern Monetary Theory

A Critical Survey of Recent Developments

Hans Visser
Professor of Economics
The Free University
Amsterdam

Edward Elgar

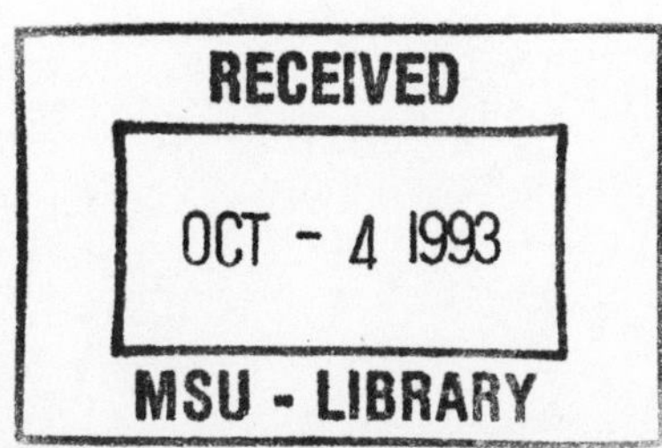

Published by
Edward Elgar Publishing Limited
Gower House
Croft Road
Aldershot
Hants GU11 3HR
England

Edward Elgar Publishing Company
Old Post Road
Brookfield
Vermont 05036
USA

A CIP catalogue record for this book
is available from the British Library

ISBN 1 85278 092 4

Printed in Great Britain by Billing & Sons Ltd, Worcester

Contents

Figures

Preface

This book is dedicated to the development of monetary theory after the heyday of the debate between monetarism and Keynesianism. Earlier developments have already been extensively surveyed (see Johnson 1962, 1967, 1970, 1974, Nobay and Johnson 1977, Smith 1970) and have found their way into the textbooks (for example Pierce and Shaw 1974, Visser 1974, 1980, Dennis 1981, Harris 1985). Nevertheless, in order to provide the necessary backdrop to the new developments a brief overview of the history of monetary theory is presented in Chapter 1.

As Clower (1969a p. 7) observed, 'The literature of monetary theory overlaps or verges on virtually every other branch of economic analysis'. The boundaries of monetary theory are not clear-cut. No selection of subjects can, therefore, be anything but subjective to a greater or lesser degree. No apologies are made for any interesting developments missing, but of course other selections would have been possible.

Chapter 2 is devoted to a subject that stems from monetarist arguments but has, one might say, become independent, an issue in its own right, namely the crowding out of private expenditure by government expenditure. Another offshoot of monetarism, New Classical Macroeconomics (NCME), is covered in Chapter 3, together with the opposing views held by New and Post-Keynesians (this chapter is an extensively rewritten version of Visser 1984). Chapter 4 discusses the search for microfoundations of monetary theory. This can be seen as an outgrowth of Keynesian analysis, fed by an increasing dissatisfaction with the absorption of Keynesian macroeconomics into the so-called neoclassical synthesis.

In NCME one finds echoes of Austrian business cycle theory. A new direction in the Austrian approach is the advocacy of competition in the money supply, treated in Chapter 5 (which earlier appeared in a Dutch-language version, Visser 1989b). In Chapter 6 we turn from money supply to money demand. The tenet of the stability of the money demand function, a cornerstone of the monetarist theoretical structure, has come under attack from at least two sides, apart from those who argue that financial innovations lead to instability in the money demand function. Firstly, even if there is something like a stable money demand function, it may take economic agents time to adjust their actual cash balances to their desired cash balances. Secondly, currency substitution may play havoc with the stability of demand functions for national currencies. This brings us to the subject of Chapters 7 and 8, exchange-rate determination, where monetary factors have come more to the fore lately (an earlier version of these chapters was published as Visser 1989a).

One subject that has very consciously been left out is the development of empirical monetary models. This has recently been surveyed by Chan-Lee and Kato (1984) and den Butter (1984, 1986 Ch. 2) and new directions are covered in Driehuis, Fase and den Hartog (1988). Where necessary, references to empirical research are made, though.

The aim has been to emphasize the economic substance of theories, with only a very restrained use of mathematics. Readers are expected to have a good knowledge of basic monetary macroeconomics.

Comments by Professor Frank den Butter, Professor Jan Willem Gunning, Jaap Koelewijn, Dr Willem Smits and Dick van der Wal on preliminary versions of various chapters are gratefully acknowledged. Unfortunately these colleagues cannot be held responsible for any remaining mistakes, gaps or clumsy phrasing.

Hans Visser

March 1991

Abbreviations and Symbols

GNP = gross national product
LOP = law of one price
NCME = new classical macroeconmics
NRU = natural rate of unemployment
PPP = purchasing power parity
RE = rational expectations

e = spot rate of exchange
g = growth rate
i = rate of interest
m = real money supply
r = risk premium
w = real wealth
y = real national income
Bd = demand for domestic bonds
Bs = supply of domestic bonds
D = domestic demand for home goods
E = expectations operator
F = forward rate of exchange
Im = imports
K = net capital inflow
M, Ms = money supply
Md = money demand
P = price level
Q = number of foreign bonds at one foreign currency unit per bond
Qd = domestic demand for foreign bonds
Qs = domestic supply of foreign bonds
R = terms of trade
S = savings
T = volume of trade
U = rate of unemployment

V	= velocity of circulation of money
X	= exports
W	= nominal wealth
Y	= nominal national income
λ	= rate of change of wages
π	= rate of inflation
*	= expected value
f	= foreign value

1. An Extremely Succinct History of the Subject

THE TRANSMISSION MECHANISM OF MONETARY IMPULSES

Arguably the roots of present-day monetary theory go back to the quantity theory of money. The quantity theory in its turn can be seen as a reaction to, on the one side, the mercantilist inclination to identify wealth with money and, on the other side, the experiments of John Law, in whose opinion a large quantity of money was a great help in attaining wealth. It was predominantly within the framework of the quantity theory that economists began systematically to pay attention to the transmission mechanisms of monetary impulses, till the present day a central theme in monetary theory. The quantity theory says that a change in the money supply *ceteris paribus* results in a proportional change in the price level. The interesting question of course is how such a result comes about. On a theoretical plane, it is not so much the comparative statics that is of interest (whether the *ceteris paribus* condition holds in a given situation or not is a matter of empirical verification, or should one say belief), but the dynamics of the impact of monetary impulses on the prices and quantities of goods and services.

The most influential early publication expounding the way in which changes in the money supply influence the real (commodity) side of the economy was David Hume's 1752 essay 'Of Money' (Hume 1955). Hume described a *direct mechanism*: an increased volume of money induces economic agents to increase their spending on goods. The demand for labour increases, wages rise, more labour is supplied and the impact is first felt in a higher level of economic activity (see also Perlman 1987). Little by little goods prices increase and economic activity reverts to its original level, until in the end it is only prices that are higher as a result of the monetary impulse.

Other mechanisms can be thought of as well. For instance, banks can keep the rate of interest below the level at which savings equal investment, which leads to higher borrowing and increased spending. In this case an *indirect mechanism*, working via the rate of interest, drives up expenditure. The most elaborate exposition of this mechanism is Knut Wicksell's *Geldzins und Güterpreise* (Wicksell 1898), but it had been expounded nearly a century before by the great Henry Thornton (1978 pp. 253-5) and soon after by David Ricardo (1965 ch. 27) and Thomas Joplin (see Humphrey 1987). Strictly speaking, it is not a transmission mechanism of a monetary impulse, though. In this case, it is the rate of interest that starts things moving, not the money supply, even if the volume of money increases as the banks step up their lending. But a monetary impulse proper can also be transmitted via the indirect mechanism. Increased cash balances will not only be spent on goods but on financial assets as well. The prices of financial assets are driven up in the process and the rate of interest falls, which boosts spending.

In the account just given, a positive monetary impulse is linked with a low rate of interest. A negative monetary impulse will of course be coupled with a high rate of interest and a reduction in spending. It is not necessarily the case, however, that a low rate of interest is an indication of a positive monetary impulse or a high rate of a negative one. If a continuing positive monetary impulse leads to inflation, the nominal rate of interest will tend to rise in step with the rate of inflation. If the interest rate lags behind, that in itself can be seen as a spending impulse via the indirect mechanism, because incomplete adjustment of the nominal rate of interest to inflation means a fall in the real rate of interest. If, conversely, the rate of inflation declines and nominal interest rates lag behind, the real rate rises. It was again Henry Thornton who developed this line of reasoning, in a speech before the House of Commons in 1811 (Thornton 1978 pp. 335-6), though Irving Fisher (1930) is generally credited with having come up with the idea of a real rate of interest distinct from the nominal rate. Of course it was only through Fisher's studies that it gained general acceptance. Fisher also took pains to explore the ways in which inflation increases the velocity of money, which again fuels the inflationary process (Fisher 1963 ch. 4). It may be noted in passing that, unlike what many textbooks assert, Fisher was far from assuming an institutionally determined quasi-fixed velocity of money in the short term.

KEYNES, THE NEOCLASSICAL SYNTHESIS AND REINTERPRETATIONS

With Keynes it is only the indirect mechanism that works. He took issue with the neoclassical idea of a self-regulating economic system in which the price mechanism sees to it that the effects of a disturbance are rapidly neutralized. In his view, the price mechanism does not work that fast, which is as well, because swiftly adjusting prices would create new difficulties (see Keynes 1961 chs 18, 19).

In principle the direct and indirect mechanisms cannot only be set in motion by an increase in the nominal money supply, but also by a decrease in the overall price level. In both cases real cash balances increase, and that is what counts. If aggregate demand diminishes - in terms of the IS/LM model: the IS curve shifts to the left - and wages and prices fall as a result, full employment could only be restored if the increased real balances would drive the rate of interest down to the full-employment equilibrium rate, that is Wicksell's *natural rate* or Keynes's *neutral rate of interest* (see Keynes 1961 p. 253). The LM curve shifts to the right, resulting in a downward movement of the rate of interest, known as the *Keynes effect*. In the case of a liquidity trap, however, an increase in the real money supply, or a shift to the right of the LM curve, would not suffice to restore full employment. A downward shift of the LM curve would be called for, but does not take place even if the rate of interest is above the minimum level, because, as Keynes put it, 'the rate of interest is a highly conventional .... phenomenon' (Keynes 1961 p. 203). Furthermore, a fall in wages and prices brings with it all kinds of side effects, some of which may stimulate employment, such as an improved balance of trade, but most of which work out negatively, such as an increase in the real burden of debt and the fact that wage and price decreases are tantamount to an increase in the real rate of interest (Keynes 1961 pp. 262-5). Apart from this, in Keynes's eyes aggregate spending may not only remain for considerable periods below the full employment level but also be subject to sizeable fluctuations (which translate into erratic shifts in the position of the IS curve). Such low and fluctuating spending results, as Meltzer (1981, 1988) emphasizes, from low and fluctuating investment, itself caused by volatile expectations and uncertainty. A large degree of wage and price flexibility would in this situation produce violent price fluctuations, such as to impair the function of money as a unit of account (Keynes 1961 pp. 253, 269). So if wages and, to a lesser extent, prices are sticky, so much the better; and if they are not, we had better make them behave that way (Keynes 1961 pp. 270-1). The Keynesian view of the world therefore does not rest on the assumption of sticky wages, as has so often been asserted. Full wage and price flexibility would not, in Keynes's view, return to us the lost neoclassical bliss of a full-employment equilibrium brought about by a self-regulating mechanism.

It did not take the neoclassics very long to find a reply to the alleged defects of the price mechanism. In 1943 Pigou pointed out, as Haberler had already done in 1939, that, if the price level as a result of competition between jobless workers falls to a greater degree than the money supply, real wealth in the hands of the public increases. Sooner or later this induces them to reduce their savings and increase their spending (Pigou 1943, Haberler 1963 p. 389). This *Pigou effect* (a term coined by Patinkin 1952 p. 271) is a direct effect of increased real balances on spending (which works out as a shift to the right of the IS curve). So even a liquidity trap would not prevent the price mechanism from restoring the system to full employment. Nobody ever seriously advocated letting price level fluctuations do the job, because fiscal and monetary policies were thought to be more efficient or less disruptive means for attaining full employment, but the neoclassical construct had been rescued from the Keynesian onslaught and Keynes's contribution to economics could be seen as essentially belonging to the field of economic policy rather than pure economic theory: 'The classics won the intellectual battle; Keynes won the policy war' (Hines 1971 p. 9). This state of affairs, dubbed the *neoclassical synthesis*, was not really satisfactory, because the neoclassical approach has its roots in the Walrasian tâtonnement model (Hoover, 1988b p. 258, tells us the term 'neoclassical synthesis' first appeared in 1955 in the third edition of P.A. Samuelson's leading textbook *Economics*). Keynes's misgivings about the effects of full wage and price flexibility were ignored. Furthermore, it was not immediately realized that tâtonnement does not go well with Keynesian notions such as liquidity preference, the macroeconomic consumption function or the multiplier, nor indeed with Keynes's allusions to 'the dark forces of time and ignorance which envelop our future' (Keynes 1961 p. 155). Uncertainty (in the sense of Knight) is in Walrasian models, or their more modern multi-period variants, Arrow-Debreu models, at best reduced to risk. With risk, unlike uncertainty, economic agents have a probability distribution of all possible future events. The worlds of Walras and of Arrow and Debreu are not inhabited by dark forces.

The neoclassical synthesis has since been undermined by Leijonhufvud who, building on Clower's *dual decision hypothesis*, has argued that one cannot make sense of Keynes within a model that presupposes Walrasian tâtonnement pricing. The dual decision hypothesis says that economic agents may draw up 'notional' buying and selling plans on the assumption that all sales and purchases will, as in the Walrasian world, be decided upon in one all-embracing, simultaneous decision process, such that nobody need take account of the possibility that sales or purchase plans cannot be effected. In actual practice, demand may be constrained by the failure of sales plans being effected. If sales plans are not realized, there will be a second round of decision making (Clower 1965). The typically Keynesian notions mentioned above only make sense if we drop the assumption of simultaneous, all-embracing tâtonnement pricing. In Clower's footsteps Leijonhufvud has pointed to the assumption of the omniscient Walrasian auctioneer, who conducts the tâtonnement process, as the essential difference between Keynes and the neoclassics (Leijonhufvud 1968, 1969). In the neoclassical approach, economic agents have full information on the supply and demand functions of other economic agents, through the activities of the auctioneer. With Keynes they are groping in the dark (it is a bit ironical that tâtonnement, a term used to indicate full information, itself means groping).

Clower's 1965 model has been objected to for being unduly restrictive (Gale 1983 pp. 17-21). It does not, for instance, allow for spending out of cash balances in lieu of current income, a failing rectified by Leijonhufvud (for example Leijonhufvud 1973). Nor is it obvious why plans that prove incompatible in the first round of decisionmaking should be consistent in the second round. On a more fundamental level, it has been argued that the Clower-Leijonhufvud approach still remains within the confines of Walrasian general-equilibrium models where goods directly exchange against other goods, but without fully flexible prices in this case (Rogers 1985). It is a kind of Walras without auctioneer. There is serious doubt that such models provide the right setting for the study of the economics of Keynes. Indeed, Clower himself (1975) later came to the conclusion that Keynes cannot fruitfully be studied within the framework of Walrasian models, but that Keynes had a Marshallian world in mind, where goods do not exchange directly against other goods, but are traded against money by middlemen, and where exchanges are costly (all very difficult to deal with in a formal model). Fluctuations in supply and demand are first absorbed by the stocks held by those middlemen and do not immediately influence prices as in the flexprice Walrasian model, nor do they immediately lead to quantity rationing as in Clower's dual decision model.

Clower (1965) opened the way to the development of a spate of fix-price general-equilibrium models, also confusingly labelled disequilibrium or non-Walrasian equilibrium models (see Gale 1983 pp. 21ff). Money may appear in the budget constraint of economic agents in those models (see for example Benassy 1975 and Malinvaud 1977), but it plays no role in the exchange process. Attempts to draw Keynesian conclusions from such models are very interesting in their own right, but it is doubtful whether they shed much light on what Keynes had in mind, or, what is more important, on what makes a monetary economy stick below full-employment level. Of course writing the *General Theory* was 'a struggle of escape from habitual modes of thought and expression' for Keynes (Keynes 1961 p. viii). The escape may not have been complete and interpretations abound. The *General Theory* was the start of a new approach and did not provide final answers (Meltzer, 1988 p. 310, not out to find fault with Keynes, nevertheless notes that there are serious analytical flaws in the *General Theory*: low investment for instance may explain a low per capita income, it does not explain unemployment). Part of the interpretation problem may not lie with Keynes, though, but with procrustean attempts by economists to prize Keynesian results out of general-equilibrium models which do not take seriously the role of money as a means of exchange. We will return to the more recent emphasis on the Marshallian strand in Keynes in Chapter 3.

MONETARISM

In the mid-1950s, when the Keynesian income-expenditure approach in its IS/LM form had become the paradigm of mainstream economics, Milton Friedman and his associates launched an attack on it, aiming at a revival of the quantity theory of money (Friedman, M. 1956). It gradually became clear that the difference between the so-called Monetarists and Keynesians, or broadly income-expenditure (IS/LM) theorists, did not really concern the analytical framework but was rather about different views, or beliefs, on empirical matters (Friedman, M. 1970, 1971a, *Journal of Political Economy* 1972, Mayer 1975). Monetarist analysis fits perfectly well into the neoclassical synthesis and Friedman explicitly referred on several occasions to the Walrasian general equilibrium system of equations (Friedman, M. 1969a p. 102, 1969b p. 3). He made allowance for stochastic variability in supply and demand and for all kinds of information and adjustment costs, implying that the system will need some time to return to a Walrasian equilibrium after a shock. A central tenet in the monetarist view of the world is that the private sector is inherently stable, in the sense that large fluctuations in economic activity are attributed to government policy, whilst the private sector absorbs shocks rather than causing them (Brunner 1970 pp. 5,6). Underlying this idea is the belief that markets, if left to themselves, function quite satisfactorily. For all practical purposes, the Walrasian construct is a fair representation of the real world. Given stability of the private sector, that is a reasonably swift return to full employment after a shock, and a stable money-demand function, it follows that a change in money supply growth can, after a transition period, only affect the rate of inflation.

The idea of an inherently stable private sector may be unpalatable for many economists, first of all those of a Keynesian bent. Other elements stressed by Monetarists are less controversial. Prominent among these is the Monetarists' view of the transmission mechanism of monetary impulses. Monetarists argue that a change in the money supply affects the economy via a great variety of channels, in addition to the interest rate effect on investment emphasized in standard Keynesian macroeconomics. An increase in the money supply disturbs the composition of asset holders' portfolios and gives rise to all kinds of substitution effects. These occupy centre stage in monetarist analysis, wealth effects (including the Pigou effect) being relegated to a minor, though not negligible, role (Friedman and Schwartz 1969 pp. 229-31, Brunner 1971. Sprinkel 1971 pp. 32-4). Similar sketches of the transmission mechanism can be found with professed non-Monetarists, notably Tobin, though with Tobin one link in the chain of effects is of paramount importance, namely the ratio of the (stock-) market valuation of existing capital goods to the supply price of newly produced capital goods, or *q ratio* (Tobin 1971a chs 13, 18). This ratio, which functions as a measure of the attractiveness of buying new capital goods, that is investment, is widely used in empirical studies of investment behaviour (Malkiel, Von Furstenberg and Watson 1979, Ciccolo and Fromm 1980, Heerkens 1983).

If the Monetarists' view on the transmission mechanism are not very controversial, their views on economic policy certainly are. With almost religious zeal they have preached the gospel of following rules for monetary policy, as opposed to fine tuning (see

Friedman and Heller 1968, Friedman, M. 1986). This is because the lags in the transmission process of monetary impulses tend to be long and variable, in their view. Given the assumed stability of the private sector, discretionary macroeconomic policy measures run the risk of working out pro-cyclically. The best the government (including the monetary authorities) can do is to keep the growth rate of the money supply within a narrow and pre-announced band, in that way minimizing the probability of any disturbance arising, or its severity.

Apart from the fact that such advice hinges on the stability of the money-demand function (see on this Chapter 6), it can only be valid or useful for large, relatively closed economies on a floating exchange-rate system. In economies on a fixed-rate system, or a managed-rate system, the money supply is hard or even impossible to control, depending on the interest elasticity of international capital flows (with infinite interest elasticity, the domestic money supply passively adjusts to the domestic demand for money through international capital flows at the world interest rate). For small and/or relatively open economies the price of free floating in terms of exchange-rate variability and its concomitant hindrance of international trade and investment will often be deemed too high. It has, furthermore, been brought up against the Monetarists that the money supply is not exogenous and that money is an elusive concept, what with financial innovations going apace (Kaldor 1982). Essentially this is a repetition of the discussion following the publication of the Radcliffe Report in 1959. The upshot of that discussion was that the money supply can to a large extent be exogenous, depending on the policy of the monetary authorities (they cannot control both interest rates and the money supply simultaneously in developed financial markets) and, in a fixed-exchange-rate system, the interest elasticity of capital flows. Another conclusion was that financial innovations can, and do, frustrate monetary policy to a certain extent, but not completely (see for a discussion and references Visser 1974 pp. 46-50, 21-4).

Less controversial has been the Monetarists' emphasis on the longer term. Following Irving Fisher they argued that, in an inflationary process, interest rates will adjust to inflation. High nominal interest rates in such a situation are a result of high money growth, that is a lax monetary policy, rather than, as in standard textbook IS/LM analysis, a result of tight monetary policy.

This emphasis on the longer run, and the associated more systematic attention to expectations, also put paid to the Phillips-curve trade-off between inflation and unemployment. The original

Phillips curve hinges on given inflation expectations. Attempts to exploit the Phillips-curve trade-off between inflation and unemployment for increasing employment at the cost of higher inflation will result not only in higher inflation, but after some time, in higher inflation expectations as well. The Phillips curve shifts upwards. Expectations adjust to inflation and a *long-term Phillips curve* can be constructed which runs vertically at the so-called *natural rate of unemployment* (NRU), dubbed *non-inflationary rate of unemployment* (NIRU) or *non-accelerating-inflation rate of unemployment* (NAIRU) by economists who take exception to the ideological undertones of the adjective 'natural'. This can be seen as an illustration of *Goodhart's Law*, which says that 'any observed statistical regularity will tend to collapse once pressure is placed upon it for control purposes' (Goodhart 1984 p. 96).

Even if the idea of an essentially vertical long-term Phillips curve is by and large acceptable to non-Monetarists, there is a fundamental difference in that Monetarists believe that the economy is a self-equilibrating mechanism, whilst others tend to take more seriously the possibility of disequilibrating movements. The economy will, in the view of Monetarists, after a shock which drives it off the long-term Phillips curve, automatically return to it within a relatively short period of time. Others believe that the economy can stay for a considerable period to the right of the long-term Phillips curve after a deflationary shock if no stabilization measures are taken by the government, or even that such a shock may shift the long-term Phillips curve bodily to the right (see the passage on hysteresis in Chapter 3). Economists of almost all persuasions will by now be agreed that any attempts to reduce unemployment below NRU or NIRU through monetary and/or fiscal policies, cannot but result in (higher) inflation (almost a platitude, given the definition of NRU/NIRU). This is not to say that NRU or NIRU itself cannot be reduced. A positive NRU or NIRU is a reflection of adjustment costs and imperfect information and/or a minimum wage level above the value of the marginal product for some kinds of labour. It follows that the government can reduce NRU or NIRU to the extent that it can improve information and help to reduce adjustment costs, including the costs of retraining, or reduce the costs of hiring labour and the attractiveness of remaining unemployed (this does not mean that trying to minimize NRU is always wise policy; it could imply an indecently low minimum wage level or level of social security benefits). Monetarists may see little scope for macroeconomic (stabilization) policy, their views certainly do not exclude microeconomic policies aimed at a better functioning of markets, the labour market in particular.

Monetarism can be seen as a variant of the neoclassical synthesis and is based on the Walrasian equilibrium system. A role for money as a means of exchange is, as has been argued above, difficult to find in this context. Some attempts to develop models where money is essential for the exchange process are described in Chapter 5.

2. Crowding Out and the Government Budget

INTRODUCTION

A long-standing problem in both economic theory and economic policy is whether, and if so to what extent, an increase in government expenditure can expand total expenditure or effective demand, and with it total employment, if the money supply is held constant and the additional expenditure is financed by capital market borrowings. The view that it cannot be trusted to do so was firmly held by the British Treasury in the 1920s and came to be known as 'the Treasury View' (Hancock 1970 p. 110). The theoretical underpinnings of this view were provided by R.G. Hawtrey, who argued that if the government borrows money to finance public works, that will in most cases be at the expense of private expenditure (Hawtrey 1925). Only if the velocity of circulation of money rose could effective demand for labour increase. This is of course unexceptionable. It simply follows from the equation of exchange, MV = PT: M is held constant and the price level can hardly be expected to fall as a result of public works. Where opinions differ is on the question whether the velocity of circulation can increase or not. In Hawtrey's view, it cannot, barring exceptional circumstances, namely when the outlook for industry is extremely unfavourable:

> The idle balances are not in general accumulated for want of attractive enough permanent investments; they are rather composed of unemployed circulating capital, often that of manufacturers who prefer not to be dependent on their bankers. (Hawtrey 1925 p. 43)

Apparently, to Hawtrey's mind the demand for money is interest-inelastic. Only with abnormally poor profit expectations would there be any idle balances in the Keynesian sense (Hawtrey's 'idle balances' seem rather to be held from what Keynes called the precautionary motive). All this translates, given the money supply, into an LM curve with a vertical section and a horizontal section, the latter hardly ever relevant.

The Treasury View implies that increased government expenditure fully crowds out private expenditure. In Keynesian analysis, complete crowding out is the exception rather than the rule. The Monetarists returned to the Treasury View. In fact, they had little choice but to do so if they wished to uphold their view that the price level is roughly proportional to the money supply. They rejected *fine tuning*, that is discretionary or activist macroeconomic policies designed to stabilize the economy. This leaves little room for activist fiscal policies. They marshalled empirical evidence for their view that (nominal) national income, and private consumption as one of its components in particular, was highly correlated with the money supply (implying a stable income velocity of money) but not with autonomous spending, including the government budget deficit (which was taken to mean an unstable Keynesian multiplier). Friedman and Meiselman (1963) found that the income velocity of money was more stable than the Keynesian autonomous expenditure multiplier or the investment multiplier. Andersen and Jordan (1968) regressed changes in GNP on changes in monetary and fiscal variables (producing the celebrated St Louis equation). These studies sparked off an avalanche of empirical work. The results of the reduced-equation estimates of the Monetarists were inconclusive. They proved sensitive to the choice of independent variables, whilst doubts were expressed as to the exogeneity of these variables: results are biased if the policy variables (in this case changes in the money supply and the full-employment budget surplus) were actively used for stabilization purposes (see Kösters 1973, Monissen 1973, Arestis 1985 p. 177). Also, Friedman and Meiselman's finding that in the years of the Great Depression the investment multiplier was more stable than income velocity could hardly be seen as damaging for the Keynesian position. Simulations with large-scale models of the American economy generally produced positive short-term results of fiscal policy, which after one year or a few years tended to disappear or even become negative when calculated in real terms, though the effects remained positive in nominal terms (see Fromm and Klein 1973, Infante and Stein 1976 section 4). In this chapter we survey the various mechanisms that can contribute to partial or complete crowding out. It may be noted that the subject is of wider interest than only economic policy; it also bears on the interpretation of historical developments, such as the question whether the debt-financed war efforts of the

British government during the Napoleonic Wars contributed to slow economic growth through leaving fewer funds available for private investment (Heim and Mirowski 1987).

The IS/LM model which will be used to analyse crowding out is essentially a model for the short term. Government budget deficits, run up in the course of a fiscal expansion, result in ever-increasing volumes of government debt, though, which in itself may influence spending and national income. The impact of an increasing government debt may be studied in a somewhat intuitive way in the framework of the IS/LM diagram, but also in a more formal way in an IS/LM model supplemented by an equation representing the government budget constraint. This constraint is the fact that all government expenditure that is not paid out of taxes, is financed either by creating money or by increasing the bond supply. This kind of model will be covered in the last section. The short-term nature of the model should not make us lose longer-term results of fiscal policies out of sight. In so far as private investment is crowded out by public consumption, future growth will be impaired. Of course, if private consumption is crowded out by public investment, or private investment in a consumption-goods industry by badly-needed infrastructural investments, it's the other way round. No a priori verdict seems possible.

CROWDING OUT

Real vs nominal crowding out

It stands to reason that at or near full employment, which is the normal situation in the Monetarist view, any sizeable expansion of real government expenditure can only occur at the expense of real private expenditure (in a closed economy). In that case *real crowding out* occurs. In a fixed-price setting, nominal and real crowding out come to the same thing, of course. But with flexible prices real crowding out may occur even if there is no, or no full, nominal crowding out. In terms of the IS/LM diagram, a positive fiscal impulse shifts the IS curve to the right until it intersects the LM curve beyond the point of full employment. Prices will rise and, given the nominal money supply, real balances will fall. The LM curve consequently shifts to the left. Lower real balances mean a fall in the private sector's wealth and may cause it to reduce spending (the Pigou effect), so that the IS curve may shift to the left too. The leftward movement will stop when both curves inter-

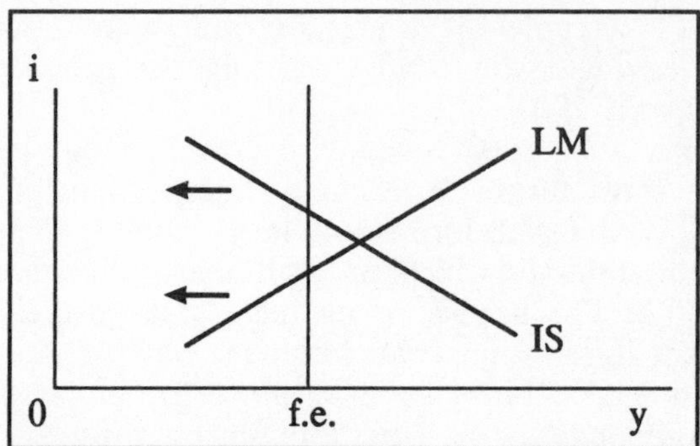

Figure 2.1. *Real crowding out without full nominal crowding out.*

i = rate of interest, y = real national income, f.e. = full-employment income.

sect at the point of full employment. Of course all the mechanisms that are at work in the case of fixed prices, to be discussed in the next section, may be at work in the case of flexibe prices as well, but even if there is no, or no full, nominal crowding out, the fall in real balances will see to it that full or quasi-full real crowding out occurs.

Even if there was real crowding out, nominal national income increased in the case just studied. Full-employment real income was restored at a higher price level. We now turn to the various mechanisms that may cause nominal crowding out. Two groups may be discerned: (i) mechanisms that act via the rate of interest and (ii) mechanisms that do not act via the rate of interest. The former cause *ex post crowding out*, the latter *ex ante crowding out*. Crowding out can of course be full or partial.

Ex post crowding out

In the IS/LM diagram, a fiscal impulse is represented by a rightward shift of the IS curve. Full crowding out will occur if the LM curve runs vertically. This means that both the money supply and money demand are interest-inelastic. The rate of interest rises to such an extent that private expenditure is reduced by the same amount as government expenditure is increased. With an upward-sloping LM curve, crowding out will of course only be partial. Full crowding out will also occur if the IS curve runs horizontally. Again, with a given money supply total expenditure cannot increase and any increase in government spending takes place at the cost of a decrease in private spending.

Other mechanisms may complicate matters. A debt-financed fiscal expansion may make people feel richer, if government debt is seen as net wealth by the public. Such an increase in wealth will on the one hand increase the demand for money, resulting in a leftward shift of the LM curve (see for an empirical estimate Butkiewicz 1979). On the other hand, it will increase spending out of a given income, resulting in a rightward shift of the IS curve. The outcome for national income is uncertain (unless the economy is in the horizontal section of the LM curve, in which case the shift of the IS curve unequivocally increases income). The rate of interest will increase (except of course if the economy is in the horizontal section of the LM curve). This in itself may have further consequences. Rising interest rates will decrease the value of financial assets held by the public, including shares, that is claims to physical assets. This *interest-induced wealth effect* reduces private spending. Private bonds are both an asset and a debt to the public, so that a price fall of such bonds leaves net wealth unimpaired. Even so, it may have an asymmetrical impact on the spending behaviour of debtors and creditors, in the sense that debtors may increase their spending by a greater or a smaller amount than creditors decrease theirs. If the price of government debt that is not seen as net wealth falls, wealth effects do not occur of course. Equity shares, though, are unequivocally net wealth and a fall in this component of wealth will depress private spending even if a fall in the market price of bonds does not.

Finally, account should be taken of the ever-increasing volume of government debt held in the public's portfolios. The LM curve depicts the equilibrium conditions in the Walrasian money market given the volume of debt. With a change in the volume of debt, the rate of interest that ensures portfolio balance at any given level of income has to change. The public will only accept higher volumes of government debt, given their wealth and the volumes of other assets, if the return on government debt increases. Put differently, the LM curve shifts upward (Hahn 1980a p. 11, Visser 1980 p. 290). The resulting crowding out may be called *portfolio crowding out*.

It has been argued that for portfolio crowding out to occur bonds and real capital must be closer substitutes than bonds and money. If, conversely, bonds and money are close substitutes, an increase in the volume of bonds may drive up the price of existing real capital without affecting the price of bonds (Buiter 1985 p. 47, Tobin 1971c p. 225). This is because an increase in the volume of one asset or group of assets disturbs portfolio balance and increases the demand for the other assets, driving up their prices; and close subsitutes can be grouped together. The price of bonds will hardly change if bonds and money are good substitutes and the bond rate of interest therefore stays put. An increase in the price of existing capital (equity shares) means that Tobin's q ratio rises (see above, chapter 1). In other words, the required rate of return on capital falls. At any given bond rate of interest the desired capital stock will increase, and with it, in the short term, the volume of investment. The IS curve will shift to the right, the LM curve does not shift upward and rather than portfolio crowding out occurring aggregate investment receives an additional boost.

Empirical research conducted by Frankel (1985a) suggests that the effects of portfolio composition on the structure of the rates of return are minor. His research does not preclude, however, an upward movement of all rates of return in tandem because of increased government budget deficits (Frankel 1985a p. 1063). One way of testing for crowding out is to look at interest rates, but that does not measure actual crowding out, that is the fall in private expenditure caused by higher interest rates and, possibly, wealth effects. Higher interest rates may affect private expenditure on consumer durables, but will mostly bear upon investment. One could try to capture the effects of debt-financed government spending on private investment directly, without the detour via interest rates, by including the change in the outstanding volume of government debt in the investment function. In this way Cebula (1978) found evidence of significant crowding out in Canada and the US, 1949-1976, even when accounting for the endogeneity of the budget deficit.

In an open economy, additional mechanisms are at work. In a fixed-rate system, the money supply cannot be supposed to be constant. A bond-financed fiscal expansion shifts the IS curve to the right. Starting from equilibrium, the current account will run into a deficit and, assuming no capital flows, the money supply falls. The LM curve shifts to the left and the rate of interest rises to cause complete crowding out (given that the current account surplus or deficit is a function of national income). With interest-elastic capital flows, however, the rise in the rate of interest caused by the rightward shift of the IS curve will induce capital imports. If international capital flows are relatively interest-elastic, increased capital imports will overcompensate the deterioration of the current account consequent on the rise in national income. There will be a balance-of-payments surplus which makes the money supply increase (provided the capital flows are initiated by the nonbank private sector). In the case of infinitely interest-elastic capital flows, capital imports and the money supply will increase to such an extent that the rate of interest stays at or returns to its original value, so that no crowding out occurs whatsoever. Knoester (1980 pp. 152-6) found for the Netherlands 1953-1975 that bond-financed fiscal impulses led to crowding out via balance-of-payments deficits. In later periods increased interest-elasticity of international capital movements seems to have changed the picture, in the sense that crowding out is shown to have been only partial (see for a roundup of Dutch studies Visser 1983, and for the results of more recent estimates using the models of the Netherlands Bank and the Dutch Central Planning Bureau den Butter 1988 and Centraal Planbureau 1987 respectively).

In a completely-flexible-rate system, international payments do not affect the money supply and the LM curve is fixed (abstracting from changes in the price level that might result from exchange-rate movements and the resulting changes in import prices; price-level changes make the real money supply, given the nominal money supply, change in the opposite direction and lead to shifts of the LM curve in the interest rate-real income plane). Exchange-rate movements that follow in the wake of fiscal policy measures may, however, weaken or strengthen the effects of such measures. A fiscal expansion increases national income, ups the import bill and tends to create a deficit on the current account of the balance of payments. The rate of exchange (in the non-British sense of the price of foreign currency in terms of domestic currency) will rise (domestic currency will depreciate), which boosts exports and drives the IS curve further to the right. In the process, the rate of interest increases. If capital flows are interest-elastic, net capital imports will increase. This in its turn exerts a downward pressure on the rate of exchange and makes the IS curve shift to the left (supposing that the Marshall-Lerner condition is fulfilled). The higher the interest-elasticity of capital flows, the more the rate of exchange is pushed down. At the limit, when capital flows are infinitely interest-elastic, the rate of interest cannot diverge from the world rate of interest. Any rightward shift of the IS curve following on a fiscal impulse immediately induces capital imports that lower the rate of exchange to such an extent that the deterioration of the current account exactly balances the increase in government spending. The IS curve returns to its original position, cutting the LM curve at the given world rate of interest. Crowding out is complete. This is of course nothing else than the conventional Mundell-Fleming result that with completely interest-elastic capital flows fiscal policy is ineffective in a flexible-exchange-rate system, whilst it is very effective (that is, no crowding out occurs) in a fixed-rate system.

In all this we have abstracted from expectations. Government policy measures may of course affect the expectations of the public.

The public may get nervous about a growing volume of government debt, fearing future corporate tax hikes because of a higher future government debt service and hence cutting down on longer-term investments. The IS curve shifts to the left. This is a different case than the Ricardian equivalence discussed below, where it is consumption that bears the brunt of higher expected future taxes and taxes are nondistortionary. Besides, in the present case, unlike under Ricardian equivalence, there is uncertainty. The fear of higher taxes may well be unwarranted as higher future income may enable interest and amortization payments on an increased volume of government bonds at unchanged tax rates. Deficit spending by the government may well result in more rosy expectations. Firms may feel secure in the knowledge that the government does its best to prevent a slump occurring and step up investment in new plant. The IS curve shifts to the right in that case.

The crowding out discussed in this section is known as ex post crowding out because it results from various mechanisms that reverse the increase in national income caused by the rightward shift of the IS curve consequent on increased government spending. In the next section mechanisms will be discussed that prevent the IS curve from shifting to the right in the first place. That kind of crowding out is called ex ante crowding out.

Ex ante crowding out

In the case of ex ante crowding out, an increase in government expenditure immediately meets with a fall in private expenditure and a higher volume of government debt can be taken up in the public's portfolios without any need for the rate of interest to rise. It is tacitly assumed that the increase in available private funds is fully directed to government bonds. That would change the composition of portfolios, though, which in itself might bear on interest rates and cause portfolio crowding out. This effect is neglected in the literature on the subject.

Two approaches can be discerned: ultrarationality and Ricardian equivalence.

Ultrarationality

David and Scadding (1974) studied the savings ratio in the United States over a 70-year period. They were struck by the fact that gross private savings, including expenditure on consumer durables, were over that period by and large constant as a percentage of

GNP, defined including the imputed annual gross rental flow on consumer durables. This constancy occurred despite changes in the distribution of private saving between personal saving and business saving and despite changes in the share of output absorbed by the public sector. They sought to explain these phenomena by the assumption of *ultrarationality*. As to the composition of savings, this means that private persons adjust their saving to changes in business saving, not so strange if private persons see themselves as the owners of the business firms. This phenomenon is not at issue here. As to the public sector, ultrarationality implies that tax-financed government services, such as schooling or medical care, are seen as full substitutes for individually bought services. Private agents lower their spending to the full amount of the tax increase and the private savings ratio as a fraction of GNP does not change. There is a certain plausibility to the notion that tax-financed education or medical care reduces private expenditure on these items by roughly the same amount, but David and Scadding (1974 p. 241) further presuppose that consumption expenditures by the government are financed by taxes and that government investment is financed by bonds. Hence, the private sector treats government deficits as public investment. In addition, it considers public investment and private investment perfect substitutes. An increase in bond-financed public spending therefore reduces private investment by a similar amount. This is what they call ex ante crowding out (David and Scadding 1974 p. 243). The private savings ratio remains constant and extra funds become available in exactly sufficient volume to absorb the new government bonds. The increased supply of bonds meets with an increased supply of funds and the rate of interest need not increase in order to draw funds away from other applications.

Apart from the question whether the gross private savings rate is really a constant over time in all countries, it is, as Tobin (1980a p. 65) notes, completely gratuitous to conclude that an extra dollar of government deficit will displace a dollar of private investment. Without David and Scadding's rather far-fetched assumptions, a constant gross private savings ratio undermines the idea of ex ante crowding out. If the private sector does not consider debt-financed government spending and private investment perfect substitutes and the private savings ratio is a constant, a battle for scarce investment funds will follow on an increase in government expenditure, driving the rate of interest up.

The Ricardian equivalence theorem

Finally, we have what is known as *the Ricardian equivalence theorem*, which was developed by Barro (1974) and given its name by Buchanan (1976). The equivalence referred to is the equivalence between taxes and debt as sources of finance for government expenditures. This results from *full tax discounting*: government debt is not seen as net wealth by the private sector, because private agents take account of the future burden of taxes that will be levied to finance debt service payments. When, with a given level of public expenditure, the public sector substitutes bond-financing for taxes, private agents will increase their savings out of their increased disposable income in order to provide for these future taxes and the higher volume of government debt is taken up by the public without any need for the rate of interest to rise. Private expenditure and consequently aggregate expenditure remain unchanged. If the way of financing public spending is immaterial (neglecting monetary financing), we have a public-finance version of the Modigliani-Miller theorem, which says that the way a firm is financed, that is the respective shares of debt and equity in total sources of funds, is of no consequence for its value. The value of a firm depends on its productive capacity. In the same way, what counts in the determination of national income is the level of expenditure, not the way it is financed (barring, again, monetary financing).

Barro (1974) showed that a shift from tax-financed government expenditure to bond-financed expenditure will leave private spending unaffected under a number of conditions (see also Buiter 1985 section 5, Leiderman and Blejer 1988, Laidler 1990a p. 188):

1. Economic agents must act as if they were immortal, maximizing utility over an infinite time period. This means that they must be able and willing to leave bequests to next generations and not let government finance affect decisions in this respect. People, older people with a short remaining life-expectancy in particular, would otherwise not discount future tax liabilities and would increase spending after a shift from taxes to bond-financing by the government, in the process reducing their bequests. It may at first sight look somewhat far-fetched to assume a bequest motive with virtually the whole population. But bequests need not necessarily be made in the form of money or tangible wealth, they can also be made in the form of, for instance, investment in education. This example serves to show that a bequest motive need not always

result in Ricardian equivalence, though. If the public responds to higher expected future taxes not by increasing their savings but by higher investment in their children's education (that is, by increasing their offspring's income-generating capabilities or human capital rather than their tangible wealth), current spending increases (Feldstein 1982 p. 5). Future productive capacity changes as well.

2. There must be perfect foresight. Without perfect foresight, an increase in future tax liabilities following a shift from tax-financing to debt-financing might increase uncertainty as to the incidence of future taxes. Risk-averse agents feel less wealthy as a result and reduce their consumptive expenditures (Dotsey 1985 p. 11).
3. Taxes and transfer payments must be lump sum, or, more generally, nondistortional. If not, they affect behaviour. Taxes on income for instance tend to discourage income-generating efforts and to reduce aggregate income below the level attained with bond-financed government expenditure. Expected future wealth taxes may stimulate present consumption expenditure. Apart from this, Tobin (1978 p. 619) notes that government obligations differ from future tax liabilities as to liquidity (see point 4), uncertainties (see point 1) and distribution among citizens. This might well cause aggregate spending behaviour to differ from a situation of tax-financed government expenditure. It is not a priori clear in which direction spending would move.
4. Finally, the rate of interest faced by the public must be the same as the rate faced by the government. In actual practice, the government's borrowing rate is usually lower than many a private borrower's rate, because of lower perceived risk and lower costs of acquiring information on creditworthiness and of monitoring the borrower. Besides, private borrowers may for the same reasons be subject to credit rationing. A debt-financed tax cut can be seen as the government borrowing on behalf of private agents and in its turn granting them a loan to be repaid by future taxation. More and cheaper funds are available to the public, allowing it to increase consumption (Webb 1981, Chan 1983 pp. 369-71, Dotsey 1985 p. 9, de Haan 1989 pp. IV:12-14).

Notice that Ricardian equivalence is quite a different animal from ultrarationality. Ricardian equivalence is about a shift in the method of financing a given amount of government expenditure, whilst ultrarationality is about changes in the level of government spending. The equivalence theorem does not in itself imply that bond-financed government expenditure leaves aggregate spending unaffected, only that its effects do not differ from those of tax-financed expenditures. Results of changes in bond-financed government expenditure on aggregate expenditure similar to the Haavelmo effect or balanced-budget multiplier effect are therefore not precluded. If, however, private spending on consumption is a function of wealth rather than of income, complete crowding out of private expenditure by government expenditure, whether bond-financed or tax-financed, is possible. In that case there is not only *debt-neutrality* or no effect of changes in government debt on aggregate spending, but also *fiscal impotence*: fiscal policy in general is without any effect on aggregate expenditure or on the IS curve. Taxes reduce private wealth and private consumption is reduced in step. The same happens when bonds finance an increase in government expenditure: the government siphons off part of the public's income stream by selling bonds that are not net wealth. The money appropriated by the government is returned to the public of course through government expenditures, but if the higher level of government expenditure is maintained, taxes or government borrowings take it away again in a next period. If the higher level of government expenditure is not maintained, the money is returned and private spending reverts to its original, higher level. This analysis does not require money to be net wealth. If money is *inside money*, that is money created against IOUs, and part of the money supply is handed over to the government, the public ends up with lower money holdings but no lower level of debt and thus with lower net wealth. It is, by the way, a moot point if inside money cannot be net wealth. Pesek and Saving (1967) maintained that inside money is always net wealth. Patinkin (1972b) argued that only if there are monopolistic elements in money creation by banks can inside money represent net wealth, but Pesek shows no signs of giving in (Pesek 1988).

As an aside, one might wonder why the public would offer money for bonds that are not net wealth. Bonds are assets whose value is offset by the capitalized value of increased future taxes. This is on the level of society as a whole. Individual agents are not made poorer by exchanging money for bonds though, as their individual future tax obligations do not increase to any perceptible degree through such a transaction. On an aggregate level (through the democratic process), society will only agree to accept bonds in exchange for money if it values the services that the government supplies out of the loan proceeds at least as high as the money sacrificed, just as in the case of tax-financed expenditure.

Keynesian deficit spending is both futile and innocuous in the case of Ricardian equivalence (in its fiscal impotence guise), as

Tobin (1980a p. 52) notes. That is, Keynesian deficit spending is ineffective as an instrument of stabilization policy. If, to repeat the argument at the end of the Introduction to this chapter, the government increases its investment spending at the cost of private consumption spending, the results may be felicitous in the long run, though.

In terms of the IS/LM model, Ricardian equivalence implies two things. Firstly, a shift from taxes to bonds or vice versa should not in itself alter the rate of interest, that is, it should not make the LM curve shift. In other words, there should be no portfolio crowding out. Of course, most applications of the IS/LM model neglect portfolio crowding out. Secondly, aggregate demand should not depend on the method of financing government expenditure. It follows that the IS curve cannot be represented by the standard textbook equation

$$Y = C(Y - T) + I(Y,i) + G \tag{2.1}$$

where Y = national income, C = consumption, T = taxes, I = private investment, i = rate of interest and G = government expenditure.

Ricardian equivalence would instead obtain (as Fields and Hart 1990 argue) with the following specification:

$$Y = C(Y - G) + I(Y,i) + G \tag{2.2}$$

Equation 2.2 expresses the idea that the current burden of government is better measured by the production capacity it absorbs than by the taxes it levies. With an IS curve defined by equation 2.2 there is fiscal impotence if the marginal propensity to consume out of disposable income is unity (disposable income in this case is either after-tax income or after-government-borrowing income). With a lower marginal propensity to consume, an increase in government expenditure would shift the IS curve to the right. Ricardian equivalence with fiscal impotence also follows if consumption is a function of wealth rather than disposable income. This requires that government bonds are not net wealth, that is, there is full tax discounting, and the marginal propensity to consume out of wealth is, again, unity:

$$Y = C(W) + I(Y,i) + G \qquad dC(W) = - dG \tag{2.3}$$

W = net wealth of the public.

Though the equivalence theorem bears his name, Ricardo himself would not have subscribed to it. He argued, in chapter 17 of his *Principles*, that if the government needs £2000 for some purpose, it should be a matter of indifference whether that amount of money be raised by taxes or by borrowings. The money is taken away from other allocations and, to paraphrase Ricardo, its opportunity cost is what really counts. Agents who are, in our parlance, 'rational', would be indifferent between paying £100 at once and paying £5 per year in taxes, as they would be doing if the government issued consols at 5 per cent. But Ricardo did not believe that agents are rational and therefore was no adherent of the equivalence theorem: an agent who would have to pay £100 at once would

> save speedily the £100 from his income. By the system of loans, he is called upon to pay only the interest of this £100, or £5 per annum, and considers that he does enough by saving this £5 from his expenditure, and then deludes himself with the belief that he is as rich as before. (Ricardo 1965 p. 163)

O'Driscoll (1977) concludes that Ricardo enunciated a *nonequivalence theorem* and Feldstein (1982 p. 2) proposes to speak of the *pre-Ricardian equivalence* hypothesis (unfortunately omitting any reference to pre-Ricardo economists who might have held this view).

Empirical tests of ex ante crowding out

It may be interesting to go into attempts to find empirical evidence of ex ante crowding out, however cursorily, because these attempts may shed some light on the theoretical issues involved in the concept of ex ante crowding out.

As an indirect test, it has been argued that the equivalence theorem would seem to imply that the public's consumption and savings behaviour is indifferent as to fully funded and unfunded pension systems (Buchanan 1976 p. 341). In particular, a shift from a funded system to a pay-as-you-go system should not increase private spending, because the public would take account of future payments. This corollary does not seem to have been corroborated in actual practice, though Barro (1976 p. 348) finds the empirical evidence against the view that future taxes or social security contributions are capitalized not convincing.

Direct tests of ex ante crowding out also focus on the consumption function. Tests of ex ante crowding out are to all intents and purposes tests of Ricardian equivalence. Ultrarationality tends not to be taken seriously. We give a quick roundup of some of the empirical research, in order to show the gist of the literature, without any claim to comprehensiveness (see for more extensive surveys of tests de Haan and Zelhorst 1988, de Haan 1989 ch. 4).

Of course the real market value of government debt does not affect expenditure on consumption if the public does not view government debt as net wealth. Most research workers try to find additional evidence. They basically apply three further tests of Ricardian equivalence, sometimes in combination:

1. Firstly, the government budget surplus is added to the consumption function. Tanner (1979) argues that the Barro hypothesis implies that a government budget surplus has a positive effect on private consumption demand. Presumably the public views such a surplus as a reduction in future tax liabilities. A surplus reduces saving just as a deficit increases saving, as we have seen. The equation which he estimated also contained, apart from disposable income and lagged disposable income, real corporate retained earnings, the rate of unemployment, the real stock of consumer durables and the net stock of fixed capital. Corporate retained earnings were assumed to lead to capital gains and thus to higher wealth and more consumption. Consumer durables were expected to exert a negative influence (part of total consumption is in the form of services of consumer durables which do not figure in national income) and the stock of capital, being net wealth, was expected to be positively correlated with consumption. For the 1947-1974 period in the US Tanner found evidence of tax discounting, with government debt not being seen as net wealth by the public.

   In the same vein, Kochin (1974) argued that high government deficits should make consumers realize that their true permanent income is lower than is indicated by the level of their current and past disposable incomes, because deficits mean future taxes. Like Tanner, he found a significant negative influence of the government deficit on consumer expenditure on nondurables and services, in his case for the 1952-1971 period in the US.

   A problem with this approach is that it does not seem to discriminate between Ricardian equivalence and the life-cycle approach, where people also take account of future taxes. The difference is only that their planning horizons are finite in a life-cycle approach.
2. Nicoletti (1988) argues that Ricardian equivalence, or the Barro model, is obtained when, in an equation explaining private

consumption, the coefficients of disposable income and the government budget surplus are equal. That would mean that

$$C = a_1(Y - T) + a_2(T - G) + a_3(Z) \qquad a_1 = a_2$$

Z = the vector of other relevant variables

so that

$$C = a_1(Y - G) + a_3(Z) \tag{2.4}$$

which takes us back to equation 2.2.

He notes that there may be direct substitutability of private and public consumption. This means that it is difficult to separate ultrarationality and full tax discounting. Indeed, if the government increases its bond-financed spending and the private sector reduces its consumptive expenditure this may be either because of full tax discounting or because of direct substitutability (this case was ruled out by David and Scadding, because they considered only tax-financed government expenditure consumptive). Nicoletti found no support for ex ante crowding out for the US, Japan, France and West Germany over the 1961-1985 period, but evidence of ex ante crowding out was found for Belgium and Italy, precisely the countries with extremely high debt as a percentage of national income and explosive debt dynamics. The most likely explanation in his eyes is that economic agents anticipate a change in fiscal policy when both the government itself and the press question the sustainability of the fiscal stance. This prompts them to increase savings, as a precautionary measure. Ricardian equivalence then occurs only in extreme situations.

Lal and Van Wijnbergen (1985) were struck by the fact that in 1983 OECD budget deficits absorbed nearly 52 per cent of gross savings, as against less than 1 per cent in 1970. Ex ante crowding out would have been a remarkable phenomenon with such a change. They argued that, if private sector agents are completely indifferent between different ways of financing a budget deficit, the measure of disposable income figuring as an argument in the consumption function should be income minus government expenditure (as in equation 2.2) whereas if they are not, the relevant measure is income minus tax revenues (as in equation 2.1). The first definition is essentially identical with Nicoletti's approach. Regressions of consumption run on both variables should show which one is more relevant. Their research did not support Ricardian equivalence, as they found no full crowding out of private consumption. They did not separately test for the influence of the volume of government debt. An alternative is to replace disposable income by income and the government budget surplus by government expenditure, that is, not to deduct taxes from either variable. In that case the coefficient for income should be equal but of opposite sign to the coefficient for government expenditure. Using still another variant, where income transfers were deducted from both income and government expenditure, de Haan and Zelhorst (1989) found that changes in government expenditure in Italy (1950-1982) and the Netherlands (1957-1982) were not neutralized by opposite changes in private consumption.

3. It has also been argued that in a consumption function which includes total private wealth including government debt (this could be called gross wealth) and government debt separately as arguments, the coefficients for these terms should be of equal magnitude but opposite in sign for Ricardian equivalence to hold (Feldstein 1982 p. 11). That is, in

$$C = a_1Z + a_2W + a_3B/i \tag{2.5}$$

where B/i = government debt (this formulation may look strange and serves no purpose here, but it is chosen with an eye to the analysis in the next section, see equation 2.6), we should have

$$a_2 = - a_3.$$

The idea is that government debt is not net wealth and that, if total wealth includes the market value of government debt, Ricardian equivalence requires the separate variable for government debt to offset any change in gross wealth caused by a change in government debt.

De Haan and Zelhorst (1989) found that for Italy (1950-1982) the coefficients for both total wealth and government debt were positive whilst for the Netherlands (1957-1982) they were of opposite sign, though not of equal magnitude. One wonders if it would not be preferable to include government debt and private wealth less government debt as arguments in the consumption function. That would preclude any multicollinearity problems and would provide a direct test of debt neutrality.

Estimates by Feldstein (1982), using a permutation of the various approaches (relevant variables) for the US 1930-1977, also failed to support Ricardian equivalence, with the exception of the test for social security. This was after Feldstein corrected for the endogeneity of taxes. An exogenous increase in consumer spending boosts both incomes and tax receipts. A positive correlation between taxes and consumer spending is found in this way, which biases the coefficient of the tax variable in the consumption function towards zero. Ricardian equivalence would receive spurious support (Feldstein 1982 p. 12).

The question of ex ante crowding out is of eminent practical interest. With Ricardian equivalence, the public would be indifferent between taxes and bond-financed government deficits. On the one hand, attempts by Ministers of Finance to increase taxes in order to cut public borrowing, given the level of government expenditure, would meet with no opposition. On the other hand, nothing would be gained by such a shift from bonds to taxes. It could be argued that politicians are inclined to promise the voters all kinds of government-supplied goods and services while deluding them into believing that they somehow will not have to foot the bill. With Ricardian equivalence the public sees through such attempts.

Ricardian equivalence also bears on explanations of the effects of macroeconomic policy. High government budget deficits, for instance, cannot be held responsible for high interest rates and its concomitant effects on exchange rates if Ricardian equivalence holds. High US (real) interest rates and the rise of the dollar in 1981 could in that case only be explained by restrictive monetary policies. P. Evans (1985) noted that there have been three periods in US history where the federal deficit exceeded 10 per cent of national income, and that interest rates showed no appreciable rise in those periods. The three periods mentioned by him were, however, war periods, during which the public probably had no choice but to cut down on consumption because productive capacity was directed to the war effort. Evans (1986) further argued that the value of the dollar expressed in a number of other important currencies tended over the period 1948II-1984III to move inversely with the federal budget deficit. Evans sees this as indirect evidence of Ricardian equivalence, but his case is weak. A budget deficit without ex ante crowding out would push the rate of interest up, induce capital imports and make the dollar appreciate in terms of other currencies. It would, however, also increase income and in its wake imports. For periods in which the current account dominates the capital account of the balance of payments, the balance could tilt towards a depreciation. Moreover, Evans found that the dollar depreciated with a fall in taxes, keeping federal spending constant. This would also point to the influence of higher income on imports.

Curiously, he also found that interest rates decreased with a fall in taxes (which of course also makes the dollar depreciate via its effect on capital exports). Ricardian equivalence would leave interest rates unchanged. Evans surmises that higher real after-tax returns on investments increased savings and thus caused interest rates to fall. All in all, his reasoning can hardly be seen as providing cogent arguments in favour of Ricardian equivalence. In stark contrast to Evans, Fischer (1988 p. 328) sees the US fiscal experiment in the early 1980s as a clear refutation of ex ante crowding out as real interest rates rose in those years and private saving did not increase. Clearly, different people read the signs differently.

It may be concluded that full ex ante crowding out finds little support in empirical tests. Still, it is remarkable that a systematic influence of government budget deficits on the rate of interest has not been established either (see also Darrat 1989 on the US 1946-1986).

THE GOVERNMENT BUDGET CONSTRAINT

IS/LM models can be augmented with an equation for the government budget constraint. Such augmented models can be used to study the behaviour of the system when the government budget is not in equilibrium and either the money supply or the volume or government bonds is changing (see Blinder and Solow 1974). Wealth effects and interest rate effects move the system to a new equilibrium, if such an equilibrium exists, which need not be the case (Infante and Stein 1976, Buiter 1985). In these models (long-term) debt and capital are perfect substitutes in the public's portfolios, so that an increase in the volume of government debt raises the required rate of return on capital.

The basic model is as follows:

$$Y = C[Y + B - T(Y + B), Ms + B/i] + I(Y,i) + G \qquad (2.6)$$

$$Ms = Md(Y,i,Ms + B/i) \qquad (2.7)$$

$$DB/i + DMs = G + B - T(Y + B) \qquad (2.8)$$

where Y = national income (added value) excluding interest on government debt, G = government expenditure excluding interest payments, B = number of government bonds, consols which each pay one unit of money per period on interest (B therefore equals the amount of interest payments per period), Ms = money supply, Md = money demand, D = the operator d/dt.

Equation 2.6 represents the IS curve. It is to be noted that interest payments on government bonds figure separately. There is a wealth effect in consumption, wealth consisting of the money supply Ms and the market value of bonds, B/i. Equation 2.7, representing the LM curve, also contains a wealth effect. Note that government bonds are net wealth, there is no debt neutrality in this model (though it can of course be introduced as a special case). Equation 2.8 represents the government budget constraint, showing that a budget deficit (the right-hand side of the equation) implies either debt financing or money creation or both. It is possible to include the stock of capital in both the wealth variable and the investment function, at the cost of some of the transparancy of the model (see Blinder and Solow 1973). This kind of analysis can also be extended to open or growing economies (see for an open economy Branson 1976 and for an economy that is both growing and has targets for the current account of the balance of payments van Ewijk 1986).

This model allows of crowding out through wealth effects and shifts of the IS curve along a sloping LM curve. Portfolio-balance effects could be introduced through including the fraction of total (financial) wealth Ms + B/i held in B/i in the right-hand side of equation 2.7. Inclusion of the government budget constraint means that the point of intersection of the LM and IS curves represents only a temporary equilibrium if there is a surplus or deficit on the government budget. Changes in the money supply or the bond supply will then lead to further shifts of the IS and LM curves. Full equilibrium obtains when

$$G + B = T \qquad (2.9)$$

or, after total differentiation, when

$$dG + dB = T_Y dY + T_Y dB$$

subscripts denote partial derivatives

or, after rearranging,

$$dY/dG = [1 + (1 - T_Y)dB/dG]/T_Y \qquad (2.10)$$

(we assume that tax rates on interest income are identical to tax rates on other income).

If increases in government expenditure are financed by the creation of money (that is both by the government paying for its purchases with newly issued bank notes and by selling Treasury notes to the Central Bank, so that interest payments flow back to the government), equation 2.10 reduces to

$$dY/dG = 1/T_Y \qquad (2.11)$$

If dB/dG >0, this means that the long-term multiplier of government expenditure is greater under bond financing than under money financing, provided a new equilibrium is indeed attained. This differs from the short-term effect. In the short term, bond-financed government expenditure will not only shift the IS curve to the right, but also move the LM curve upward (given the money supply, with an increase in the bond supply equilibrium on the money market will at any level of income only obtain at a higher rate of interest; this is because of a wealth effect which increases the demand for money and is possibly reinforced by a portfolio balance effect). On outstanding bonds, however, interest has to be paid. The government sees itself forced to issue new bonds in order to be able to pay interest. Total wealth therefore increases further, and against a further upward shift of the LM curve the IS curve shifts further to the right. Depending on the relative degrees of shifting of the curves, the net effect on aggregate spending and national income may be positive (if not, it seems that no new equilibrium can be reached in the model, for if national income does not increase tax receipts will never catch up with interest payments).

The term dB/dG may have a negative value. This can happen if the short-term effects of dG are very strong. With a high propensity to consume and strong reactions of investment to changes in national income, national income may grow fast enough for the increase in tax receipts to surpass the increase in government expenditure. For the money supply to be held constant, government debt has to be bought in rather than sold (again, the system is unstable). A curious implication is that open-market operations have a contractive rather than an expansive effect in that case: the fall in the number of bonds outstanding reduces interest payments and leads to budget surpluses which are used for a further reduction of the outstanding volume of bonds, private wealth is reduced in the process and the resulting contraction by far outweighs the effects of the increased money supply (Mayer 1984 p. 374).

It should be realized that the outcomes of the above analysis hinge on the premise that non-interest government expenditure is unaffected by the amount of interest payments and that tax rates are held constant. Furthermore, the model is a Keynesian fixprice one, which restricts its usefulness for long-term analysis. A diagrammatical analysis by Mayer (1984) with flexible prices threw up the same results as the fixprice algebraic model, though. Also, full equilibrium should be made contingent on zero net investment as well (Arestis 1985 p. 111; see for simulations with a model with flexible prices, equity shares, the stock of capital and explicit expectations Nguyen and Turnovsky 1983 and for a growth model, of course admitting of net investment in equilibrium, van Ewijk 1986).

3. Rational Expectations, New Classical Macroeconomics and Alternative Views

INTRODUCTION: THE PHILLIPS CURVE, RATIONAL EXPECTATIONS AND NEW CLASSICAL MACROECONOMICS

The textbook IS-LM model of macroeconomics did not provide a satisfactory account of wage and price movements. In essence labour supply was assumed elastic until full employment was reached, after which point it was wages rather than employment that adjusted to changes in aggregate expenditure. The relationship between unemployment and wage or price changes known as the *Phillips curve* was welcomed because it appeared to provide the missing equation in the standard macroeconomic model (Phillips 1958). One implication was that a trade-off between employment and price stability was possible, that more employment could be 'bought' at the price of more inflation. However, Milton Friedman (1969a) and E.S. Phelps (1971) soon put a damper on those propagating active macroeconomic policies based on this trade-off. Friedman introduced the concept of the *natural rate of unemployment* (NRU), as an analogue to Knut Wicksell's natural rate of interest. At NRU, a kind of Walrasian equilibrium prevails, which does not exclude unemployment of the structural and frictional varieties, but does not allow of Keynesian unemployment following from a lack of demand. For all practical purposes, NRU means full employment. Starting from NRU, unemployment can indeed be reduced in Friedman's view by expansive macroeconomic (monetary and/or fiscal) policies, but only for a comparatively short while (a few quarters). Higher aggregate demand pushes prices up. Employers perceive better market conditions and hire more labour. Workers interpret rising wage offers as relative wage increases and supply more labour. As time passes workers discover that the higher nominal wages are offset by higher prices and businessmen discover that the price increases for their products are not relative price increases. Both realize that they are not better off than before and employment and GNP return to their NRU values, though at a higher rate of inflation. People take account of expected inflation when making decisions. The wage equation representing the Phillips curve

$$\lambda = a_0 + a_1/U \tag{3.1}$$

was extended by an argument representing expected price increases:

$$\lambda = a_0 + a_1/U + a_{2\pi}^* \tag{3.2}$$

with λ = rate of change of wages, U = rate of unemployment, π = inflation rate, an asterisk denotes expected values.

In Friedman's view, economic agents do not suffer from money illusion, that is, they will not, if full information is available, confuse nominal and real movements. Thus, π^* will converge to λ (abstracting all the time from productivity increases) and $a_2 = 1$. NRU, or the equilibrium value of U, therefore is

$$NRU = -a_0/a_1 \tag{3.3}$$

Demand-management measures induce a movement along a short-term Phillips curve which is followed by a move of the short-term Phillips curve. That move occurs when expectations adjust. The short-term curves all cut the long-term Phillips curve, which runs vertical at NRU.

Phelps's reasoning differs only slightly from Friedman's. In Phelps's island parable workers may accept work at a certain wage rate on their own island, but may also row to other islands in order to collect information on wages prevailing there. They weigh up the income forgone if they spend time on collecting information and the additional future earnings that may be the fruit of their search activities. Unlike Friedman's workers, who increase their labour supply if (perceived) real wages rise, Phelps's workers simply seek the highest wages at which they can work for a given number of hours a week. Like Friedman's workers, they will first mistake increased nominal wage offers following on an expansionary impulse for better relative wage offers (in Friedman's case: better real wage offers) and cut short their search activities. When the higher nominal wage turns out to be a lower relative wage, they (or rather some of them) start rowing again and unemployment returns to NRU.

In the Friedman-Phelps story, unemployment is voluntary, it is search unemployment or frictional unemployment (barring structural unemployment of workers whose marginal productivity is too low ever to find work). It would be suboptimal, from a welfare-theoretic point of view, to attempt to reduce unemployment below NRU. A reduction can only be brought about by deceiving workers. It is another thing to reduce NRU itself, by removing frictions in the labour market, such as incomplete job information, minimum wage laws and housing controls (which impede regional mobility).

Restrictive macroeconomic policies should in principle work out in a similar way: a temporary reduction of employment and real production, followed by a return to NRU at a lower rate of inflation. Also, random shocks should not set in motion deviation-amplifying mechanisms. This implies that markets work satisfactorily. If not, there is a possibility that a positive shock still works out as described by Friedman and Phelps, whilst a negative shock leads to protracted unemployment, which in this case is of the involuntary variety. Even so, the lasting contribution by Friedman and Phelps is that expectations receive a systematic treatment in economic theory. Their *adaptive expectations hypothesis*, which says that expectations of wage and price growth rates adapt to actual growth rates, can be seen as a manifestation of Goodhart's Law. It tells us that the short-term Phillips curve relationship breaks down when policy makers try to exploit it to boost employment.

The logic of Friedman's adaptive expectations implies that unemployment can be held below NRU at the cost of ever-increasing inflation, because with adaptive expectations, that is a weighted average of past and current inflation rates, expected wage or price rises lag actual increases and people continue to over-estimate their relative or real income:

$$E_t \pi_{t+1} - E_{t-1} \pi_t = b(\pi_t - E_{t-1} \pi_t) \qquad 0 < b < 1 \qquad (3.4)$$

E is the expectational operator, subscripts denote periods.

Rational economic agents will, however, notice that their forecasts are systematically wrong. They will take account of the ever-increasing inflation and not stick with adaptive expectations once they understand how the economy really works (Friedman 1976 pp. 230-1). This idea of rationality builds on a 1961 article by Muth, who proposed that expectations are 'essentially the same as the predictions of the relevant economic theory' (Muth 1961 p. 315). His hypothesis was, more precisely, that

> expectations of firms (or, more generally, the subjective probability distribution of outcomes) tend to be distributed, for the same information set, about the prediction of the theory (or the "objective" probability distribution of outcomes). (Muth 1961 p. 316)

Predictions may be wide of the mark, but they are not systematically wrong. Put differently, errors are not serially correlated.

Muth applied this concept of *rational expectations* (henceforth RE) to speculative behaviour and to the cobweb cycle. It has since with more or less success been applied to single markets, such as the stock market or the foreign exchange market (see Chapter 7). Lucas (1972) introduced the idea into macroeconomics. In a macroeconomic setting, the Phillips curve has been reinterpreted as a supply function - which was sorely missing in the IS-LM framework - and RE plus this supply function coupled to the idea of continuous market clearing gave *new classical macroeconomics* (NCME). In NCME, economic agents base their decisions on real factors and they are, given the information they possess, always in equilibrium. RE ensures that they do not commit systematic errors. All this means that there will only be random deviations from NRU, or from any other equilibrium for that matter.

NCME was first used to outdo Friedman and other monetarists in their stand against policy activism. Though governments would be well-advised, in the monetarist view, not to exploit the short-term Phillips curve trade-off between inflation and employment, because they would as likely as not intensify cyclical movements instead of counteracting them, it is in principle not impossible for them to affect real variables such as employment and production. NCME went one better and denied that governments could systematically affect real variables. Tobin therefore coined the term 'Monetarism, Mark II' for NCME (Tobin 1980a p. xiii). If the criterion for classification is not policy prescription, as in Tobin's case, but methodology, NCME can be seen as a break with Monetarism rather than as a continuation of it. Hoover (1984) argues that new classical economists have a Walrasian view of the world, whilst Monetarists have a Marshallian view, or at least Friedman has. Marshallians accept the idea that everything depends on everything else, but for practical purposes, that is, to keep an investigation manageable, they examine one problem at a time and partition reality: the relationships that are deemed by the researcher to be the most important ones are modelled in detail, the rest is summarized. Walrasians by contrast do not wish to partition reality, they stick to general equilibrium analysis and consider any model used to explain empirical phenomena to be below par if it lacks consistent assumptions about economic agents' objective functions and does not provide explanations based on first principles (Hoover 1984 pp. 67-8). Keynesian macromodels are a case in point. The term 'new classical' by the way is at least misleading, as neither classical economists (such as Ricardo) nor neoclassical economists held views corresponding with NCME (witness Ricardo's rejection of the rationality of agents, discussed in Chapter 2, see also Niehans 1987).

POLICY INEFFECTIVENESS

Monetary policy

NCME started out by emphasizing the ineffectiveness of stabilization policies, first of all of monetary policy, though it has later been argued by NCME proponents that this *neutrality proposition* has been overemphasized and that they never intended to take it seriously but meant to show that monetary policy measures may have quite different effects than one would expect under nonrational expectations (Sargent in Klamer 1984 p. 70, Minford 1986 p. 327). A common point of departure is the so-called *Lucas supply function* (here in a form that Minford and Peel 1981 call the Sargent-Wallace aggregate supply function):

$$y^s_t = y_n + a_1(P_t - E_{t-1} P_t) + u_{1,t} \qquad a_1 > 0 \qquad 3.5$$

where y^s_t denotes real output at time t, y_n the natural rate of output, corresponding with NRU, P_t the price level at time t, and $u_{1,t}$ is a serially uncorrelated random disturbance with mean zero. All magnitudes are expressed in logs.

Essentially, equation 3.5 is a reformulation of the Phillips curve. If actual prices equal expected prices, unemployment is at NRU and production is at its 'natural' level, apart from random disturbances. The economy is on the long-term, vertical Phillips curve. When price surprises occur, that is, actual prices differ from expected prices, output differs from its natural level, as in Friedman and Phelps's microeconomic approaches.

The supply function is complemented by an aggregate demand function:

$$y^d_t = M_t - P_t + u_{2,t} \qquad 3.6$$

where y^d denotes the log of aggregate real demand.

If goods markets clear, $y^s_t = y^d_t$ and P_t can be solved from equations 3.5 and 3.6:

$$P_t = (M_t + a_1 E_{t-1} P_t - y_n)/(1 + a_1) \quad 3.7$$

We now introduce rational expectations. First assume that the money supply is known to be held constant or to follow a fixed rule, such that $E_{t-1} M_t = M_t$. Given that $E_{t-1} u_{1,t} = 0$ and $E_{t-1} u_{2,t} = 0$, the rational expectation of P_t in period t - 1 is

$$E_{t-1} P_t = (M_t + a_1 E_{t-1} P_t - y_n)/(1 + a_1) \quad 3.8$$

Combining equations 3.7 and 3.8, we find that

$$P_t - E_{t-1} P_t = (u_{2,t} - u_{1,t})/(1 + a_1) \quad 3.9$$

or, in words, that deviations of actual prices from expected prices are completely random; and so are deviations of output from its 'natural' level, as shown by equation 3.5.

We now assume that the monetary authorities resort to an activist monetary policy. They decide to follow a proportional feedback rule, increasing the money supply when output falls short of the natural level and decreasing it when output exceeds the natural level:

$$M_t = M_n + a_2(y_{t-1} - y_n) + u_{3,t} \quad 3.10$$

M_n is the trend value of the money supply. An error term is added because the authorities are assumed not to be able to completely control the money supply.

With rational expectations, economic actors will lose little time in finding out what rule the authorities are following. At the end of period t - 1 they form a rational expectation of the money supply in period t:

$$E_{t-1} M_t = M_n + a_2(y_{t-1} - y_n) \quad 3.11$$

Substituting equation 3.11 in equation 3.6 and taking expectations, we find that

$$E_{t-1} P_t = [M_n + a_2(y_{t-1} - y_n) + a_1 E_{t-1} P_t - y_n]/(1 + a_1) \quad 3.12$$

and

$$P_t - E_{t-1} P_t = (-u_{1,t} + u_{2,t} + u_{3,t})/(1 + a_1) \quad 3.13$$

Because economic actors take account of the monetary policy rule, prices do not systematically divert from expected prices and monetary policy does not systematically affect real variables. The monetary authorities can only influence real output and employment by engineering surprise shocks in money growth. The more frequently they change their policy rule, the less easily the public is led to revise its decisions. A short-term Phillips curve may exist after all, but it tends to disappear if the authorities try to exploit it. The more often the authorities change the money supply rule, the less easily will the public be fooled and the more vertical will the short-term Phillips curve be (see Lucas 1973).

Strictly speaking, there is little sense in monetary policy as depicted above, because disturbances are not serially correlated. Measures taken to correct an output shock in one period only take effect in the next one. Nevertheless, the example serves to show that monetary policy cannot bring unemployment systematically below NRU. One is inclined to say that this is as well, because NRU represents a kind of macro-equilibrium and a systematically lower rate of unemployment requires economic agents to be deceived, which can hardly be optimal from a welfare point of view. It is another thing whether active economic policies can help to reduce fluctuations of employment around NRU. If they do, welfare may well increase.

Policy effectiveness under NCME

NCME does not rule out a positive contribution of monetary policy to economic stabilization. First of all, the authorities may have prior knowledge of economic disturbances. The measures they take will then have real effects, that is, affect volumes in lieu of prices. But an informational advantage really makes a weak case for active policy-making. Either the information will be available to the public without much delay (Grossman 1980 p. 13, Wagner 1981 p. 5) or the authorities could make the information freely available (McCallum 1980a p. 43).

It has been shown that slight modifications to the model discussed above may suffice to give the authorities the opportunity to reduce output fluctuations, at the cost of an increase in price fluctuations. Asako (1982) for instance developed a model where current prices and expected future prices are mutually dependent, while expected future prices also depend on the money-supply rule. Current supply and demand depend upon the difference between current prices and expected future prices. Different money supply rules then result in different values for the variance of output. In nonlinear models, the authorities can even influence the average value of output and employment: if they are able to manipulate the variance of the difference between actual and expected prices, and output depends in a nonlinear way upon this difference, average output is affected by the money supply rule (see Shiller 1978 p. 10, Snower 1984).

In an open economy on fixed exchange rates macroeconomic policies are bound to be non-neutral, even if they had been expected by the public. This is because at least one price, the price of tradeables, is not free to move with the domestic price level. For a small country, this price is even fixed. An expected increase in the money supply will increase the nominal demand for both tradeables and nontradeables, raising the price of nontradeables in the process. Production of nontradeables will increase and production of tradeables will fall as producers of nontradeables draw workers away from the tradeables industries. Nominal wages will rise in terms of tradeables and fall in terms of nontradeables (otherwise equilibrium in the labour market could not be maintained). If the aggregate price level is not very sensitive to the price of nontradeables, and nominal wage demands therefore do not rise to a great extent when nontradeables' prices increase, aggregate employment may rise, provided labour demand in the nontradeables sector reacts relatively strongly to a fall in the product wage (that is the nominal wage level relative to the price of the product of the industry) and labour demand in the tradeables sector is relatively insensitive to an increase in the product wage (Montiel 1987).

In a model with asset holdings monetary policy will generally be non-neutral too. Unforeseen price movements change the real value of nominally denominated government assets, provided they are considered to be net wealth (Minford 1986 p. 231). As for private debt, distribution effects may occur, that is, creditors and debtors may react asymmetrically to changes in the real value of debt consequent upon unexpected price level changes. The same goes for foreseen price changes which economic agents could not hedge against in time. If, for instance, the government now embarks on an economic programme that everybody understands will bring inflation within a couple of years, holders of bonds carrying a fixed rate of interest suffer a loss. Only new bonds will carry a higher or a variable rate of interest that compensates holders for inflation.

Many rational-expectations models admit of nonunique or multiple solutions. This may be the case when the values of today's endogenous variables depend on today's expectations of tomorrow's endogenous variables. Optimism and pessimism may then be self-fulfilling, which opens the way for government policies (Fischer 1988 p. 325, Diamond and Fudenberg 1989). A belief fostered by government pronouncements that it will promote future economic growth, for instance, may stimulate current private investments and thus not only make for sustained future growth but also for high current income and employment (see for the mathematical aspects of nonunique solutions Shiller 1978, Pesaran 1989 section 5.3 and McCallum 1989 section 8.7, who plays down their importance).

Fiscal policy

The argument that the government might be able to influence expectations concerns government policies in general, not only monetary policy but also fiscal policy, not to mention infrastructural policy, trade policy, competition policy and so on. As we have seen in Chapter 2, under strict conditions full crowding out or fiscal impotence can occur. In the case of ex ante crowding out, this requires a high degree of rationality. If the strict conditions are not met, fiscal policy can in principle be deployed for stabilization purposes. In one respect, more can be expected from it than from monetary policy: automatic stabilizers work automatically and are not dependent for their effectiveness on an informational advantage on the part of the authorities. Tax receipts for instance react automatically to variations in sales. Consequently, by varying the characteristics of the built-in stabilizers the authorities should be able to influence output variability.

Of course, even in cases where fiscal policy does not contribute to short-term economic stabilization, it can hardly be neutral. After all, it affects on the one side government expenditure and therefore the system's demand functions, and on the other side tax rates and therefore labour supply and savings or the supply of loanable funds.

Superneutrality

Even if macroeconomic stabilization measures were ineffective, policy measures might bear on the long-term growth path of the economy. A change in the rate of money growth and the concomitant change in the rate of inflation may affect investment by virtue of the *Tobin* or *Mundell-Tobin effect* (Tobin 1965, Mundell 1963a, 1971 ch. 2). Higher inflation for instance makes real capital more attractive to hold relative to money. Investment is stimulated and per capita production increases. This effect can be included in rational-expectations models by making the demand for capital an increasing function not only of the expected real return on capital but also of the expected rate of inflation (Fischer 1979). Alternatively, a real-balance effect can be introduced in the consumption function. Higher inflation will induce people to reduce their real balances, which in turn affects consumption and in its wake the desired capital stock and therefore investment (McCallum 1980b, Begg 1982 pp. 147-9). In case long-term growth is not affected, there is *superneutrality*.

Fiscal policy is even less likely to be subject to superneutrality than monetary policy. Fiscal actions that change investment ratios or the allocation of investments cannot but affect future economic growth.

NONCLEARING MARKETS AND POLICY EFFECTIVENESS

If markets are not assumed to clear continuously, that is, if NCME is not maintained, policy effectiveness need not at all be impaired by RE. Some form of price stickiness is called for in RE models to prevent markets clearing. One way of achieving this is to introduce contracts that fix prices or wages for a period during which the monetary authorities can react to new information. The public can then perfectly well forecast what policies the authorities will follow but, being bound by contracts, is not able to react to these policies.

A case in point is a model developed by Fischer (1977), in which at the end of each period new wage contracts are drawn up for one half of the work force for the next two periods. There is some serial correlation in the disturbances, which means that policy measures that take effect only next period still make sense. The variability of output and employment can be reduced in this way. In a linear model the mean levels of those real variables cannot be reduced, as that would still imply that workers would be fooled, which they will only accept for the duration of the contracts. Repeated attempts to fool them would be answered by a revision of the contracts.

In another model, developed by Phelps and Taylor (1977), prices and wages are fixed before the money supply is decided upon. Inventories carry disturbances from one period to the next. Monetary policy thus is both possible and useful. In cases such as these, it is not true that a fixed money supply rule is optimal when the expectations of the public are rational, nor is it true that monetary policy which follows a feed-back rule is only optimal when the public's expectations are not rational (see for such a proposition Korteweg 1976 p. 500).

It is true that models have been built where stabilization policy is ineffective, even without instantaneous market clearing (McCallum 1977, McCafferty 1982). This only proves the ingenuity of model builders. Of more importance is the question why agents should conclude contracts that fix prices in the first place. This problem is tackled below, in the section headed **NCME and RE: an appraisal.**

BUSINESS CYCLES

A remarkable feat of NCME has been the construction of models that purport to explain business cycles within the framework of continuously clearing markets. If markets clear continuously, business cycle movements imply cyclical movements of equilibrium output and employment. One might try to explain these movements by introducing exogenous shocks, such as technological changes (which make marginal productivity curves and labour demand move) and changing preferences as to consumption and leisure (which makes labour supply move). But, as Tobin (1980a p. 37, 1981 p. 37) notes, there is no reason why such moves should be autoregressive (see also Lucas 1977 p. 20).

NCME adherents have found several ways to explain the parallel movements of prices and quantities that characterize the business cycle. They have to fall back upon a confusion between changes in relative prices and changes in the general price level or a confusion between permanent and transitory shocks, or both, plus some mechanism for transmitting disturbances from one period to another. Such a mechanism can be found in time delays in information, costs of adjusting output decisions once taken or the influence of durable goods or inventories on production during next periods (Laidler 1981 pp. 11-12).

Starting from the idea that the supply of labour is not very elastic with respect to real wages, Lucas (1977) argues that workers will increase their labour supply if there is a (perceived) real wage increase that they believe to be only temporary. In his view, leisure in one period is a good substitute for leisure in other, nearby periods, witness the small premium required to induce workers to shift holidays and vacations. Otherwise prolonged unemployment can only be explained in an NCME framework by unwillingness to work at low real wages, which again means that unemployment is voluntary, or by prolonged search for work by labour suppliers who adjust their reservation wage with long lags to new economic realities, which does not seem to accord with RE. Introducing durable goods, Lucas observes that current relative price movements have their maximal effect on capital accumulation if they are regarded as permanent, for investment decisions will not be taken on the basis of price movements that are believed to be only short-lived. Hence, in order to have both investment and employment move systematically with relative price movements, those movements must be viewed as a mixture of permanent and transitory relative price changes.

If investment is increased as a result of incorrect price perceptions, there will be a downturn during subsequent periods, because producers wish to reduce capacity again and therefore invest less for a time (Lucas 1975, Sargent and Wallace 1975). Adding inventories to the model will give similar results. An unanticipated change in the general price level, interpreted at least in part as a relative price change, will make firms increase sales and raise both production and sales out of inventories. In subsequent periods inventories are gradually built up again and output will be higher for a time than would have been the case otherwise (Blinder and Fischer 1981, Brunner, Cukierman and Meltzer 1983 p. 283). More generally, persistence effects can be explained by introducing adjustment costs, including the cost of bringing the capital stock and inventories back to their equilibrium or trend values. The aggregate supply function then may take a form like

$$y_t = a(P_t - E_{t-1} P_t) + \sum_{i=1}^{n} b\, y_{t-i} + u_t$$

or, if y_n follows a trend,

$$y_t - y_{n,t} = a(P_t - E_{t-1} P_t) + \sum_{i=1}^{n} b_i(y_{t-i} - y_{n,t-i}) + u_t$$

(see McCallum 1979 p. 241, Oxley 1983 p. 185).

An interesting model with heterogeneous goods was developed by Long and Plosser (1983). They describe an economy with a variety of commodities where production of any commodity requires positive inputs of other commodities and labour. If the output of any one commodity is unexpectedly high (say because of a good harvest), inputs of this commodity in the production of other commodities is also unexpectedly high. A higher than usual amount of those other commodities becomes available for use in the next period, leading to higher than usual production for most or all commodities. This explains the persistence of a shock. The model does not include durable goods, there is no investment. It scores over the models usually encountered in NCME business-cycle analysis in that it is not restricted to one commodity. (Stockman 1990 shows some of the difficulties that one-good models have in explaining empirical facts of international business cycle propagation.)

A problem with equilibrium business-cycle models, apart from the fact that involuntary unemployment is denied, is that they do generate positive serial correlation in consumption and production, as happens in real-world cycles, but that they fail to generate positive serial correlation in investment (Dotsey and King 1988 p. 5). Another very serious problem for empirical testing of the NCME hypothesis is that with lagged income in the aggregate supply function it tends to become observationally equivalent with Keynesian models.

It may be noted in passing that these equilibrium business-cycle models have much in common with Austrian business cycle theory (Lucas 1977 p. 23 n. 15, Laidler 1981 p. 12). In either approach, business cycles are caused by spurious price signals. Austrians of course confine themselves to interest rates and the implied relative price of capital goods and consumption goods. For the rest, the way Austrians look at the world differs considerably from that of NCME economists (van Zijp 1990). They do not view business cycles as equilibrium phenomena. Further, Austrians such as Hayek do not expect individuals to be able to gain perfect knowledge of the 'true' model of the economy, nor do they believe that the relevant system is characterized by well-behaved random disturbances (with no serial correlation and zero mean). That would mean that there is only Knightian risk, not uncertainty: the probability distribution of disturbances would be known beforehand, which is not the world that Austrians find interesting to study. In line with this distinction, NCME economists see economics as a predictive enterprise, they want to deduce from their models predictions about the behaviour of an economy which is subjected to various shocks (Laidler 1990c p. 61, Hoover 1988b ch. 10). Such an aim goes against the grain with Austrians, who are very sceptical of the possibility of predicting human behaviour. Austrians see human behaviour essentially as acts of conscious choice in ever-changing circumstances, which by their very nature are no mere repetitions of acts in the past and the results of which are consequently hard to predict (see Reekie 1984 ch. 3). Finally, NCME tends to neglect the distinction between individuals and the collectivity of economic agents, whilst in Austrian analysis coordination problems between economic agents occupy centre stage.

EMPIRICAL IMPLICATIONS OF NCME

In equilibrium business cycle models, fluctuations in employment are not deviations *from* NRU, but movements *of* NRU, apart from random disturbances. This leads to at times rather startling interpretations of economic history. Darby (1976) for the US and Benjamin and Kochin (1979a, b, 1982) for the UK, for instance, stated without blinking that the unemployment that plagued the 1930s was nothing to worry about. Darby rested his case on a postwar finding that the government spending multiplier was very small over a period of two or three years. In other words, the 5 to 7 per cent of the labour force employed in public construction work in the US between 1934 and 1940 and officially counted as unemployed, would in his view have been employed by private enterprise had the government not taken them on. But of course the real government-spending multiplier can hardly be anything else than near-zero in a near-full-employment economy as characterized much of the 1950s and 1960s. This finding is totally irrelevant for the 1930s. Moreover, even not counting those on public construction work, unemployment was abnormally high (never lower than 9.2 per cent, a figure reached in 1937, as against 14.3 per cent including those on relief work, using the same figures as Darby).

Benjamin and Kochin argue that, had the British unemployment insurance system in the interbellum been no more generous than it was in 1913, official unemployment would have averaged 7 per cent instead of 14. Without denying that unemployment benefits may have played a role, it must be said that Benjamin and Kochin seem rather to underestimate the severity of the eligibility criteria and to overestimate the attractiveness of being on the dole (Metcalf, Nickell and Floros 1982 pp. 387-93) whilst, on top of that, their results were not very robust (Ormerod and Worswick 1982, Collins 1982). Worse still, Benjamin and Kochin left no place for aggregate demand in their research strategy, but in some models at least, deficient demand seems to explain British unemployment in the interbellum quite satisfactorily (Broadberry 1983, Hatton 1983).

It is impossible to review the huge literature on empirical testing of RE and NCME here. We will just give an idea of what is involved in such tests. For expectations to be rational they must be both efficient and consistent. Expectations are *efficient* if one-period forecasts and realizations share a common autoregressive pattern:

$$X_{t+1} = \sum_{i=1}^{n} a_i X_{t-i} + u_{1,t} \quad 3.14$$

$$E_t X_{t+1} = \sum_{i=1}^{n} b_i X_{t-i} + u_{2,t} \quad 3.15$$

Efficiency requires that $a_i = b_i$ for all i, meaning that expectations are generated by the same process that generates the variable to be forecast. Otherwise, expectations are biased. Forecasts are *consistent* if the multiperiod forecasts are obtained recursively, with the rational forecasts being substituted for the as yet unobserved realization of the series. Forecasts made in period t, say, of inflation in period t + 1 (the next year) and of inflation over the periods t + 1 and t + 2 (the next two years) yield an implicit forecast of inflation over period t + 2. Forecasts or expectations are said to be consistent if the forecast made at the end of period t + 1 of inflation in period t + 2, expectations of inflation in period t + 1 held in period t having proven correct, do not systematically differ from the implicit forecast of period t + 2 inflation made in period t. Put differently, if one-period forecasts show no bias and two-period forecasts show a systematic bias, forecasts are inconsistent. On top of that, rationality requires *orthogonality*, that is absence of serial correlation of forecast errors u with known past errors. Using inflation expectations data from surveys conducted over a long period of time by the *Philadelphia Bulletin* journalist J.A. Livingston, Pesando (1975) found that the information used in the six-month forecasts was not applied consistently to generate twelve-month forecasts. It was also found, not only by Pesando but by others researchers as well, that agents made systematic forecast errors (see Carlson and Parkin 1975, Sheffrin 1983 pp. 17-23; an update of Carlson and Parkin by Batchelor and Orr 1988, however, was inconclusive). The outcome on orthogonality was mixed (Batchelor and Orr 1988). Similar results have been found for interest-rate forecasts (Friedman, B.M. 1980).

Rational expectations have been very extensively applied in models of financial markets. The idea is that markets are efficient, which means that expectations are rational and arbitrage is quick. In other words, frictions are minimal and all available information is rapidly reflected in prices.

One upshot of RE and NCME is that expected changes in money growth affect the rate of inflation, whilst unexpected changes first of all affect real variables. Tests based on this idea give a mixed picture. Reasonably positive for NCME were tests conducted by Wogin (1980) for Canada 1927-1972, by Attfield, Demery and Duck (1981) for the UK 1963-1978, by Barro (1977, 1978) for the US 1941-1973 and by Bomhoff (1980 ch. 4) for the Netherlands 1953-1976. Less positive outcomes were reported by Barro and Rush (1980) for the US 1941-1980 and negative results by Driscoll, Ford, Mullineux and Sen (1983) for the UK over the postwar period to 1979 and Paleologos (1986) for postwar Greece. In such tests much depends of course on the way expectations are modelled. Apart from that, there is the problem of *observational equivalence*, that is the fact that the time series are compatible with several rival theories (Sargent 1976; see for an especially lucid discussion of the econometric issues involved Attfield, Demery and Duck 1985).

If anticipated changes in money growth only affect the rate of inflation, it should be possible to reduce inflation by means of a restrictive monetary policy without serious side-effects in the form of unemployment. Eckstein (1981) concluded from simulations with the 800-equation DRI-model for the US that there is great resistance of factor prices to demand management, including monetary policy. It appeared that changes in long-term expectations take time (Eckstein 1981 pp. 60-2, 79). Gradual price adjustment was also reported by Gordon (1982) for the US, 1890-1980. This might explain why disinflation policies in the US starting in 1979 (Mankiw 1986 p. 218), in Britain under Mrs Thatcher, also starting in 1979 (Attfield, Demery and Duck 1985 pp. 195-7), and in Chile under Pinochet after 1973 (Corbo and de Melo 1987) initially caused a sharp rise in unemployment. The public possibly first sits back to see if the government's policy is credible, that is, will not be reversed.

NCME AND RE: AN APPRAISAL

NCME imposes not only RE but also continuously clearing markets. We have seen above that initially policy ineffectiveness was postulated but that it was later admitted that this idea was oversold. Shocks may cause multi-period deviations from trend output and employment. This could, however, be explained without abandoning the continuous-clearing postulate. Continuous market clearing seems hard to defend, though. We have already cited evidence of gradual price adjustment. Price stickiness was also found by Silberston (1973) and Rotemberg (1982). Sticky wages and prices were found by Gordon (1983) for postwar USA, but not for postwar Britain and Japan. Carlton (1986) studied individual transactions price data collected by Stigler and Kindahl and found that prices can be quite rigid, prices to individual buyers in some industries remaining constant for several years. Price rigidity was positively correlated with the degree of concentration in the industry concerned, which points to imperfect competition. In the final section of this chapter we shall go further into this phenomenon. We shall also see there that unemployed workers may offer their labour services below the going wage rate and still be refused employment. Employers may quite rationally prefer to hire employees at a fixed wage rate and ration the posts offered. In other words, there are quantity constraints and the system does not function like a Walrasian general-equilibrium system where all agents are price takers and the auctioneer sees to it that transactions are made at equilibrium prices and all agents are on their demand and supply curves. Nor would it do to introduce nonmarket clearing and retain the other aspects of the Walrasian model (Lucas 1987 ch. 5). Such fixprice models yield price vectors that do not clear the market, but they do not admit of involuntarily unemployed people remaining unemployed even if they offer their labour services at a rate below the going market rate (Keynesian involuntary unemployment). There are no quits and dismissals, only hours of employment and wages are determined in the model.

In the real world goods markets too are quantity-constrained. Firms are price setters which set output targets on the basis of expected sales. Deviations of output from its trend result from faulty sales forecasts, not from incorrect price expectations, as in NCME models (Forman 1980 p. 38). Furthermore, in the real world communication and coordination between markets is time-consuming and costly (Gordon 1981 p. 526). Decisions made in one market during one period may affect other markets only during the next period, and economic agents in any one market are constrained by conditions prevailing in other markets which lack the flexibility of Walrasian markets. Firms may be unable to lower their selling prices at short notice after a negative demand shock, for instance, because their suppliers will only after a lapse of time be willing to adjust the prices of inputs. A demand shock therefore first affects quantities and only after a period of time will prices react. In such a non-NCME world stabilization policies may be quite effective. Rational expectations are not precluded and may even strengthen the effectiveness of stabilization measures. Agents may, for instance, hold that with a higher money stock the demand for goods will be higher. Higher expected demand for the next period may improve employment expectations for the next period, depress savings for the current period and in that way increase demand and employment for the current period. Again, there is in that case not a unique RE equilibrium (Hahn 1982, Tobin 1980a p. 45; see also Begg 1982 section 6.4 and Neary and Stiglitz 1983 for models in this vein).

Arguably real monetary economies are characterized by the very properties that NCME leaves out, such as transaction costs, apart from information costs to some degree, and economies of scale that preclude perfect competition. Essentially, NCME models, often one-good models with representative agents, describe a world with perfect competition where money is inessential. Some of them at least have to rely on quite improbable mechanisms to explain economic fluctuations. Neither firms nor workers for instance are likely to confuse price-level changes and relative price movements for other than restricted periods of time or small changes. The Friedman-Phelps approach and the Lucas supply function are not well-founded. To be meaningful, NCME will probably have to find ways to incorporate coordination problems between economic agents.

The RE hypothesis in itself has a lot going for it. RE as such do not imply policy ineffectiveness (as we have seen, not even NCME precludes policy effectiveness). RE have, though, brought home the fact that expectations concerning policy measures affect the outcome of those measures. This led Lucas (1976) to make short shrift of econometric model simulations of economic policy measures. He argued that, as agents take account of the government's policy, the structural parameters of the model cannot be assumed to be stable. The logic of this *Lucas critique* seems unassailable. More generally, RE have made us aware that models where economic agents make systematic mistakes offer unexploited opportunities for profit-making. This runs counter to economic insights and intuition.

Still, the applicability of RE seems restricted. RE presuppose a 'true' probability distribution of outcomes which is known by agents. This means that it only fits situations characterized by Knightian risk, not uncertainty, that is, it fits systems characterized by recurrent stochastic processes or random shocks (Lucas 1977 p. 15). One might try to 'rescue' RE by introducing subjective or Bayesian probability, but different people may hold widely diverging beliefs about the future, whereas RE models usually postulate identical beliefs about probability distributions of future events (Bray 1985 p. 167). It has been shown by Haltiwanger and Waldman (1989) that different expectations held by different agents need not cancel out in the aggregate. Let the cost of participating in some activity on the labour market vary over individuals. In addition, let some people (pessimists) undervalue and other people (optimists) overvalue the true benefit of participating. Some pessimists will not participate, incorrectly, given the true benefit, and some optimists will, also incorrectly, participate. In the aggregate the participation ratio may be equal to the participation ratio in a representative agent model, where those individual differences are assumed to even out. But if the cost of participating is described by a nonlinear function showing increasing marginal costs, the number of optimists incorrectly participating will be lower than in the case of a linear cost curve. The number of incorrectly nonparticipating pessimists is no longer offset by the number of incorrectly participating optimists. In general, nonlinearities in the system will make the outcomes of exercises in multi-agent models differ from those in representative-agent models. This is an interesting conclusion but does not repair the restricted usefulness of RE.

If, because of unforeseen shocks, the structural parameters of the system change, it seems reasonable to expect a learning period during which agents assemble information about the new structure. In that case we are back with a kind of adaptive expectations (Friedman, B.M. 1979 p. 36, Sijben 1980 p. 92). It is not of the naive adaptive kind, though, where agents make systematic errors of the kind described by Milton Friedman in his attack on the idea of a long-term Phillips-type trade-off between inflation and employment. An obvious case is when a new government announces that it will reverse the pernicious policies of its predecessor. Especially if similar policy intentions in the past, like so many good intentions, only paved the way to hell, agents will tend to adopt a wait-and-see attitude first. Only after it has become clear that a new regime, for instance a liberalized foreign-trade regime, is there to stay, will investors change their behaviour accordingly and, in this case, move from import-competing industries to export industries.

In the course of a learning process, economic agents take decisions based on incomplete information, that is, a false model of the system, and in that way make the system itself change. Convergence to a RE equilibrium requires agents to improve their forecasts faster than the model changes (Runde and Torr 1985). There are some obstacles standing in the way of the implied feedback. It often takes considerable time before the outcome of a decision is known and then it may be difficult to attribute it to a particular action, and there is often no information about what would have happened had other decisions been taken (Tversky and Kahneman 1986 p. S274). On a more fundamental level, a learning process to discover the 'true' system implies an inductivist approach to knowledge, which is debatable from a methodological point of view (see on this Boland 1982, especially ch. 4). Of course Milton Friedman's 'as if' approach offers a way out:

> it is frequently convenient to present [...] a hypothesis by stating that the phenomena it is desired to predict behave in the world of observation *as if* they occurred in a hypothetical and highly simplified world containing only the forces that the hypothesis asserts to be important'. (Friedman, M. 1953 p. 40)

Another thing is that some models admit of multiple equilibria, as noted earlier. To complicate matters, agents may quite rationally expect other agents not to base their decisions on so-called market fundamentals, such as real growth, money growth and interest rates, and base their own decisions on those expected decisions by others. This opens up the possibility of rational speculative bubbles (see Chapter 7). These problems associated with RE models need not, though, be seen as defects of those models, but rather reflect a bewildering empirical, or real, world.

Finally, there is disturbing evidence from psychological tests that people judge the likelihood of a future event by its similarity to current events, ignoring both prior information and the quality of current evidence (for instance, sample size) and underestimating uncertainties (Tversky and Kahneman, cited by Arrow 1982 p. 5). Also, it was found that alternative descriptions of a problem often influence decisions (Tversky and Kahnemann 1986 p. S251).

It seems fair to conclude that NCME neglects some of the basic features of a monetary economy, but that RE have a useful, though limited role to play, such as providing a research strategy for some kinds of markets. Even if the applicability of RE is restricted, it can stand comparison with other methods of modelling expectations. In general it improves on the ad hoc assumptions of other methods and if it can only satisfactorily cope with risk, not with uncertainty, that is a universal problem. There is no way of moulding Keynes's 'dark forces of time and ignorance' so as to fit them into an elegant expectations model (Keynes 1961 p. 161).

NEW KEYNESIANS AND POST-KEYNESIANS

New Classicals start from the assumption of *tâtonnement* pricing. Others by contrast study the results of a price mechanism that does not guarantee continuous market clearing. They are often labelled *New Keynesians*, but unlike New Classicals they do not follow one distinguishing analytical approach to the exclusion of others. Prominent amongst them was Arthur Okun (1981 ch. 4), who has shown that, with imperfect information, it can be rational (in the sense of profit or utility maximizing) not to let markets clear. He distinguished between *auction markets* and *search* or *customer markets*. Continuous market clearing, as in Walras's model, implies the universality of organized auction markets, with every economic agent being a price taker. Such markets can only exist for products that are standardized and can be viewed as homogeneous by a prospective buyer who places orders through a broker. Markets for heterogeneous goods by contrast are search or customer markets where the costs of acquiring information are relatively high and a certain degree of price stickiness may be advantageous for both buyers and sellers. The buyer remains true to his or her supplier, and is rewarded by prices that are kept relatively stable by the supplier. It could be said that buyer and seller have an *implicit contract*. In Chapter 4 we shall see that this line of reasoning gains further plausibility of we introduce middlemen between suppliers and customers. It will be cheaper for those middlemen to absorb fluctuations in supply and demand to some degree than hectically to adjust prices in order to equate (fluctuating) supply and (fluctuating) demand at every moment in time.

The idea of an implicit contract has also been applied to the labour market (Okun 1981 chs 2, 3). A satisfying and coherent wage theory does not seem to have resulted from such attempts, though (van Hulst 1984 pp. 44-7). An implicit contract on the labour market would seem to imply that employees prefer the risk of unemployment over the risk of a wage reduction, which is highly improbable (Thurow 1983 ch. 7). Still, imperfect information has proved to be a promising starting point. For instance, New Keynesians tend to explain wage rigidities from the imperfect information which employers have about prospective employees, together with the costs of taking on new personnel, including the costs of screening and training (Greenwald and Stiglitz 1987 pp. 123-5). It may then be advantageous for employers to pay relatively high *efficiency wages* as a reward for a relatively high level of productivity in order to motivate the existing labour force, even if outsiders are willing to accept work at a lower wage. Employers ration jobs and the labour market does not clear. Employees in their turn contribute to wage rigidities because searching for other jobs may be costly (Hahn 1980b p. 288). This may prevent not only downward but upward wage adjustments at times. Nominal wage rigidities, as in Fischer's 1977 model mentioned above, can of course also be explained by the costs of changing nominal wages or of indexation (Corden 1987 p. 173, Minford 1986 p. 321). Nonetheless, if inflation is high and variable, indexation clauses are likely to be included in wage contracts and contracts will have a shorter duration. New Keynesian explanations may not exclusively explain all instances of wage rigidity, but they seem to be able at least to explain some cases where other approaches fail.

The New Keynesian approach applied to the credit market implies that the rate of interest does not ensure equilibrium. Rationing credit may be more advantageous for financial institutions in the case of excess demand for credit than raising the rate of interest. At a higher rate of interest relatively riskless demand for credit may priced out of the market whilst more risky debtors are attracted with possibly dubious promises of a high return. This *adverse selection* might lead to lower expected returns for the financial institution, even if the rate of interest were higher (Stiglitz 1988, Koelewijn 1989; see for an application to interest deregulation policy in developing countries Villanueva and Mirakhor 1990).

A phenomenon at odds with New Classical views, though not specifically of a (New) Keynesian nature, is *hysteresis*. There is hysteresis if the equilibrium value of some variable, such as the natural rate of employment, depends on the values of that variable in the past. To fix ideas, if a random shock causes mass unemployment at some moment in time, that unemployment may itself cause the natural rate to increase over time. This is because the human capital of the unemployed in the form of skills and motivation deteriorates, or employers think it deteriorates. Besides, a protracted economic depression implies a long period of low investment, which causes a loss of jobs (Cotis 1988, Cross 1988).

In passing, some attention may be paid to the *Post-Keynesians*, though their publications do not really date only from the period after the Keynesians-Monetarists debate. They somehow have hardly ever been in the limelight and deserve some attention if only because they offer an alternative to the dominant views. Post-Keynesians believe that there are inherent instabilities in the capitalist economic system (Minsky 1988 p. 24). In the monetary field, Post-Keynesians concentrate on the role of money in an uncertain and unstable world, which role in their view tended to get obscured in the dominant neoclassical synthesis and monetarist approaches. There is no unified Post-Keynesian monetary approach, but a central tenet is that the money supply cannot be used by the authorities to control the economy, because it is endogenous, depending on the volume of credit creation (Rousseas 1986 p. ix, Arestis 1988 p. 2 and chs 2 and 4). Arguably the most notable contribution of Post-Keynesians in the monetary field is Minsky's theory of *financial instability*. As Minsky sees it, at the start of a cyclical upswing entrepreneurs find it advantageous to contract cheap short-term debt in order to finance investment goods. As both investments and profits keep on increasing, the volume of debt grows and firms become more and more dependent on frequent refinancing. In the course of time the rate of interest will rise, so that the costs of production increase and profits are squeezed. The financial structure becomes more fragile. Firms face increasing difficulties meeting their debt service obligations and some see themselves forced to sell some assets or even entire divisions. This helps to depress the demand price for capital goods, whilst at the same time the supply price or cost of production is rising. Even firms that are still financially sound prefer to retire debt or to take over parts of other firms rather than to invest in new capital equipment. Tobin's q becomes smaller, investment in new capital goods dwindles and a cyclical downswing starts. The central bank may provide liquidity enabling the banks to lend to business firms, so that they can continue to pay their creditors. Also, expansionary fiscal policies may curb a downswing. A severe depression may in this way be prevented, but at the cost of an increased possibility of (higher) future inflation (Minsky 1982, 1986, 1988).

On a more general level, NCME neglects the possibility of coordination failures between economic agents, while a central Post-Keynesian tenet is that a market economy cannot be assumed to be automatically stabilizing (Arestis and Skouras 1985 p. xi). Like Minsky's credit market, any market may be destabilizing. Post-Keynesianism and NCME are poles apart.

4. Microfoundations of Money and Finance

MONEY IN FRICTIONLESS GENERAL-EQUILIBRIUM MODELS

Money and banking textbooks have little difficulty explaining the use of money. Money facilitates the exchange of goods and the division of labour by lowering transaction costs. There is nothing wrong with that story, but when it comes to incorporating money in microeconomic general-equilibrium models, it proves extremely difficult to explain why people would be willing to hold a non-interest-bearing asset (or low-interest-bearing asset) whilst riskless assets with a positive return (or a higher positive return) are available in the form of time or savings deposits and why the use of such an asset could lower transaction costs. All kinds of plausible models have been developed to explain the volume of money demanded, but they presuppose an economy where money does already exist in the first place. In the textbook story money does away with the need for a double coincidence of wants for a transaction to take place or, in the absence of such a coincidence, with the need for a series of transactions. More generally, the use of money reduces the transaction costs which a seller incurs in order to find a buyer and which a buyer incurs in order to find a seller. Those transaction costs are predominantly of an informational character: they result from the need for communication between prospective buyers and sellers, from gathering information on the market and inspection of goods but also from the keeping of records and the drawing up of accounts (Niehans 1969 p. 709). These costs must be distinguished from the minimal costs of physically transferring goods from seller to buyer, which should really be seen as production costs.

Walrasian equilibrium models with money are not very satisfactory because they provide no reason why goods shouldn't exchange directly for other goods (Hahn 1973 p. 23). The Walrasian auctioneer ensures costless information processing and transactions are decided upon in one all-embracing decision, which easily permits of multilateral trading. Arrow-Debreu models, where transaction decisions are taken in a similar way at one moment for all future dates, provide no place for money either (see Debreu 1959, Geanakoplos 1989). The Walrasian auctioneer or the *tâtonnement* mechanism that regulates the buying and selling process in these models is a device expressly introduced to abstract from information costs, the very rationale of the use of money. Money is *inessential* in these models: the exchange process is not in the least hampered if money is absent. Note that this is not synonymous with *neutrality of money*. If money is neutral, equilibrium quantities and price ratios in the system are independent of the volume of money, but not of the use of money as such. In a quantity-theoretic comparative-static analysis, for instance, different volumes of money result in different absolute prices with quantities and relative prices remaining unchanged. It is not implied that quantities and relative prices would be the same in a moneyless economy. As David Hume put it, money

> is the oil which renders the motion of the wheels [of trade] more smooth and easy (Hume 1955 p. 33)

and its use can only stimulate trade. If information processing is costless and money is inessential, it is not only money as medium of exchange that is superfluous. Money as a unit of account can also be dispensed with (Laidler 1990d p. 104). Money as a unit of account after all only serves to make calculations easier to perform and to simplify bookkeeping. Money could still function as a store of value, but that would not distinguish it from other assets, apart from its low or zero rate of interest.

Patinkin's attempt to integrate monetary and value theory in his painstakingly written *Money, Interest, and Prices* (Patinkin 1965), which can be seen as the culmination of the Walrasian tradition, is a glaring example of the ultimate futility of introducing money in a general-equilibrium model where all goods exchange against all goods. Patinkin tries to

> conceive of a barter economy as the limiting position of a money economy whose nominal quantity of money is made smaller and smaller. (Patinkin 1965 p. 75)

This attempt was doomed to failure, because prices go down in step with the nominal money supply so that the real quantity of money is not reduced. Patinkin realized full well that one cannot compare a barter economy with a monetary economy in this way. His argument was that

> in a barter economy there is obviously neither an excess-demand equation for money nor a dependence of commodity excess-demand equations on real balances (ibid.)

which would to his mind make a comparison between a barter economy and a monetary economy more or less impossible. But a comparison between a monetary economy and a frictionless barter economy would serve no purpose, even if it could be done without any technical difficulties. The rationale of using money is absent in frictionless barter models and the consequences of the introduction of money can never be analysed with such models as a point of reference. The only meaningful comparison is with a barter economy where transactions are costly because of the higgling and haggling involved. Patinkin neglects the fact that the exchange technology in a monetary economy is more efficient than in a barter economy. A given initial supply of resources will result in different amounts of goods and services and, in a production economy, in different paths of capital accumulation under the two systems. In monetary growth models, to which Patinkin incidentally also contributed, this is taken account of by adding real balances as an argument to a macroeconomic production function (Patinkin and Levhari 1968). Such a procedure may intuitively be more appealing than adding real balances to utility functions, which is an alternative way of explaining a demand for money in frictionless general-equilibrium models. Still, both procedures suffer from the lack of a microeconomic foundation, which is hard to supply in models such as these monetary growth models where markets are assumed to work without frictions (these models are surveyed in Sijben 1978). If macroeconomic models assume a productive contribution of money balances or an increase in agents' utility, microeconomics should provide an explanation why this is so.

MONEY IN A SINGLE-PERIOD MODEL

A step forward was made by writers who constructed general-equilibrium models with transaction costs, prominent amongst them Niehans (1969, 1971, 1975, 1978 ch. 6). Niehans (for instance 1978 p. 101) simply posits that there are no IOUs or more generally that there is no credit (with the exception of Niehans 1975, but in that article bonds are added to the system only in order to explain the rate of interest). This effectively precludes triangular trade or multilateral trade in general. Under a Walrasian auctioneer system, A could sell goods to B and B goods to C while C sells goods to A. In a system where transactions are not concluded in an all-embracing single decision as in the Walrasian world, A demands a *quid pro quo* from B instead of agreeing to wait for delivery of goods by C. C may have to pay C-goods to B, who has no need for them and uses them to pay A. In a multi-agent world without a generally accepted medium of exchange long chains of transactions may be called for before a preferred redistribution of goods will have taken place. If instead some goods, say C-goods, are used as a medium of exchange, transaction chains can be drastically shortened (notice that the *medium of exchange* may also, but need not, be a *means of payment*: the transfer of a means of payment cancels outstanding claims, it functions as ultimate payment, whilst the transfer of a medium of exchange need not in itself cancel a debt; it may, as in the case of a cheque, only be a means for bringing about the transfer of a means of payment).

The reduction in the number of exchange transactions achieved by deploying a generally accepted medium of exchange and the consequent reduction in transaction costs is analysed in a model developed by Jones (1976). Jones argues that indirect exchange can be cheaper than direct barter because fewer search contacts are on average needed between prospective sellers and buyers before an exchange is made (see for a further development of Jones's model Oh 1989). In contrast to transportation, storage and inspection costs, the information costs of finding a trading partner may be assumed to be nonadditive. Indirect exchange may double transportation costs, but not information costs, over direct barter. Let a supplier of good i enter the market and search for a supplier of good j. All agents in the market hold one unit of a good and demand one unit of another good. Note that prices are given in this model and that the market is assumed to clear eventually at these prices. The (subjective) probability that a randomly met trader in the market demands good i is denoted by p_i. The probability that he or she supplies good j is denoted by p_j. The probability that an agent offering good i and demanding good j meets another agent who demands good i and supplies good j therefore is p_ip_j. The number of search contacts which the agent expects to make before the desired transaction can be concluded consequently is $1/p_ip_j$. With indirect exchange through the medium of a good n, there is first a search for an agent demanding i and offering n and then a search for an agent offering j and demanding n. The expected number of search contacts is $1/p_ip_n + 1/p_np_j$. The expected number of contacts, and with it the expected search costs of exchange, is smaller with indirect trade than with direct barter if

$$1/p_ip_n + 1/p_np_j < 1/p_ip_j$$

or

$$p_i + p_j < p_n.$$

This may the case for some goods but not for others. Jones's model leaves open the possibility of direct barter and indirect exchange existing side by side. This is not only because indirect exchange does not always yield lower search costs, but also because any savings on search costs may be nullified by the higher transportation costs involved in indirect exchange. The assumption of additive transportation and related costs also precludes chains of barter transactions.

The question of which good becomes the money commodity was taken up by Brunner and Meltzer (1971). In their view, transaction costs are, apart from costs of transfer and storage (which can best be seen as production costs), in fact costs of acquiring information on assets or, more precisely, the costs of identifying qualities of a good, including the location and identity of other traders (see also Alchian 1977). Repeated use of some assets and some transaction sequences will lower the marginal cost of acquiring information. This means that patterns of indirect exchange emerge in which some specific assets are deployed as media of exchange.

The assets used in indirect trade evolve into money. Their function is to enable individual agents not to balance the value of sales and the value of purchases at every moment of time. In the absence of a Walrasian auctioneer, money enables agents to demand goods without being certain of the quantities they will be able to sell and the prices at which these will sell. In a timeless Walrasian economy it may be somewhat difficult to imagine repeated use of assets and, consequently, of learning processes, but time could be thought of as consisting of separate periods within each of which all purchases of goods and services are paid for by payments of goods and services. This implies that money must either be a good that ends up as a producer or consumer good with an economic agent at the end of each period, or be a claim to such goods, or that it is credit money which is destroyed when all claims are settled at the end of each period. Goods and services are ultimately paid for by goods and services. In terms of Niehans's example,

C could pay A by transferring a claim in the books of a financial institution, a bank, to A against the creation of a debt to the bank. A would transfer the claim to B against receipt of B-goods and finally B transfers the claim to C, after which C's claim and C's liability both vanish through compensation. This implies that for every individual agent the total value of sales (expressed in the numeraire or unit of account) must equal the total value of purchases within every individual period. Forced sales (in order to make up net debit positions at the bank) or forced purchases (in order to get rid of a net credit position) are conceivable. With the demise of the Walrasian auctioneer, perfect markets and price-taking economic agents are gone too. (Jones's model, among others, assumes that prices are given to agents, but that is only because combining the central idea of information costs as a stochastic variable depending on chance meetings between prospective trade partners with flexible prices proved a technically insurmountable task.)

Within self-contained periods of time, it is hard to conceive of agents who would wish to hold end-of-period balances of intrinsically worthless pieces of paper, or more generally of fiduciary money, rather than goods. The holding of fiduciary money, such as bank notes or book entries, that is not destroyed at the end of each period only makes sense in models of *sequence economies*. Sequence economies differ not only from Walrasian economies where the future does not figure (except perhaps in a roundabout way through expectations). They also differ from Arrow-Debreu economies where all decisions are made in one fell swoop at the dawn of (model) time. From then on till Kingdom Come nothing happens but the realization of plans, if not with certainty then with known probabilities. Without uncertainty, but with a known probability distribution of future 'states of the world', that is of exogenous circumstances such as the weather, claims on contingent commodities can be exchanged. To fix ideas, an order may be placed for umbrellas to be delivered at a certain date if it rains and for parasols if the sun shines (see for an extremely lucid, nontechnical exposition of such an Arrow-Debreu economy, Meade 1970). The risks this involves for the producers can be insured, as probability distributions are known. As in Walrasian one-period economies, there would be no point in holding money beyond the span of time during which contracts are being concluded, even if we send the auctioneer packing and introduce information (search) costs. It would serve no purpose after the decisions for all future periods had been made. In contrast, sequence economies require new decisions to be taken and new transactions to be made every new time period. It appears that sequence economies provide a better setting for analysing the foundations of monetary economies than single-period models, as single-period models are hard put to it to explain the continued holding of money.

MONEY IN A SEQUENCE ECONOMY

Niehans (1978 ch. 6) does not confine himself to a one-period model but also considers a multi-period situation. Transaction and storage costs, again, are simply assumed to exist, with the money commodity having the lowest cost of all. The suggestion that these costs are mostly search and information costs is all that is given by way of explanation (Niehans 1978 pp. 63-3; again, he rules out credit). Brunner and Meltzer's analysis on first sight does not take us much further, as it leaves one somewhat in the dark about the nature of the information sought. A clue is given in a footnote, which says that

> If there are no costs of acquiring information, differences in the timing of receipts and payments are adjusted by issuing verbal promises in exchange for goods and, later, delivering goods. (Brunner and Meltzer 1971 p. 785 n. 4)

Though Brunner and Meltzer's idea was not taken up at the time, recent developments follow a similar track. Gale for instance argues that in a world without a complete Arrow-Debreu system of markets, trading continues after the first date. The value of sales will not at every moment in time equal the value of purchases for all individual actors. Money holdings then serve to absorb the difference, at which point Gale, like Brunner and Meltzer before him, observes that if agents were really trustworthy, there would be no need for a sequence of budget constraints (Gale 1982 p. 186, see also pp. 197, 235, 245). Or, as Niehans notes, if one could be perfectly certain that everybody would always stay within his budget constraint, everybody could be allowed to obtain goods without a specific *quid pro quo*, which would make exchange otiose (Niehans 1978 p. 63 n. 4; as with Brunner and Meltzer, the most fundamental observations are relegated to footnotes; see also Ostroy 1973 p. 597, Ostroy and Starr 1974 p. 1093). In that case agents could, in a one-period model, issue debt (IOUs) or entries could be made in an accounting system in the understanding that after a round of dealings the claims would be cancelled. Every agent would be both willing and able to meet his or her budget constraint. In a sequence economy, A could sell to B at time t and be certain of receiving something in return at time t + 1 from C (Goodhart 1975 p. 3).

The point of trustworthiness is also stressed by Illing (1985). Even if agents were immortal, his argument runs, there would be no complete Arrow-Debreu system of contingent future markets, if only because of moral hazard problems which follow from asymmetric information (Brunner and Meltzer 1971 p. 786, also stress the uneven distribution of information between buyers and sellers as a reason for seeking alternatives to barter). In other words, trade would not only take place at the initial date, but there would also be spot markets at future dates. Illing develops the following thought experiment. Households are at the start of every period supplied with endowments of perishable consumption goods. These endowments are risk variables, with a known probability distribution. Households do not know beforehand how much they will exactly receive. They could even out the fluctuations in individual endowments by concluding insurance contracts. But there is asymmetric information. At any moment in time, households know their own endowment. Others do not, which means that the insurance company has to incur costs to collect information on individual endowments. There is, therefore, an incentive for households to cheat. It may in these circumstances be advantageous to hold money as a substitute for costly insurance, because of a moral hazard problem. But why, again, money rather than IOUs? Illing here follows Gale: because financial assets other than money imply information costs (Illing 1985 pp. 81-2). An idea of the information costs involved in actual practice is given by the commission paid by retailers to the credit card company when payment is made through a credit card, which is of course a form of credit (Gale 1982 p. 187). It should also be obvious that only a subset of transactions can be settled in this way, and that only some fraction of the set of agents can make use of this kind of credit, precisely because of the costs involved.

It might be objected that a model such as Illing's is far removed from reality, but such an objection would be beside the point. The aim is to find the essential or minimum requirements for a monetary economy, not to give a realistic description of a monetary economy. It is, moreover, not difficult to think up variations on the theme of moral hazard. It is conceivable, for instance, that contracts would be concluded for the immediate delivery of goods against the future provision of labour services, but then the difficulty arises of ensuring that the work be done well (Hahn 1988 p. 971). The use of money as a means of splitting this intertemporal barter transaction into two separate transactions does away with that difficulty.

It is not surprising to find that transaction costs and, if money is to be more than the rather bloodless construct it is doomed to be in a timeless model or a one-period model, a time duration are minimum requirements of a monetary economy. Apparently the use of money does not have to be predicated on uncertainty as to prices or interest rates, which looms so large in standard Keynesian and other money-demand functions. These phenomena may explain the volume of money demanded once a monetary economy exists, but not why money is demanded in the first place. And of course the basic models of the transactions demand for money, notably the Baumol-Tobin inventory-theoretic model, assume full certainty as to prices and interest rates.

It has been argued by some that there will only be monetary exchange if there are costs of negotiating exchange transactions and if some commodities have certain physical characteristics, such as low storage costs and divisibility (Clower 1977), but that begs the question why IOUs could not do the job. The conditions mentioned may be necessary, but are by no means sufficient. Money is, in the above analysis, useful because it saves on transactions costs. More precisely, the use of money saves on the costs of acquiring information (King and Plosser 1986). The crucial characteristic in this connection is the trustworthiness of the issuer (Gale 1982 p. 189). Hence, fiduciary money can only be the result of a long development. People accept intrinsically worthless paper money only because they expect other people to accept it in their turn at a later date. Their readiness to accept it can be fostered by the government announcing that people may pay taxes in that kind of money (Starr 1980 p. 262; in line with this approach, de Roos, 1989 p. 30, proposes to further the use of the Ecu through European governments doing their spending and collecting their taxes in Ecus). If money were restricted to commodity money, enormous amounts in terms of the unit of account would be needed, which would entail high costs in terms of resources and would drive up the relative price of the money commodity to the detriment of its function as a production or consumption good.

It seems that a sequence economy not only results from moral hazard but also from the costs of making decisions. In an Arrow-Debreu world, where incidentally households are infinitely lived, preparing for all possible future 'states of the world' by exchanging claims on contingent commodities would imply an infinite number of decisions. If we drop the fiction of a costless Walras/Arrow-Debreu auction mechanism, an infinite number of decisions implies infinite costs. Because of computational limitations of economic agents, it is impossible to write contingent contracts or resort to insurance (providing, for instance, for the case of illness of an agent who is bound by contract to provide labour services at a future date) for every possible transaction (Radner 1968 p. 31, Hahn 1988 p. 971). It is cheaper not to decide on all future dealings and postpone most decisions to later dates. Even if it were conceivable to conclude contingent contracts for all future dates and all future 'states of the world', with positive costs of concluding contracts it would surely not be welfare-optimizing to concentrate all efforts at the initial date (Hahn 1985b p. 76). Factors of production would be used up in the decision-making process, leaving few or no resources avaliable for production nor much time for consumption. If households are not infinitely lived, or if the future is not only risky but also uncertain in the sense of Frank Knight, decisions for all future dates and all possible 'states of the world' are not even conceivable. Present generations cannot have knowlegde of the preferences of future generations or the range of products and services available in the future.

Not all factors that make for a sequence economy also explain the use of money. Computational limitations would not in all cases exclude the use of IOUs if there were no moral hazard problems, but the decision-making process would in general become more expensive with a widespread use of IOUs instead of money because of the additional risk involved in using IOUs. They are promises that may not be fulfilled, for example because of illness, and hence call for a multiplicity of additional contingent contracts. Besides, it would not be easy to provide the public with small-denomination debt. The production of small-denomination IOUs might not be overly expensive, but the costs of paying interest and amortization on large amounts of small-denomination debt would surely be prohibitive. This also seems to preclude the use of low-interest government debt, in particular Treasury bills, as money.

The last word has certainly not been said on this subject. There is certainly no lack of fine ideas, but to model these ideas is no mean task. One thing at least is clear: timeless general-equilibrium models won't do if we want to explain not only the use of money during the process of concluding contracts but also the holding of money. We need models that provide for sequences of trades, as emphasized by people such as Gale and Illing.

Having found the minimum requirements of a monetary economy, the next step should be to incorporate production in the model and to take account of the better specialization made possible by the use of money, which means that the productive capacity in monetary economies differs from that in barter economies. But this poses enormous technical problems. On top of that, there seems at present to be no way to model the scale economies implied in an economy without a costless (Walrasian/Arrow-Debreu) transaction technology (Hahn 1985a p. 2, Niehans 1969 p. 106). With transaction costs at least in part independent of the magnitude of transactions, that is, with fixed set-up costs (as in Jones's model and also as involved in probing the trustworthiness of agents), transaction (information) costs do not rise in step with the scale of individual transactions, nor with the number of transactions for that matter, as repeated contracts with the same trade partner are likely to imply diminishing marginal information costs. It would be difficult to conceive of a Pareto-optimal competitive equilibrium in such an economy, to mention one problem. With scale economies, if internal to firms and households, pure competition is impossible and with perfect markets gone as well, no tidy general-equilibrium model can be applied.

It is to be noted that the transaction costs and scale economies that explain the use of money also explain the rise of middlemen, as indeed they explain why firms exist. Reverting to Jones's model, search costs can be substantially reduced if specialist traders stand ready to buy and sell certain goods (Clower and Howitt 1984 p. 182, Clower and Leijonhufvud 1984 p. 212). These specialist traders or middlemen absorb fluctuations in demand and supply volumes and adjust buying and selling prices only if inventories change in one direction over an extended period (Clower 1975 p. 17). This could explain price stickiness, expanding the imperfect-information theme underlying Okun's implicit contract approach (see Chapter 3) and takes us even further away from Walras/Arrow-Debreu models where markets continually clear. However, to explain why traders do not generally accept IOUs in payment and use these to pay their suppliers, we again have to resort to the issues of trustworthiness (moral hazard) and risk and uncertainty (illness or untimely death of a debtor), which make money a superior device for settling transactions.

OVERLAPPING-GENERATION MODELS

Economists associated with the Federal Reserve Bank of Minneapolis in particular have made attempts to find the essential characteristics of money with the help of overlapping-generation models (Kareken and Wallace 1980). In overlapping-generation models, there are at any moment in time two generations of people, an older one and a younger one. Older people must have saved resources or claims to resources in order to survive after retirement. Storing resources over a number of decades is a costly affair and society can achieve considerable savings if people build up a store of claims to resources instead. Those claims could be intrinsically worthless pieces of paper, that is, fiat money. A generation then first works and sells part of its produce to the older generation against money and when it in its turn has become the older generation it uses up its money treasure and receives consumption goods from the then younger generation, and so on (see for an extremely formal model, in which the young are at the start endowed with consumption goods and the old with both consumption goods and money, Wallace 1980).

Intrinsically worthless fiat money is certainly one means of transferring resources from one generation to another. There seems, however, to be no compelling reason why it should be more efficient or convenient than other means, such as claims to ownership of land which has the benefit that the acceptability of the claims by next generations can hardly be in doubt. It might be asked why commodity money could not be used, but that would mean that people store commodities, which the use of money was supposed to make otiose in the first place. In a world with multilateral trade, where exchanges are not restricted to intergenerational transfers (and agents may even be immortal), money first may take the form of commodity money and fiduciary money may gradually come into use as trust in its acceptability by other agents grows, until at some point in time intrinsically worthless fiat (paper) money gains currency. Overlapping-generation models restrict severely the class of exchanges and consequently the possibilities of a medium of exchange to save on transactions costs. In fact, transactions costs are conspicuous by their absence in these models, because there are no search or other information costs, there being only one (consumption) good. In fairness, it must be mentioned that the proponents of this line of attack themselves see the assumption of costless communication, that is the absence of information (transactions) costs, as a major problem. They only wonder how such costs can be adequately modelled (Kareken and Wallace 1980 p. 9). But mentioning a problem is no substitute for solving it.

It may be concluded that overlapping-generation models fail to capture the medium-of-exchange function of money adequately (Ostroy 1989). Money has only a distinct role to play in the world pictured in those models if it is fiat money and it is not explained why money exists alongside other claims to commodities, or why it would be superior as an intergenerational transfer mechanism to a social security scheme. Besides, overlapping-generation models do not admit of agents that are immortal or behave as if they were (as in Barro's Ricardian equivalence model, see Chapter 2) and, as we have seen, a case can be made that even in such a world money as a medium of exchange finds a place (see Tobin 1980b). Overlapping-generation models do not provide a satisfactory rationale for the use of money and preclude situations where money could be useful.

CASH-IN-ADVANCE MODELS

Patinkin struggled with the problem of finding a rationale for the use of money in a general-equilibrium model. Clower attempted to cut the Gordian knot that Patinkin failed to untie by simply positing that, in a monetary economy, 'money buys goods and goods buy money; but goods do not buy goods' (Clower 1969b pp. 207-8). That, though, is not much better than adding money as an argument to the utility function, which Clower incidentally does too, as it leaves the contribution of money to welfare unexplained. In Patinkin's case money is held even if transactions could easily be made without money; Clower sets out to correct this situation by putting an arbitrary restriction on the system. For it is quite an arbitrary procedure to postulate the use of money in each and every transaction, as is common practice in this kind of model (other examples are Lucas 1980 and Eden 1986). In the real world, many transactions are still concluded without the use of money, not only within small groups such as households (where the division of labour usually does not involve money payments) but also on a larger scale, as in the case of compensation trade between business firms. Furthermore, in cash-in-advance models there is the restriction that at the beginning of any trading period the total demand for goods, expressed in the unit of account, cannot exceed the total volume of money, which excludes purchases paid for by receipts of money against goods and services sold during the period in question (Clower 1969b pp. 208-9).

The introduction of money can hardly be shown to have welfare-increasing effects if a cash-in-advance restriction is simply grafted on an already existing system of demand and supply equations. Nonetheless, if the aim is not to compare barter and monetary economies but to explore the effects of the use of a generally accepted medium of exchange, the procedure might be of some use. It can be of no more than limited use, though, as an inflexible transactions technology is imposed on the system which leaves no room for alternatives to the generally accepted medium of exchange, such as trade credit. Even if the capital market is not so perfect as to give borrowers an unlimited access to it at constant costs, to exclude trade credit altogether is swinging to the other extreme.

Lucas (1987 ch. VI) uses a moderate variant of the cash-in-advance procedure in order to introduce both the Tobin portfolio demand and the Baumol-Tobin inventory-theoretic demand aspects in his money demand model. He assumes that goods on any day can be bought with money acquired before, for instance in the securities market, but he provides for the possibility of obtaining trade credit. His model is a general-equilibrium model where the relative price of cash goods (goods paid for in cash on the spot) and credit goods (goods to be paid for one period later) is exactly equal to one plus the rate of interest. In other words, trade credit costs you exactly the same amount of interest as selling securities now in order to pay spot and forgoing the interest on these securities. IOUs apparently carry no risk premium in this model and the introduction of money can hardly be shown to increase welfare, because it does not save on information costs. It is simply postulated that agents have specific preferences over cash and credit goods.

Even with Lucas's addition of a credit market, cash-in-advance models still beg the question of why money is used, though they may be useful for studying the results of the use of money (as regards, for instance, the money-demand function).

FINANCIAL INTERMEDIATION

Money is used first and foremost because it saves on information costs. Financial intermediaries have come into being for similar reasons. If an economic agent needs a big loan, a number of investors will be involved. If every investor separately invested in the production of information on the borrower, there would be an enormous multiplication of costs. Alternatively, there could be a *free-rider problem*, as every investor would try to make use of the information produced by other investors, which might even lead to the absence of any information production (Diamond 1984 p. 393). Financial intermediaries specializing in information production can spare the investors the trouble and expense of gathering information themselves, just as middlemen reduce the costs of search in merchandise trade. Another service that financial intermediaries can provide is monitoring without disclosing the information found to a wider public, which firms may demand for reasons of competition strategy (Diamond 1984 p. 395).

If investors delegate information production to financial intermediaries, problems of a *principal-agent* type arise. The financial intermediary, acting as the agent of the investors, is inclined to spend as little as possible on information production. Again, we run into a moral hazard problem. Ramakrishnan and Thakor (1984 p. 417) suggest that the compensation each information producer receives (intermediaries in their model being made up of a number of individual information producers) should be contingent on some *ex post* indicator of the quality of the information. The market could be trusted, though, to provide incentives for intermediaries to give investors reliable information: investors who employ successful intermediaries make high returns. Such intermediaries build up an intangible asset: a good name; and if they want to stay in business it is in their own interest to maintain that name. Still, there is a problem here which suggests that fixed payments to investors are often the optimal arrangement (Diamond 1984 p. 404). Arrangements that give the investors a fixed payment and provide the intermediary with a residual income provide strong incentives for intermediaries not to let things slip. In order to secure a satisfactory residual income from debtors financial intermediaries would be saddled with the need to supervise their debtors' doings closely, though. Debtors have an incentive to withhold information. This problem seems to plague some Islamic banks, who grant credit in return for a share of the profits of their clients' activities (Tourani Rad 1989 p. 304). Closely monitoring borrowers of a financial intermediary may well be more difficult than monitoring the financial intermediaries themselves (which is, in the case of commercial banks at least, done by the monetary authorities in most countries, relieving depositors from the task). In cases where detailed information on a debtor's dealings is not easy to get, a fixed return for both the intermediary and the investors or the financial intermediary's depositors appears to be the optimal arrangement. For investors who are after a high return rather than low risk, a fixed return need not be optimal, but their need for monitoring the financing intermediary will be reduced if the intermediary (in this case an investment company rather than a commercial bank) contributes its own funds to the projects in question. The intermediary then has an additional reason, apart from maintaining its good name, for prudent behaviour. Of course many investors prefer fixed-income investments to variable-income investments. Financial intermediaries may either provide fixed-income assets by themselves investing for a fixed return or provide these and accepting themselves the risks of having variable-income assets and fixed-income liabilities. In both cases monitoring the borrowers is left to the intermediary.

Apart from their contribution to a reduction in total information costs, financial intermediaries of course provide investors with the opportunity of spreading risks at low transactions costs. Diversification of the intermediary's loan portfolio increases the probability that it will be able to pay the agreed returns to its investors or depositors. Like the principal-agent or moral-hazard problem, this results from market imperfections. Transaction costs are at least partly independent of the amount of the investment and small investors themselves can only diversify their portfolios at prohibitive cost. Market imperfections not only explain the use of money but also the existence of financial intermediaries.

CONCLUDING COMMENTS

It has proved quite a struggle to break loose from the Walras/Arrow-Debreu world in building monetary models. If money is simply added to a frictionless general-equilibrium system, it is well-nigh impossible to find a rationale for the holding of money. Nothing in terms of the consumption set available or the volume of production is gained by using money. Walrasian and Arrow-Debreu models do not provide a satisfactory framework for a meaningful study of money. They provide no room for introducing alternative transactions technologies other than restrictions on the possible set of transactions that can only be seen as arbitrary within the context of those models. General-equilibrium models with transaction costs that favour the use of a generally accepted medium of exchange, as developed by Niehans, leave unexplained what has to be explained first of all. Though they may be a step forward, still the use of money is imposed on the model rather than explained from the model, which takes us not much further than does the inclusion of real balances as an argument in the production function or the introduction of a cash-in-advance restriction. Explanations of the use of money, and of financial intermediaries for that matter, by the saving they provide on information costs resulting from moral hazard look much more convincing.

In single-period models, money is useful because it saves on information costs. In sequence models, money of course fulfils the same function, but in addition a sharp distinction between money and debt (IOUs) can be made there. Money is generally preferred over debt to settle transactions. In single-period models, no such distinction seems possible because the book entries deployed to keep track of the transactions can be viewed as inside money, that is money created against IOUs. Outside (fiat) money, which continues to be held by agents after claims are settled, can only find a satisfactory place in sequence economies. Sequence economies without a Walrasian auctioneer also provide an additional rationale for the use of money, namely the reduction in the cost of decision-making made possible by the use of money rather than IOUs, apart from any moral-hazard problems.

Models that assume the use of a generally accepted medium of exchange without explaining its use can in principle be useful in analysing the effects, if not the causes, of the use of money. Yet it is not clear to what extent, if at all, macromodels should take account of the work done in this area (Barro and Fischer 1976 p. 155, Fischer 1975 p. 158). Postulating a general cash-in-advance restriction for instance is a rather crude procedure. Possibly less account has to be taken of it the smoother the monetary mechanism functions. In cases of poorly functioning financial markets a cash-in-advance restriction might come in useful to characterize the working of the system. One remaining problem involves price setting, as a monetary economy must do without a Walrasian auctioneer and prices may be set out of equilibrium (Hentschel 1976 p. 93). Promising approaches, based on imperfect information, have been discussed in Chapter 3. More insight can probably be gained by highlighting the role of middlemen.

It is worth noticing that the function of money as a medium of exchange is really that of an asset that people prefer to hold between transactions. The medium-of-exchange quality follows from its quality as an asset. This fits in quite well with the standard textbook proposition that money is an asset, namely the asset with the highest degree of liquidity (for instance Ritter and Silber 1970 p. 17). Attempts by Hicks (1967) to construct a system with a money that lacks the asset or store-of-value character thus were bound to fail. His system resembles Niehans's one-period model, with agents who buy before they have been able to sell, running up a debt with a bank that has to be settled before the period ends. Now against agents who buy before they sell there are agents who sell before they buy. They are credited by the bank and can use their claim on the bank to buy goods and services, indeed are obliged to do so. Even if the claims on the bank can only be used within one period and cannot be carried over to the next period, they represent purchasing power during that period and hence must be considered assets, that is a store of value, if only for a restricted period of time. The concept of money without store-of-value character appears contradictory.

Finally, it goes without saying (or nearly so) that money and financial institutions presuppose imperfect markets, where agents, unlike in a Walrasian or Arrow-Debreu world, are not all price-takers and cannot be sure that the market will always accept or supply at the going price the full amount of goods or financial instruments they offer or demand. The possibility that within a geographic area more than one type of money circulates and the problems involved will be discussed in the next chapter and in Chapter 6.

5. The Monetary Order

PROPOSALS FOR FREE BANKING

Introduction: the existing monetary order

Even the Monetarists, however strong their championship of *laissez-faire* and competition, have never questioned the government monopoly of the supply of base money and have always stressed the need for the monetary authorities to regulate the total money supply. Where they differ from economists of a more interventionist bent is in their opposition to discretionary policies and, conversely, in their advocacy of following rules. This pertains not only to monetary policy but is characteristic for their view of the role of government in general (see Friedman 1962 ch. 2, on The Role of Government in a Free Society). In all this they, like virtually everybody else, have taken the existing monetary order for granted.

For our purposes we may describe the existing monetary order as a two-tiered system, one tier consisting of the central bank or the monetary authorities and the other made up of commercial banks. The monetary authorities provide base money, supervise the banking system, act as lender of last resort and conduct monetary policy (that is, they try to control the money supply and/or interest rates). The commercial banks run the payments system, grant credit and accept deposits. These deposits are denominated in a unit of account which is tied to the government-supplied base money. Deposits are of various kinds, one of which functions as the means of exchange. The banks stand ready to supply currency, that is, base money, to their depositors at par. One can, if one wishes, discern a third tier, made up of nonbank financial institutions. These institutions provide their clients with noncheckable deposits and other financial instruments. They themselves hold deposits in the commercial banks and payments made or received by their clients are effected through the intermediary of the commercial banks. Small banks in the US that use the payments facilities provided by larger correspondent banks with whom they keep deposits can also be seen as belonging to the third tier.

Alternatives for the existing monetary order

Latterly alternatives have been developed for the existing monetary order, coming from two directions. There are those who advocate a deregulated system with different currencies competing against each other, but with banks performing very much the same functions as in the present system. A second group of people sketches the outlines of a drastically deregulated system where the differences between banks and other financial institutions get blurred and money as such hardly exists. Unlike the first group they are, one feels, not so much driven by a wish to reform the present system as by intellectual curiosity (though the free banking reforms proposed by Glasner 1989 go far in the direction of the system sketched by this second group). In this chapter we describe these systems, which both are characterized by the absence of supervision by the monetary authorities or even the absence of monetary authorities and hence are cases of *free banking*. At the end of the chapter we shall also pay some attention to a less extreme form of free banking, namely a system of commercial banks using a common currency within a given geographical area but operating without supervision by monetary authorities.

Competing currencies

The present monetary order has come under attack from Friedrich Hayek, followed by Vaubel (see for instance Vaubel 1985). One of Hayek's main preoccupations has always been the debasement of the currency which may result, and in his view hardly ever fails to result, from the government's power over the money supply. Governments are under constant pressure to increase the money supply in order to ensure full employment or to fulfil other wishes of pressure groups (Hayek 1978b p. 21). This cannot but end in inflation, which in Hayek's Austrian analysis causes distortions in the production structure that can only be remedied through a depression. In Hayek's eyes Keynesian macroeconomics is the main culprit and in a sideswipe at Keynes he describes him as a kind of reincarnation of John Law, though he does not go so far as to blame him for the postwar inflationary policies carried out in his name, for which, in the British case, he tends to hold Kaldor responsible instead (Hayek 1978c p. 230). Governments cannot be trusted to provide people with sound money. They 'have incessantly and everywhere abused their trust to defraud the people' (Hayek 1978b p. 26). Money is 'a tool of government for fleecing us and for "managing" the economy' (Hayek 1984a p. 325; 1984b p. 31).

Hayek's solution is not the abolition of the right of goverments to create money, but the introduction of *competing currencies* or *currency competition* (hereafter CC), also labelled *parallel currencies* (Vaubel 1978 p. 90). In such a system different money units function in the same geographical area. Private firms should be allowed to create their own kind, or brand, of money, alongside governments or central banks. Besides, countries (first of all within the European Community) should leave their citizens free to use foreign currencies (Hayek 1978c p. 225, see on this subject also the detailed study by Vaubel, 1978). Hayek expects that CC would hardly affect retail transactions, but would most of all bear on the willingness to hold money (Hayek 1978c p. 227). Competition between issuers will lead to the solution that best fulfils the wishes of the public, possibly even to the use of ounces of gold (ibid.). It is worth noting that Hayek, even though for most of his life he sung the praises of the gold standard, already toyed with this idea before the Second World War (Hayek 1937 p. 77, see also Visser 1988). Hayek's ideas seem to have been embraced by the then British Chancellor of the Exchequer, Mr John Major, who in 1989 first proposed to introduce currency competition between all the national currencies in the European Community and later to introduce a 'hard' Ecu that would compete with the various national currencies and, if a success, could eventually replace these.

Hayek did not provide a detailed blueprint of a competitive system (Fischer 1986 p. 434, calls Hayek's proposal, 1984b, 'messianic, not analytic'). That would of course run counter to his philosophy of society, which holds that competition is incomparably superior to government planning as a means to find or invent the best solution to a problem (see Hayek 1944 and, on the subject of the monetary order, Hayek 1984a p. 324; 1984b p. 31). Nevertheless, the idea can be analysed and it will be contrasted in this chapter with the other extreme form of free banking, to which we now turn.

New monetary economics

The other strand in the clamour for freedom from state interference, known as the *New Monetary Economics* (NME), envisages a system where money as we know it hardly exists. NME, with Black (1970), Fama (1980) and Hall (1982) as its main originators and Greenfield and Yeager (1983) as its propagandists (who call it the *BFH system* after its originators), draws a picture of a financial system where banks are completely unregulated, apart possibly from the imposition of capital requirements (of course, if one is out to find predecessors, they are found; see Cowen and Kroszner 1987). There are no reserve requirements and there is no central bank. Banks create deposits as part of their loan-making or investment business. These deposits are rather like shares in a money market mutual or an investment fund and therefore in principle have no fixed value in terms of the unit of account. The dividing line between demand deposits and other liabilities of the financial institutions gets blurred. Payments are made as in the existing system by writing cheques against deposits or by making remittances. For some kinds of payments, currency is more convenient than deposits. NME does not exclude the creation of coins and banknotes (Yeager 1989 p. 370). These could be provided by the financial institutions themselves or by the government, which could stand ready to provide currency against payment into its accounts with the banks.

Banks have two main functions in this system. Firstly, they provide a book-keeping system whereby claims held on them by the public are transferred from one depositor to another, that is, they provide a payments mechanism. Secondly, they manage portfolios of financial instruments; they are financial intermediaries. A common unit of acccount is used. Unlike CC proponents, NME adherents tend to set great store by the informational advantages of using a common unit of account. Such a unit may be determined by the government (on a noncoercive basis) and may be defined, for instance, as a certain amount of a good or a bundle of commodities. It could also be left to the market to agree on a unit of account. Note that only a definition is involved; there is no convertibility of the deposits into the bundle of goods making up the unit of account. NME is quite different from a commodity reserve standard, it is meant to be a one-tier system and the goods making up the bundle consequently need not be storable. If the unit of account is defined as a bundle of a large number of goods, prices of individual goods may of course fluctuate, but the general price level in terms of the unit of account will be quite stable. The unit of account and the means of payment are entirely separated.

From the viewpoint of the NME, the usual views on money supply do not apply in an unregulated environment, if only because the quantity of money is not defined. Constructs such as the quantity theory are only considered valid in a system with government regulation and as a result of government regulation (Hall 1982 p. 1552). In order words, the behaviour of the money supply as depicted in economics textbooks is a result of legal restrictions.

MORE ON THE WORKING OF FREE-BANKING SYSTEMS

Currency competition

Under CC the principles of a free market would be applied to money production as it is to any other private industry. The owner of a certain 'brand' of money, say the dollar, could offer them to the public all over the world and could sell licences to produce and sell this product. This is unlike the present situation, where Eurobanks can produce dollars without the American monetary authorities having any say in it (Salin 1984 pp. 13-4).

Money producers would be held back from creating too much money by the fear of depositors withdrawing their funds. But Hayek admits that banks face a problem when trying to keep the purchasing power of their deposits constant. A purchasing power guarantee of sorts is involved. This implies that the banks must stand ready to supply the public in exchange for one unit of their own money with such an amount of other kinds or brands of money as would be needed to buy the bundle of commodities which defines that unit (Hayek 1984b pp. 37ff.). Friedman rightly observes that for such a guarantee to be given, the banks should hold assets carrying a fixed purchasing-power guarantee, which is hard to imagine unless governments issue securities with a purchasing-power guarantee (Friedman 1984 p. 43). A peculiar problem could arise if depositors want to change large amounts of other brands of money for one particular bank's money. That bank would be saddled with the problem of finding sufficiently attractive investment outlets for the funds received. If it did not freely accept the other kinds of money at fixed rates of exchange *vis-à-vis* other currencies, its own money would appreciate in terms of other monies. This would make loans supplied by that bank less attractive, as borrowers would in effect face a rise in the real rate of interest charged. In order to keep the purchasing power of the money they create roughly constant and to curb an excessive inflow of funds lest difficulties arise in the future, banks would have to adjust their deposit and lending rates or to vary the margin between the buying and selling rates of other monies (refusing to accept new deposits would amount to inconvertibility and would endanger the system; hence, it is ruled out).

Hayek expects that such a system would lead to a number of monies that all have a relatively stable purchasing power and are also stable in terms of each other. If they are stable in terms of each other, that would be the result of the banks' attempts to keep the purchasing power of their monies constant, not of any agreement to maintain fixed rates. Consequently, there need be no fear of the working of Gresham's Law (Hayek 1984a p. 326, Starbatty 1982). 'Bad' money, that is money which depreciates in terms of goods, will not drive 'good' money from circulation, as it will depreciate in terms of 'good' money. It is quite possible, though, that 'bad' money stays in circulation notwithstanding this depreciation, provided deposits pay a high enough rate of interest to compensate for the fall in purchasing power. Nor is there any certainty that exchange rates could not fluctuate violently.

New monetary economics

In the NME system, there is a common unit of account. The government would not itself create money, except possibly for currency to meet the need for small change. Its budget deficit would in its entirety have to be covered by borrowings from the public or the banks. It would conduct its financial affairs like any other economic agent through its accounts with the banking system.

Deposits can be seen as claims on or shares in the investment portfolio of a bank (including IOUs bought by the banks in the course of granting credit). Fluctuations in the value of the bank's investments, expressed in the unit of account, are reflected in changes in the value of the depositors' claims. Greenfield and Yeager (1983 p. 308) feel that the financial institutions could provide the public with currency in the form of shares. It is not quite clear how they could adjust the circulating shares for losses and profits, though. Admittedly payment of interest on paper circulating as medium of exchange has not been unknown in history, but such paper bore a fixed rate of interest (the use of bills of exchange as a medium of exchange in eighteenth-century and early nineteenth-century England is well known, but there were many other cases; see Goodhart 1988a p. 31 for references). The idea of Fama (1983 p. 11) to issue currency with a fluctuating value, reported daily by the media, does not look very practicable either. Alternatively, financial institutions could issue debt instruments with a fixed value in terms of the unit of account (Fama

1980 p. 41). The investment portfolio of such an institution could consist of relatively riskless assets or, alternatively, other depositors would have to bear a higher risk.

Money growth and the price level

Under CC there are identifiable money assets. It is claimed that their volume need not be controlled in order to keep inflation in check; no such thing as a Friedmanian money growth rule is needed. This is because money issuers will in their own interest try to maintain the purchasing power of their monetary liabilities. In an NME world, the very idea of a money growth rule, or of any other way of monetary control, is irrelevant, because the dividing lines between money and other assets are fluid (Yeager 1985 p. 103). It may nonetheless be asked if overissue of money or bank deposits is really impossible. Do bankers under CC always behave according to their enlightened self-interest as defined by Hayek and is a constant price level under NME always ensured given that there is no identifiable money supply? Bankers are of course constrained by the fact that an overly enthusiastic credit expansion leads to their depositors making net payments to other banks' clients, but that does not necessarily keep the whole banking system from granting credit too easily. When all banks increase the volume of outstanding credit in step, the increase in total spending can conceivably outstrip the increase in the supply of goods and services, causing inflation.

We have seen above that under CC banks can offer their depositors an interest compensation for any depreciation of the money they supply *vis-à-vis* other monies. If no fixed exchange rates are maintained, overissues result in depreciations and are not stemmed. In that case, we have a system resembling Wicksell's *pure credit economy* (Wicksell 1965) and Gurley and Shaw's *inside money economy* (Gurley and Shaw 1960 pp. 253 ff, see also Visser 1974 pp. 138-40, 150-1). In those systems banks can, by lending at rates differing from the *natural rate*, that is the equilibrium rate of interest at which the volume of savings equals the volume of lending, make the price level rise or fall without limit (apart from the lower limit of zero, of course). In Hayek's view, this cannot be a serious problem, as other suppliers would step in to satisfy the public's desire for stable money. Interest payments are a poor substitute for stable purchasing power, the more so as demand (chequable) deposits generally carry no interest rate that fully compensates for inflation and taxes are normally levied on nominal interest rates, with usually no full adjustment for inflation being made. Hence, interest payments are probably no satisfactory substitute for a stable medium of payment and only an imperfect substitute for time and savings deposits denominated in a stable money.

Under NME, deposits with banks are claims on a fraction of the bank's investment portfolio which will generally have a fluctuating but not systematically rising or falling value in terms of the standard bundle defining the unit of account. If a bank grants too much credit, that can only mean that the IOUs it obtains are viewed with suspicion by the market, resulting in a fall in the value of the deposits of existing depositors, expressed in the unit of account. Put differently, the price level would not be affected.

So far, we have abstracted from the impact of notes and coin. If deposits are issued to excess under CC by an individual bank, this results in net payments to clients of other banks, which forces the bank to exercise restraint. Under NME, overenthusiastic buying of IOUs (that is, credit creation) also leads to a deficit in the clearing with other banks, but net payments can be effected by selling off part of the investment portfolio. No inflation need result. Notes and coin however, unlike deposits, remain in circulation. By issuing notes financial institutions have at their disposal a cheap means of acquiring interest-bearing assets. Nonetheless, if banks under CC aim at a stable purchasing power of their money, they will take care to restrict the volume of notes and coin they bring into circulation.

As for NME, McCallum (1985 pp. 35-6) expresses the fear that, if financial institutions bring notes into circulation, they will be tempted to issue these to excess. Prices, even those of the standard bundle, would in his view rise in terms of the unit of account. Put differently, the unit of account would be at a discount in terms of the standard bundle. Against this, it can be argued that the summed value of a bank's liabilities, expressed in the unit of account, equals the market value of the bank's investment portfolio. Any excessive issue of banknotes with a fixed nominal value (in terms of the unit of account) would be at the cost of the value of the deposits or claims on or shares in the investment portfolio. Contrary to McCallum's view, it seems that an excessive note issue need not put the standard bundle's use as the unit of account in jeopardy. It may be expected, furthermore, that the depositors and shareholders of an overexpanding bank would correct its management or that depositors would withdraw their deposits, which would force the banks to shut up shop if they refused to mend their ways.

CLAIMED BENEFITS OF FREE BANKIING

New monetary economics

Advocates of free banking claim that it would do away with a number of the problems plaguing economies with a heavily regulated two-tiered financial sector. In this section we start with NME instead of CC, because a systematic enumeration of the advantages of NME has been given by Greenfield and Yeager and the exposition will benefit if we reproduce their listing first. The advantages claimed by Greenfield and Yeager (1983 pp. 308ff) for NME, resulting from the absence of money as we know it whilst the disadvantages of a barter system are yet avoided, are the following:

1. There would be a stable unit of account, which has obvious benefits for borrowing and lending, calculation etcetera.
2. The government would come under financial discipline. It could no longer resort to inflationary finance.
3. Unrestricted competition between financial institutions would exert discipline on them and would provide the much-vaunted spur to innovation which in Hayek's view is what characterizes a market economy, whilst wasteful attempts to get around regulations would be a thing of the past.
4. The absence of base money, that is, the reduction of the financial system to one tier, would bring more stability. There would no longer be multiple contractions or expansions of the money supply in response to changes in the base money supply. Nor would there be runs on the collectivity of banks as occurred during banking crises before the Second World War (or before the introduction of deposit insurance; in this respect the situation would not differ much from the existing system). Put differently, there would be no *internal drain*, that is, no substitution of bank money into base money and banks would not face any liquidity problems. Runs on poorly-managed financial institutions could of course occur, buth these would not spread to other institutions (again not much different than the existing situation, where the central bank fulfils its role as a lender of last resort in accordance with Walter Bagehot's famous advice to the central bank to lend readily in times of panic, see Bagehot 1920 pp. 48, 298).
5. With the disappearance of money as a clearly defined separate

entity, macroeconomic monetary disorders would disappear as well. There could be no excess supply of or excess demand for money rocking either the general price level or the level of real activity.

Currency competition

Hayek's competing-currencies world lacks a common unit of account, but units of account could be stable in terms of purchasing power. Individual banking firms may fail and their depositors may suffer a loss, but creditors holding claims on other economic agents expressed in the unit of account in which the failed banks' money was expressed do not see the value of their claims impaired (Hayek 1984b pp. 40-1). The credit system would not suffer, therefore, as it would in a situation where bank runs are contagious and develop into a deep depression. Governments would under CC come under financial discipline, too. If the government resorted to inflationary financed budget deficits, it would bloat the money supply. The money it created would fall in value and consequently run the danger of being driven from the market. Vaubel (1985 p. 550) believes that competition between central bank monies could help to abate inflation in still another way. People in inflation-ridden countries would hold their governments responsible for the fall in the value of money, both in terms of purchasing power and in terms of other currencies. For these effects to occur it does not, however, seem necessary to allow full-fledged currency competition. The third and the fourth points in favour of the NME system would go for the competing currencies case as well. As for the fifth point, though Hayek does not expect a blurring of the boundaries between money and other assets, his system might conceivably be less prone to macroeconomic disorders from monetary sources than a two-tiered system. Multiple money supply expansions and contractions in response to changes in the base money supply would not occur. Substantial changes in the volume of any type of money in circulation would not have far-reaching consequences because holders would fear a fall in the purchasing power of the money concerned or, in the case of a contraction, debtors would fear a rise in the purchasing power and in both cases a substitution by other types of money would follow (unless of course interest rates provide full inflation or deflation compensation).

POSSIBLE PROBLEMS WITH FREE BANKING

Economies of scale in the use and the production of money

On a very general level, a case can be made for the abolition of government regulation if the means of payment can be seen as in no way different from other goods. But that is a very big 'if'. In a way money as a means of payment resembles a telephone exchange, and the use of money as a unit of account resembles a language. Comparisons like these suggest that a kind of monopoly might be useful (Hellwig 1985 p. 572). There are external economies in the use of money. With more people using a certain type of money, the utility of using that kind of money increases. Increased use of a certain type of money tends to reduce its transactions costs, including information costs (Brunner and Meltzer 1971, Tullock 1975). It is much easier to have to use one language than several languages; anyone who has experienced the American telephone system will understand that it is easier to live with one network than with a greater number. More currencies mean higher transaction costs, prominent among them information costs, the more so if exchange rates between the various currencies are not well predictable. These costs include the costs of investigating the solidity of the money supplier (Illing 1985 p. 124). People may be of course be interested in investing their wealth in financial instruments denominated in different units of account, in order to better spread their risks. When they are free to do so, as they are in a number of countries, that does not imply the use of various types of money simultaneously as means of payment (which Hayek admittedly did not expect).

Another question is whether there are also economies of scale in the production of money, which would imply a natural monopoly. The disappearance of very small banks suggests that scale economies indeed occur, but probably only over a certain range. Nor do these economies seem to be very strong (see for empirical research Benston 1972, Gilbert 1983, Humphrey 1987).

In a completely deregulated system, another aspect comes to the fore. With no lender of last resort, economic agents will be more careful in choosing a financial institution with which to hold their deposits. Those institutions will have to invest in creating a good name, in what Claassen (1984 p. 51) calls the *quality of money*, first of all by good behaviour, but bigness also helps to create confidence. There are, it appears, strong forces that restrict competition.

Money and a government monopoly

Even if money were a natural monopoly or if economies of scale in the use of money would justify a restriction of competition, it does not follow that a government monopoly is called for. The government may instead regulate a private monopoly or auction a monopoly licence. In a two-tiered system as we know it the government of course only has a monopoly for the supply of base money. In a one-tier system a natural monopoly might induce the government to throw up impediments to other potential suppliers. However, we do not, as Hayek and Vaubel stress, know what an optimal type of money looks like, and a government monopoly denies the market the opportunity to find out which solution is best (Hayek 1978b p. 24, Vaubel 1984 pp. 46-7). If the government does have a natural advantage in the production of money, that should become apparent in the market place, without restrictions on entry for other potential producers and without subsidies for the government money supplier (Vaubel, ibid.).

Instability

Another moot point is the claim that a lender of last resort is superfluous under free banking. Is it really that far-fetched to imagine that a failure of one banking institution could lead to runs on others? (See for a model of bank runs showing the impact of deposit insurance, Diamond and Dybvig 1983.) Banks can only function if they are able and willing to change the claims their clients hold on them for claims on other banks on demand. If banks hold claims on problem banks, a failure of those problem banks would obviously undermine their solidity in the eyes of the public. Banks that do not hold claims on a failed bank might be affected as well. The result would be a scramble for currency provided by the monetary authorities, if that is available. In other words, a classical internal drain would occur; a typical case for central bank intervention. But that would in effect mean that we were back to a two-tiered system. In a system without currency provided by the central government the public would have no choice but to stick with their bank money, though they might try to substitute claims on problem banks with claims on a safer one. Bigger banks would probably be preferred and the tendency for an oligopoly or a monopoly would be reinforced.

With various currencies vying for the public's favour, there is a danger of another kind of instability, especially under CC. The confidence of the public as regards the future purchasing power of a currency may be weakened or increased by a multitude of causes. This may lead to erratic behaviour of the exchange rates between the currencies, as we have seen on international currency markets after 1973. Hayek, however, expects exchange rates under CC to remain quite stable and it is, indeed, well conceivable that money suppliers seek to create confidence in their products by guaranteeing convertibility into another currency or other currencies at fixed rates. But this could lead to the emergence of a *dominant currency*, held by banks as a reserve against deposits, or of a small number of dominant currencies, each one concentrated in a certain geographical area. In that case we are back with a two-tiered system, which might consist of a few blocks of currencies, cutting across national frontiers.

Deposit money is created by a stroke of the pen or rather by touching a few keys on a keyboard. We have already considered the question if there is no danger of private money suppliers trying to expand money production to the point where marginal revenue equals the putative zero marginal cost. The answer was no, because the marginal cost of overexpansion, in terms of loss of confidence on the part of the public in the stability of the purchasing power of money, would be very high. Banks then have an incentive to overexpand only if the monies produced by the different suppliers are indistinguishable homogeneous products. This would mean that they issued identical notes and coins, which they could do under NME but obviously do not need to do. In case they do, individual banks can reap the benefits of overissue (that is, cheap funding) themselves and shift the costs for the most part to others (but if every bank acts in this way, they will all ultimately suffer).

The public will only be willing to hold a bank's liabilities if the bank has created sufficient confidence in its product. For this it must have a clean record of noninflationary money creation and, especially at entering the business of banking but later as well, it must hold a supply of other means of payments and stand ready to convert the public's deposit holdings on demand into other kinds of money or financial assets or even bundles of commodities (Klein 1974 p. 434). There remains the possibility that banks in a Hayekian world first create confidence and, next, use the good name they have created to harvest a rich profit by suddenly expanding the volume of their deposits, producing a high rate of inflation that nobody had expected. This phenomenon is called *dynamic inconsistency*. A bank will only act in this way if the short-term profit expected from deceiving the public outweighs the resulting long-term loss from eating into its 'brand-name capital'. With the public having the choice to demand other currencies at will, such behaviour can, however, never be long drawn out. The money issued by an overexpanding bank depreciates not only in terms of goods but in terms of other currencies and clients defect to other banks. Or, with fixed rates of exchange, other banks see their claims on the overexpanding bank increase and will demand payment. The overexpanding bank is in this way forced into discipline or fails. In the latter case, depositors lose their money. There will always remain a principal-agent type of problem in the relationship between a bank and its clients (as stressed by Illing 1985 p. 125, and Summers 1983 p. 161). A bank's creditors cannot closely monitor the activities of banks as intermediaries in the credit system and the risk that they will be deceived by a bank is never entirely absent.

Further problems

The separation of the unit of account and the means of payment under NME may not be to the public's liking. Claims on a part of a financial institution's asset portfolio vary in value, which is tantamount to saying that the value of one's balance with a financial institution fluctuates in terms of the unit of account. In other words, the public may prefer to hold demand deposits; which, as we have seen, the financial institutions could provide along with other liabilities if some of the public were willing to run higher risks. Another point, advanced by White (1984 p. 707), is that a payments system with demand deposits is probably much cheaper to run than a payments system where shares in mutual funds have to be transferred.

It has also been suggested that if there are more money suppliers, there is a greater danger of counterfeit, which creates higher social costs. In the free-banking literature little attention is paid to notes and coin, but the problem cannot be ignored. It is doubtful, though, whether it would be more serious than in the present situation where bank branches accept foreign banknotes. Because of the economies of scale in the use and the production of money referred to above, the total number of money suppliers would most probably be relatively low, which would keep counterfeit problems within manageable proportions.

IS A ONE-TIERED SYSTEM CONCEIVABLE?

The discussion so far is predicated on the idea of a one-tiered financial system. But is it conceivable that such a system, if it were ever introduced, would remain unchanged in its main characteristics? The answer is probably no. There are strong reasons for believing that a one-tiered system would of itself develop into a two-tiered system.

The main reason is that both under CC and under NME, financial institutions need a means of payment to settle net positions *vis-à-vis* each other. As for NME, Greenfield and Yeager (1986 p. 848) draw a picture of claims being settled at a clearinghouse with 'issuers transfer[ring] not quantities of the standard bundle itself, but redemption property *worth* as many standard bundles as the number of units to be settled'. But what makes up that redemption property? It may mean claims held by one bank on another, but banks will only be willing to open credit lines to other banks on a limited scale. It may also mean financial assets held by the remitting bank as part of its investment portfolio. The latter solution is suggested by Greenfield and Yeager (1983 p. 307), though they hardly address the question seriously. But settlement of clearing balances by means of transferring a bundle of financial assets would imply relatively high transaction costs, not least because one bank's preferred portfolio differs from another bank's preferred portfolio and negotiations are needed for each transaction. Problems would also arise because the prices of the securities fluctuate over a day and the parties involved could try to influence these (White 1986 p. 851). It is highly probable, then, that one type of asset evolves into a dominant money, be it a currency created by a monetary authority or a big private money issuer, or gold or other commodities; and in that case we are back with a two-tiered system.

A dominant money arises precisely because banks feel a need for a means of exchange with a fixed nominal value (under NME). Hence, prices will be expressed in terms of that dominant money. The price level may fluctuate again, depending on the demand for and the supply of the dominant money. Even a stable supply of the dominant money would not guarantee a stable price level or the absence of multiple credit contractions and expansions. Shifts in the proportion of transactions conducted with bank deposits relative to those conducted in the dominant money (in the form of notes and coin) could very well occur (Helpman 1983), that is, the familiar problems of a variable money multiplier could crop up again.

The tendency for banks to hold a dominant money as a reserve against deposits will be further strengthened because international payments, or payments between currency areas, have to be made. As in the present world, economic agents could save on transaction costs by routing transactions between two currencies via a third one. This is because the spread between selling and buying rates tends to be much smaller for such transactions than for direct exchange between currencies for which there is only a thin market (McKinnon 1979 ch. 2).

It is not only the banks that will tend to use a dominant money. The public can also be expected to set store by it. It may prefer to hold deposits with banks that guarantee convertibility into a dominant money with a proven low tendency to lose purchasing power. It seems as if a two-tiered system can hardly be avoided.

CONCLUDING REMARKS

Deregulation and inflation

It has been claimed that the devaluation of money is a result of governments pursuing ill-conceived short-term macroeconomic aims (apart from Hayek, see also Tullock 1975 p. 497). This in itself does not seem sufficient reason for a shift to NME or CC. Free financial markets imply competition in the sense that economic agents are free to choose any currency for their payments, investments and contracts. But competition between currencies might still remain within the boundaries of a two-tiered system with government- or central-bank-created base money. The problem then remains of how to keep inflationary policies by the monetary authorities in check. If, as has been argued, the seat of the trouble is the short time-horizon of the policy makers, one solution is to leave monetary policy with people who have a vested interest in keeping inflation low. This is an argument in favour of having relatively independent central banks, as in Germany, Switzerland and The Netherlands and as proposed by the Delors Committee for the European System of Central Banks. Central bankers generally are judged on their success in keeping inflation at bay. Moreover, their tenure is generally longer than that of cabinet ministers, so they are less likely to pursue expansionary policies and saddle their successors with the resulting problems.

From this point of view, there do not seem to be compelling reasons to forbid experiments with private financial institutions supplying money with a more stable purchasing power. Indeed, in many countries banks are free to do so. The private Ecu is a point in case. Experience suggests that such alternative monies will not play a large role. Even in the turbulent 1970s the public was not much interested in deposits denominated in units devised by private banks (Lomax 1983 p. 274). Freedom of choice for the public may help, though, to stimulate good behaviour by governments or at least to give economic agents the opportunity to shift to other currencies. Sizeable shifts apparently only occur in countries plagued by very high and fluctuating inflation rates or by uncertainty with regard to the rate of exchange (see the examples mentioned in the last section of Chapter 7, on currency substitution). Still, it is not uncommon in EC countries to find 10 or 20 per cent of deposits held by residents in resident banks denominated in foreign currencies, but as these holdings seem motivated largely by interest-rate considerations and interest rates may compensate for inflation, a moderate inflation need not frighten depositors away.

Given the increasing liberalization of financial markets, competition between various national currencies may well intensify. This can happen without a radical transformation of the present system, which is undesirable anyway. To take a leaf from Hayek's book, the present system is the result of a development spanning centuries rather than decades. It should be open to further evolution, but a radical transformation could only do harm. It seems likely that, with a move to a more competitive system, the public will prefer an existing currency with a stable purchasing power over a new currency created by a private institution. This, however, is no reason to prevent them from trying.

The world pictured by NME seems unlikely ever to emerge. It is unrealistic in its assumptions about the preferences of the public, which probably prefers deposits with a fixed nominal value and it may be expensive to run. Some versions of NME, notably the one developed by Fama (1980), seem theoretically flawed. In his model, anything can serve as the unit of account. The model is in essence a Walrasian system in which the real sector determines relative prices and financial institutions are irrelevant to the general equilibrium solution of the system. Illing (1985 p. 116) argues in his critique of this model that perfect capital markets do not provide the right framework for analysing banks, just as the Arrow-Debreu intertemporal general equilibrium model leaves no place for money. With a perfect capital market, the public does not need banks for the provision of finance (Hoover 1988a pp. 157 ff, 1988b ch. 5). Debts could be settled by a direct transfer of financial instruments from debtors to creditors and even the payment mechanism provided by Fama's banks seems superfluous.

Less extreme forms of free banking

CC and NME can be seen as attempts at creating a one-tiered financial system. Less extreme forms of free banking are conceivable as well. These would boil down to a system like the present one, but without central bank or other monetary authorities. There would be commercial banks that create money and use a common unit of account. Such a system existed in Scotland from the beginning of the eigtheenth century until 1846 and in at least some states of the United States during various periods before the creation of the Federal Reserve System in 1913, to name the two most famous cases. It was seen by Bagehot (1920 pp. 101, 104, 275-7) as the best system to make bankers behave responsibly, because there would be no central bank to bail them out, and by Mises (1966 pp. 443-8) as the best system to prevent inflation, because governments only interfere to expand credit. No ideals to create a one-tiered system would be involved. The question then is how the system would deal with such problems as inflation and financial crises. There would be no monetary policy, which bears on the inflation problem, and no prudential supervision, which brings the possibility of liquidity problems and financial crises to the fore.

It seems that inflation before the First World War was hardly ever a problem in countries where the government refrained from inflationary finance. The possibility of financial crises was a more common threat. A case can be made for the proposition that, if there is a danger of a panic spreading to many financial institutions, rational bank managers would decide to help their brethren in difficulty. This happened in Scotland. When the Ayr Bank failed in 1772, two of the three big banks announced that they would accept the notes of the failed bank, which helped to avert a panic (Gorton 1985 p. 270).

In the Scottish case, there was a small number of big institutions that could easily act in concert and each of which could to a large extent internalize the benefits of a rescue operation. With a bigger number of banks and no dominant big banks, history shows that other mechanisms to stem a crisis can develop. In the United States, banks set up clearing houses that in times of crisis evolved into lenders of last resort, even creating their own paper money, whose legality was dubious but whose effects were felicitous (see Dwyer and Gilbert 1989 on how the clearing houses coped with bank runs). Prudential supervision of a kind was involved as well, in the cases where the clearing houses only admitted banks observing a certain minimum capital ratio. A large literature on free banking in the United States has developed. The upshot seems to be that the system kept the losses to the public from the note issues by private banks to a minimum, but probably more in New York (Timberlake 1984) than in other states, notably the frontier states with a much lower degree of financial sophistication (Rockoff 1985).

Two cases where free banking functioned satisfactorily may be sufficient to show that a financial system can in principle do without prudential supervision or a lender of last resort, but they do not prove that it is always the best solution. Examples such as the secondary banking crisis in the United Kingdom in the early 1970s and the 1981 financial crisis in Chile (Harberger 1986 p. 237, Corbo and de Melo 1987 p. 137), let alone the American banking crisis in the early 1930s when the Fed just let it run its course, suggest it is not. Besides, as Friedman and Schwartz (1986 p. 50) argue, free banking in Scotland profited from special circumstances: shareholders of banks assumed unlimited liability for the obligations of banks and generally were wealthy people well-known in their local communities and with a reputation for honouring their obligations. Nonetheless, banks did fail and, moreover, the big three banks restricted competition (Cowen and Kroszner 1989; see on the Scottish banks also Cameron 1967). The record for the US seems less satisfactory, even if the excesses of *wildcat banking* may not have been as bad as is sometimes alleged (in the words of Hammond 1948 p. 6: 'It was typical of the free banks that they monetized the state debts by purchasing bonds with their own circulating notes and then disappeared in order to avoid having to redeem the notes. They had to be hunted for in the woods, among the retreats of wildcats'). Bank failures were quite common and holders of the notes issued by these banks were not always paid the par value (Kahn 1985).

Both the Scottish system, where banks held reserves with London banks and gold functioned as base money, and the American system in the free banking states, where clearing houses sprang up and government paper money circulated, were in effect two-tiered systems. Indeed, a one-tiered system would of itself develop into a two-tiered one because of the fact that small banks would needed the services of bigger ones (correspondent banks) for effecting payments and clearinghouse associations would spring up (Selgin and White 1987). In two-tiered systems where a common unit of account is used and the liabilities of one institution are to be exchanged at par for those of another one, liquidity crises can appear and a lender of last resort is next to indispensable. As Kindleberger (1978 ch. 11, 1987 pp. 294-5) perhaps more than anybody else has emphasized, a lender of last resort provides stability to the financial system. In the international sphere this role could be played by a hegemonic power, whose currency could function as a dominant money; within one currency area either a central bank or an institution set up by the banks themselves is called for. But which would provide the better solution? Hellwig (1985 p. 538) is of the opinion that economic theory has too little to say on these matters for any firm conclusions to be drawn on the question whether government regulation of the banking system should be abolished, yet there are good arguments in favour of supervision by monetary authorities. As Goodhart (1988a pp. 37ff) argues on the basis of historical evidence, in the case of private banks with which other banks hold deposits or a clearinghouse dominated by a small number of large banks there is always scope for conflicts of interests. A central bank which is not driven by the profit motive, or does at least not compete with the commercial banks, is much better placed to help the banking industry run the payments mechanism and act as a lender of last resort. If close supervision is deemed necessary because of the moral hazard problem, that is, to prevent swindling, again a public authority such as the central bank of course is the appropriate institution. If deposit insurance in practice covers all deposits without limits and in that way increases moral hazard problems, because depositors only go after high interest rates and have no incentive to worry about the solidity of financial institutions, close supervision is even more called for. This was forcefully brought home by the crisis in the American savings and loans industry. That crisis suggests that full deposit insurance is not such a good idea. The Dutch system, where only the deposits of private persons and some nonprofit institutions are guaranteed up to a modest amount, appears preferable, with an eye to reducing moral hazard. Under free banking the public would more actively monitor the financial institutions.

Finally, to revert to the question of monetary policy, free banking in the sense of commercial banks creating money (unlike NME) and using a common unit of account (unlike CC) is hardly conceivable without some control on the volume of base money, as in the existing system. Given that a two-tiered system is likely to develop, control of the volume of base money (the money created in the top tier of the financial system) is necessary in order to check inflationary pressures, or deflationary forces, for that matter, unless that money is freely convertible into a basket of commodities. For practical purposes, a unit of the money could be made convertible into a fluctuating amount of one good, say gold, representing the value of a fixed basket of commodities (depending on the relative price of gold and the basket). If there is a stable demand function on the part of the banks and the public for the base money, in the sense that the relative demand for base money and bank money and hence the money multiplier is stable or predictable, it suffices for the monetary authorities to control the volume of base money if they wish to prevent inflation or deflation (or, alternatively, they can control the rate of interest).

6. The Demand for Money

STABILITY AND INSTABILITY

One cornerstone of monetarist thinking has been the stability of the money-demand function. If money demand were not a stable function of a restricted number of variables, stabilization of the growth rate of the money supply would be of little help in stabilizing the real sector of the economy. An enormous amount of research effort has gone into estimating money-demand functions, which for the two decades or so up to about 1974 gave little cause for doubts about their stability (see for discussions of research on money demand Laidler 1969 ch. 8, Bank of England 1972, Boorman 1972). But in that year money-demand functions seemed to go haywire, particularly for the United States. Projections based on money-demand functions estimated on pre-1974 data overpredicted money demand by unprecedented margins (Goldfeld 1989 p. 138). Also, around 1980 money demand forecast errors for the US became very large and there were problems with the demand for money function for other countries as well (Hafer 1985, Laidler 1990b). Research for the post-1974 period has not succeeded in answering all the questions thrown up by the apparent breakdown of the conventional money-demand functions. It was found that some specifications of the money-demand function and some definitions of money perform reasonably well for some countries and some periods, while others do for other countries or other periods (Andersen 1985, Atkinson, Blundell-Wignall, Randoni and Ziegelschmidt 1984, Den Butter and Fase 1981, Quintyn 1986 p. 80). Often, considerable instability, that is, shifts in the coefficients of the money-demand function, is found, with financial innovations usually seen as the main culprit (see Akhtar 1983, with a survey of empirical research, Judd and Scadding 1982, also with such a survey and Bank for International Settlements 1986 for a detailed analysis of the innovations involved). Other possible causes of instability mentioned in the literature are changes in the exchange rate regime and institutional changes (Boughton 1981). Institutional changes resulted in particular from the deregulation movement in financial markets that started in the 1970s and gathered momentum in the 1980s (Lamfalussy 1990). Examples are the lifting of deposit rate ceilings in Japan and the United States, the ongoing abolition of restrictions in many countries on the kinds of activities which financial institutions are allowed to engage in and the kinds of assets they may hold or the kinds of deposits they may offer, and the liberalization of international capital flows in 1979 in the United Kingdom, in Japan over the years and in France and Italy during the run-up to the first phase of the Economic and Monetary Union that started on 1 July 1990. Such measures are likely to change the relationship between money demand and its explanatory variables, as they translate into revisions of decisions on portfolio composition and into different reactions to interest rate changes, to name the most important effects.

Only the Federal Reserve Bank of St Louis seemed to cling to the idea of stability through thick and thin. As for the 1970s, its research workers argued that stable money-demand functions could be found by including long interest rates and redefining money (Hafer and Hein 1979 p. 14). Further, it was asserted that shocks such as the imposition of credit controls by the Carter administration in 1980 and the nationwide legalization of interest-bearing chequable accounts in 1981 had caused the increased forecast errors (or increased variability in the income velocity of money) found round those years, but that the errors tended to cancel out in the longer run (Hafer 1985 p. 24). Exclusion of interest-bearing chequable deposits was found to reduce the instability of income velocity and hence the instability of the money-demand function (Hafer 1984; see for similar conclusions on US money demand in the 1980s Darby, Mascaro and Marlow 1989). But even the Federal Reserve Bank of St Louis did not succeed in explaining all instability away. On one occasion it was concluded that the US money-demand function had shifted downward in 1974 without affecting the income and interest elasticities (the constant a_0 in equation 6.1 below was found to have jumped to a lower value; Hafer and Hein 1982). More recently, they have been wrestling with a puzzling drop in the velocity of narrow money: money demand-functions estimated on pre-1982 data seriously underestimated narrow money demand (Stone and Thornton 1987). A combination of financial innovations, a sharp increase in the volume of interest-bearing components of the money supply and cyclical movements in GNP is thought to account for this phenomenon, with possibly an increased interest-elasticity of money demand at work as well. The introduction in the US of chequable or demand deposits that pay interest, for instance, induced people to hold narrow money not only for transactions purposes but also for savings purposes, according to one researcher (Mehra 1989). Other research, though, failed to find any significant effect of innovations other than an increase in the demand for broad money, which resulted from the introduction of money market deposit accounts and money market mutual funds (Tatom 1990).

The cyclical movements call for further comment. Stone and Thornton (1987 p. 17) argue that an increase in money supply growth will increase nominal income growth, after a lag. During the transition period income velocity will decline. This need not, however, affect the fit of the money-demand function, for during the transition period the rate of interest will be relatively low, which could account for the relatively high money holdings relative to GNP. Only if interest rates failed to fall sufficiently to explain the volume of money held, would excessive money growth provide a separate explanation of velocity changes.

This brings us to another possible explanation, with interesting theoretical implications. It is conceivable that the Walrasian money market may be out of equilibrium at any one moment, or, alternatively, that there may be a temporary equilibrium not in consonance with the actual values of the arguments in the money-demand function, due to buffer stocks. Finally, domestic demand for foreign money may impinge on the demand for domestic money, that is, currency substitution may occur.

Not all these possible causes of instability of money-demand functions necessarily undermine the monetarist position. First of all, Monetarists never maintained that money demand is stable in the short run, and secondly, if financial innovations lead to discrete changes in money-demand functions and those innovations occur concentrated in time, policy-makers can take account of those shifts. The monetarist view that monetary policy should not be used for fine tuning is only strengthened by these developments and it is probably too early to discard the idea that a stable and low rate of money supply growth is worth striving for in the interests of a low rate of inflation. The fact that money supply growth cannot be closely controlled and that the boundary lines between money and other assets have tended to become blurred to a greater or lesser extent as a result of monetary innovations, likewise argues against fine tuning but not necessarily against a policy of low money growth with an eye to keeping inflation at bay. Nonetheless, if Wenninger (1988) is right in maintaining that the apparent stability from the 1950s to about 1973 was a unique phenomenon and is not likely to be repeated, a monetarist money supply growth rule would lose some of its effectiveness.

Before returning to the above-mentioned explanations of empirically found instability of the money-demand functions, we first discuss some problems associated with estimating money-demand functions.

THE MONEY DEMAND FUNCTION

Inclusion of the lagged dependent variable; interpretations

In empirical research, money-demand functions have usually been estimated by regressing real cash balances on 'the' rate of interest and on gross national product or a related concept. The rate of interest, in most instances a short rate, serves to represent the opportunity cost of holding money whilst GNP is a proxy for the 'work' that (narrow) money has to perform as a medium of exchange. Alternatively, if the demand for broad money is estimated, GNP may serve as a proxy for wealth, as wealth holders are assumed to hold some fraction of their wealth in the form of liquid assets. It turned out that the addition of a lagged dependent variable gave a significant improvement of the goodness of fit of the equation. What could be called the standard money-demand function therefore looked like this:

$$md_t = a_0 + a_1 i_t + a_2 y_t + a_3 md_{t-1} \tag{6.1}$$

where md = Md/P and Md = volume of money demanded, P = general price level, i = rate of interest and y = real GNP.
If the equation is written in logarithms, the coefficients represent elasticities. For estimation purposes, a disturbance variable should be added, of course.

From a theoretical point of view, there are some problems with this money-demand function. First of all, the variable measured is not money demand but the volume of money actually existing, that is, the money supply. Equating money demand with money supply implies the assumption of swift adjustment after a shock in either money demand or money supply. The addition of the lagged dependent variable md_{t-1} then serves to capture a lagged adjustment of money demand to its long-term equilibrium value:

$$md^*_t = b_0 + b_1 i_t + b_2 y_t \qquad (6.2)$$

where md^* = long-term money demand.

Equation 6.1 follows from equation 6.2 by adding a partial adjustment mechanism :

$$md_t - md_{t-1} = \theta(md^*_t - md_{t-1}) \qquad (6.3)$$

so that

$$md_t = \theta.md^*_t + (1 - \theta)md_{t-1}$$
$$= \theta b_o + \theta b_1 i_t + \theta b_2 y_t + (1 - \theta)md_{t-1} \qquad (6.4)$$

from which equation 6.1 follows after relabelling $\theta b_0 = a_0$, $\theta b_1 = a_1$, $\theta b_2 = a_2$ and $(1 - \theta) = a_3$.

The empirical data fed into money-demand functions generally are calculated on a quarterly basis. Now lags in adjustment running to many quarters are highly questionable in financial markets, as these are characterized by low transactions costs. Goodfriend's argument (Goodfriend 1985 p. 210), that portfolio adjustment costs cannot account for a gradual adjustment because those costs are largely fixed and adjustment would be made at one stroke, seems flawed, however: in an economy with a large number of agents, aggregate adjustment can well be spread over time as different economic agents adjust at different points in time. Some people argue that adjustments are indeed slow and that money balances serve as buffers. Their views will be taken up in the section on buffer stocks below. First we mention Goodfriend's (1985) rather subtle explanation. Goodfriend assumes that income (and possibly interest) is generated by a first-order autoregressive process. Money demand tends to depend more on expected variables than on realized variables, which differ from expected variables by a serially uncorrelated error. If money demand is regressed on realized rather than expected variables, money demand will be under(over)predicted when expected income is above (below) its mean value. As expected income is positively autocorrelated, lagged money in Goodfriend's view will tend to be above (below) its mean value when expected income is above (below) its mean and a_2 is biased downward as an estimate of b_2. Lagged money therefore enters the money-demand function with a positive coefficient, offsetting the under(over)prediction of money demand when expected income is above (below) its mean value. This implies that the coefficients in the money-demand function may change not only as a result of changes in the 'true' money-demand function (money demand as a function of expected variables), but also because of a shift in the income (and/or interest) generating process. Goodfriend (1985 p. 223) suggests that such a shift might result from a change in monetary policy. Note that money demand does not, in Goodfriend's view, in reality depend on lagged variables; the lagged variable only picks up what he calls a measurement error, or the effects of a random disturbance in measured income (and/or interest). His solution is predicated on a number of rather strong assumptions as to the income and interest generating processes.

In the case of broad money, the relevant scale variable is not so much current income as permanent income, as a proxy for wealth. As in Goodfriend's approach, current income is not the 'true' scale variable. Replacement of current income by permanent income in the money demand equation might remove a large part of the discrepancy between short-term and long-term money demand (Laidler 1985 p. 244). An unexpectedly high current income would not at first affect broad money demand, but if it continues permanent income and therefore the volume of money demanded will increase. If then current income in lieu of permanent income is retained as an argument in the money-demand function, this leads to a function very similar to equation 6.4. Let permanent income be generated through a partial adjustment mechanism:

$$y_{pt} = y^{p}{}_{t-1} + \Phi(y_t - y^{p}{}_{t-1}) \qquad (6.5)$$

Let the money-demand function be similar to equation 6.2, with y_t replaced by y^p, so that

$$md_t = b_0 + b_1 i_t + b_2 y^{p}{}_t \qquad (6.6)$$

Substitution of equation 6.5 in equation 6.6 then yields

$$md_t = b^0 + b_1 i_t + b_2(1 - \Phi)y^{p}{}_{t-1} + b_2\Phi y_t \qquad (6.7)$$

and substitution of $y^{p}{}_{t-1}$ with the help of equation 6.6 finally yields

$$md_t = b_0\Phi + b_1 i_t + b_2\Phi y_t - b_1(1 - \Phi)i_{t-1} + (1 - \Phi)md_{t-1} \qquad (6.8)$$

which, but for the inclusion of the lagged interest rate, is identical to equation 6.4. Permanent income perceptions of the public through partial adjustment mechanisms could therefore account for the good performance of lagged money in the money-demand function (as emphasized by Kohli 1987, though Laidler 1982 p. 52 is less sanguine on empirical grounds). If expectations of current income are generated by a similar process to that described in equation 6.5, equation 6.8 could also be deployed for estimating the demand for narrow money as a function of expected current income. More sophisticated adjustment mechanisms and expectations formation schemes can be tried too, of course, but fall outside the scope of this book (see, for instance, Kool 1989).

All this may be relevant to cases where the arguments in the money-demand function change and money supply adjusts passively to money demand or, as Laidler (1982, 1984, 1985) has it, when we perform conceptual experiments at the level of individual economic agents that are confronted with exogenous shifts in the determinants of the demand for money. But the results of such individual experiments cannot be generalized for an entire, say national, economy: economic agents can individually reduce or increase their cash balances, on an aggregate scale they cannot (at least not in an economy under a free-floating exchange-rate system). The analysis does not cover the situation where money market equilibrium is disturbed by a money supply shock or where the money supply does not fully adjust to changes in demand. In principle the rate of interest could ensure equilibrium, but that might imply frequent and wild fluctuations in these rates. Even if such fluctuations can easily be imagined to happen in the call money market, it is hard to see how the rates on any but extremely-short-term time deposits and on savings deposits, both highly relevant for money demand, could move fast enough and frequently enough to restore equilibrium immediately after a money demand or supply shock occurs. Laidler (1984 pp. 24-5) suggests that the rate of interest first of all serves to equilibrate the market for debt instruments (incidentally, he thus subscribes to a loanable-funds rather than a liquidity-preference explanation of interest rate changes). The rate of interest could not do this if it was called upon to neutralize each and every manifestation of excess demand or supply in the (Walrasian) money market. The upshot is that disequilibria in the Walrasian money market can exist for non-negligible time periods. This point will be taken up again in the section on buffer stocks.

Notes on the arguments in the money demand function

Apart from the form and the interpretation of the money-demand function, there are also question marks over the individual arguments in the function. First, if the money-demand function is expressed in real variables, it is implicitly assumed that money demand adjusts without delay (or rather with a short delay, given that quarterly data are used) to price level changes. Quintyn (1986

p. 280) found that lags actually do occur, and that these tended to increase over the 1970s.

Next, the use of a rate of interest or a few rates of interest to represent the opportunity cost of holding money is in itself not controversial, but the usual assumption that narrow money carries no or at the most a very low rate of interest seems mistaken. If interest is paid on narrow money, the opportunity cost of holding money should not be measured by the rate of interest on money substitutes, but by the difference between the two rates. As banks offer payment facilities at no or a low cost to deposit holders, demand deposits earn an *implicit interest rate*. For Belgium and The Netherlands, these implicit interest payments have been estimated to amount to 7 to 8 per cent (Eizenga 1972 p. 18, Acx and Quintyn 1982 p. 79). As the interest rate on money substitutes, such as savings deposits, is higher and seems to fluctuate more widely than the interest differential, it is to be expected that interest elasticities calculated on the level of savings interest rates are lower than those calculated on interest differentials. This idea was borne out in empirical research conducted by Barro and Santomero (1972) for the US with respect to the period 1950-1968.

A related problem is that money is not only a substitute for other financial assets, but also for goods. This would imply that, especially in times of high inflation, the (expected) rate of inflation should be included as an argument in the money-demand function. The rationale is that the higher the rate of inflation the less attractive holding money is relative to holding physical goods. Difficulties for empirical research could arise from multicollinearity between the rate of interest and the expected rate of inflation, though. A possible solution is to replace the nominal rate of interest as an argument in the money-demand function by the (expected) real rate of interest, through deflating the nominal rate of interest by the (expected) rate of inflation.

When estimating the demand for broad money, one has to face the problem that the dependent variable is built up of disparate elements, some of which carry explicit interest while others do not. The demand for some elements will react positively to interest rate changes, the demand for others negatively. Also, the demand for non-interest-bearing money is likely to be more closely linked to the level of economic activity than the demand for interest-bearing components, which tend to be held more for savings than for transactions purposes. In its calculations of broad money or liquidity (M2), The Netherlands Bank therefore includes short-term time and savings deposits with a correction for the velocity of circulation or speed of turnover (total withdrawals divided by average balances over a year). The lower the velocity (between an upper bound of 2 and a lower bound of 0.5), the lower the fraction included in M2. In this way, the difference in degree of liquidity or 'moneyness' is taken account of. This is one way of solving the problem of aggregation over imperfect substitutes. Another attempt that has lately been made to take account of the differing degrees of liquidity of the various components of the broad money supply is through the construction of so-called *Divisia-indexes*. The degree of liquidity is measured by the difference between the interest yield on a high-yielding illiquid asset and the interest yield of the monetary asset in question, representing the opportunity cost of holding that asset. The various components of the monetary aggregate are weighted by this difference to arrive at the Divisia money supply index. The idea behind this procedure is that the interest differential which the holder of the monetary asset is willing to forgo represents the utility of that asset's liquidity to the holder. It is the price paid for liquidity. Changes in the Divisia index are calculated by summing the percentage changes of the individual components of the monetary aggregate weighted by their share in the aggregate. At reasonably high levels of aggregation Divisia indexes for the US tend to give a better statistical fit than unweighted aggregates (see Porter and Offenbacher 1984, and Barnett, Offenbacher and Spindt 1984 for the period 1959-1982, see also Fase 1985 for The Netherlands), but not dramatically so. One problem (which has become less relevant in recent years) is that if interest rates are regulated, interest rate differentials give a distorted measure of the liquidity of a monetary asset. Besides, there is still the implicit interest on demand deposits in the form of the payments mechanism which can be used free of charge or at low cost.

Finally, gross national product is a poor measure of the 'work' that money as a medium of exchange has to perform. The same goes for related concepts, such as gross domestic final demand equalling GNP minus inventory adjustments and net exports. The idea underlying this concept is that spending on goods drawn from inventories or on imports calls for transaction balances without affecting GNP directly. Substitution of GNP by gross domestic final demand does not seem to make much of a difference in outcome, though (see Stone and Thornton 1987 p. 7). Money demand has also been related to gross national expenditure, made up of GNP plus imports minus exports, on the ground that people may hold domestic money to pay for imports, especially in the United States, but also in other countries. Bomberger and Makinen (1980) report a better fit, as measured by R^2, with this concept for 12 out of 16 countries studied for the two decades ending in 1975. Such concepts do not represent the total money value of transactions. Variations in the degree of vertical integration in industries and in the turnover of second-hand goods, given GNP, have an impact on the volume of money demanded independent of changes in interest rates and GNP or related concepts. The same goes for variations in the volume of financial transactions or what Keynes called the *financial circulation* (analysed in Ch. 15 of *A Treatise on Money*, vol. 1, Keynes 1971b). The Netherlands Bank for instance suspects that the recent significant increase in broad money as a percentage of national income may have something to do with these financial transactions (De Nederlandsche Bank 1990 p. 71). All this means that the parameters of the money-demand function may shift, that is, the money-demand function as conventionally measured becomes unstable. Furthermore, the statistical measures of the concepts discussed generally underestimate their true values because of the phenomenon of the black or underground economy. If value added in the underground economy as a percentage of total value added varies over time, the stability of the money-demand function is impaired again. The true money-demand function, as a function of total GNP including value added in the underground economy, need not be unstable for this phenomenon to occur. The causes of instability mentioned here differ in nature from the one to be discussed in the next section, which concerns the technology of the payments mechanism.

Parameter instability in conventional money-demand functions should come as no surprise. Instability over longer periods is of course to be expected, as the underlying relationships change continuously. Even if they did not but the true money-demand function were nonlinear, linear estimates would show parameter instability (see on the econometrics of parameter instability Kool 1989).

One can, of course, always try to improve the statistical fit of money-demand functions by including additional independent variables, at the cost of simplicity and suitability to be used as a base for economic policy. A little-used but promising method is to separately estimate money demand by households and money demand by firms. Households and firms are likely to react differently to changes in the economy. Specifically, firms can be expected to react more strongly to interest rate changes and changes in inflation rates, as active cash management is probably more important for them than for households. These ideas have been borne out in research on money demand in The Netherlands (Fase and Winder 1990). Earlier research for the UK suggested that firms tend to react in particular to the short rate of interest and households to the long rate. Besides, adjustments were made faster in the case of firms (Price 1972). Another variable that presents itself is wealth. Following the lead provided by Milton Friedman, permanent income as a proxy for wealth has often been used in demand functions of broad money, instead of current income. It is also possible to include both current income or GNP and a wealth variable. Standard monetary macroeconomics suggests that both income or GNP (as a proxy for the work to be done by money as a means of exchange) and wealth (as a scale variable in portfolio composition) play a role (see the section on ex-post crowding out in Chapter 2). Wealth variables might explain part of the underestimation of money demand found with conventional money-demand functions in the 1980s. Financial wealth appears to do so for The Netherlands (Fase and Winder 1990) but Rasche (1987) failed to find a significant contribution of wealth variables to the explanation of the shift in the US demand-for-(narrow-)money function occurring in the early 1980s. Finally, portfolio analysis suggests that in times of uncertainty economic agents will tend to keep a larger fraction of their wealth portfolios in the form of liquid assets. Milton Friedman included uncertainty (as part of a portmanteau variable) in his seminal 1956 study on the quantity theory of money (Friedman 1956), but the idea can at the very least be traced back to the *Bullion Report*, presented to the House of Commons in 1810 (Cannan 1969 p. 57; the passage in question from the Bullion Report was cited with approval by Alfred Marshall 1965 p. 42, who however erroneously ascribed the *Report* to David Ricardo instead of Francis Horner, Henry Thornton and William Huskisson; see Fetter 1953 on the myth that Ricardo was responsible for the *Bullion Report*). It appears that uncertainty is hard to model econometrically, but perhaps a cyclical indicator, as applied by Den Butter and Fase (1981) to money-demand functions from the early 1960s to the mid-1970s for eight European countries and by Fase and Winder (1990), can be interpreted as reflecting uncertainty. This indicator captures the tendency of money demand to increase relatively in a downswing and to decrease in a boom and its addition was found to reduce instability. By nature a cyclical indicator can only be applied to short-term demand functions. If current income is deployed as an argument in the money-demand function while permanent income or wealth is the 'true' variable and there are no lagged variables as in equation 6.8, it is conceivable that a cyclical indicator picks up the influence of the lags in the adjustment of permanent income perceptions. This would seem to be more relevant for broad money-demand functions than for the narrow money variety. Still, we are not spared the problem of observational equivalence, for the cyclical indicator could as well pick up the influence of lagged expectations formation of future income (again, see equation 6.8) as of uncertainty.

Not to be neglected in empirical research, of course, is the question of the form of the money-demand function, as distinct from the variables to be included. If, for instance, a loglinear form is applied, constant elasticities are implied. For these problems the reader is referred to the specialized literature (for instance, Den Butter and Kuné 1976, Den Butter and Verbon 1982).

FINANCIAL INNOVATIONS AND INSTITUTIONAL CHANGES

Money as a medium of exchange helps to facilitate transactions involving goods, services and financial assets. Payments are not only made by handing over currency but also by transferring deposits held with financial institutions. As the technology of monitoring those deposits and of effectuating those transfers evolves over time, the quantity of (narrow) money demanded for given values of determinants such as income (as a proxy for the volume of transactions) and interest is likely to exhibit a long-term tendency to fall. Transactions costs diminish.

It has been suggested that a kind of ratchet effect is at work. When interest rates are high it pays to spend time and effort on the development of financial innovations. Cases in point are *concentration accounts*, to which funds deposited in other accounts are automatically transferred at the end of every working day, *zero balance accounts*, which allow a firm to do without transaction balances at banks, yet giving them the opportunity to write cheques, and *EFTPOS* (Electronic Fund Transfer at Point of Sale). Having been introduced, these innovations are not reversed when interest rates fall again, because the costs involved are mostly set-up costs, such as thoseTobin of putting in computer hardware and software (Dotsey 1984). This could be one way of explaining a shift over time of the parameters of the money-demand function. Not only is the constant likely to have fallen in value, it is also to be expected that the interest elasticity of narrow money demand (exclusive of interest-bearing deposits) has increased as a result of financial innovations, as these have made shifts between demand deposits and high-interest-bearing deposits that much easier.

Institutional changes have also been mentioned as a cause of money demand instability. Boughton (1981 p. 593) mentions the introduction of interest-bearing checkable deposits in Canada in 1967, the prohibition of interest on demand deposits in France in the same year and the reduction of compensating-balance requirements in Japan in 1977 (this is the requirement to hold positive amounts in demand deposits against loans). And of course interest rate controls on US bank deposits have been progressively relaxed. Such changes may affect measured interest elasticity if explicit interest payments are substituted for implicit ones.

It might be argued that financial innovations and institutional changes have been going on as long as there has been money. Over the years, Bordo and Jonung (1981) discern on the one hand a downward trend in velocity, caused by increasing monetization (a decline in barter trade and in payments in kind) and the rise of commercial banks, and on the other hand an upward trend in velocity (or a downward shift in the money-demand function), caused by financial innovations and improved economic stability and security. Similar developments have been found by other research workers, such as Tobin (1971b pp. 481-7) and Milton Friedman (1971b p. 152). If such developments are in one direction, the forces at work could be captured in, for instance, an income elasticity of money demand greater than 1 (in the case of a falling velocity) or smaller than 1 (when velocity shows an upward trend). Changes in the trends in velocity are not surprising, but what sets the post-1973 period apart is the sudden nature and the quick succession of the changes. Akhtar (1983 p. 33) for instance finds a downward medium-term trend in money demand, but with shifts varying in size and uneven and unpredictable over time for five out of seven large industrial countries since the early 1970s.

As for the foreign exchange rate regime, it is, in Boughton's view, not so much the regime itself as changes in exchange rate expectations that might affect domestic money demand, through capital flows that at least partly bear on money holdings. In a few cases some influence was indeed found: after the 1969 devaluation, for instance, funds seem to have been repatriated to France which were placed in interest-bearing deposits. Yet, over the period 1960-1977 neither the collapse of the Bretton Woods system nor severe exchange rate crises in the UK nor switches between pegging and floating in Canada seem to have had any significant impact on money demand (Boughton 1981). The evidence is not conclusive, though. Arango and Nadiri (1981) found that exchange rate expectations and changes in foreign interest rates significantly improved the fit of the money-demand functions for Canada, Germany, the UK and the USA for the 1960-1975 period. These demand functions proved stable, even for the turbulent early 1970s. Against this, Batten and Hafer (1986) and Baade and Nazmi (1989) found only a limited influence of foreign variables in general on domestic money demand for the leading industrial countries.

BUFFER STOCKS

Given a situation of equilibrium in the Walrasian money market, a monetary impulse or a real impulse without accompanying adjustment of the money supply leads to an excess demand or excess supply. Adjustment processes will get started that in a flexprice economy take place via the price mechanism. Economic agents adjust their portfolios to the changed volume of money, which means that they will try to buy or sell other assets, in the process driving the prices of those assets up or down. In actual practice frictions occur. Time and money are involved in adjusting one's portfolio and in gathering and processing the information needed for making decisions. This means, as Knoester (1980 pp. 19-22, 1984) argued, that banks and the public may absorb a disequilibrium between money demand and money supply through nonprice quantity adjustments, that is, through the use of their money holdings as *buffers*. In the case of banks, these adjustments take place in the form of changes in the volume of free reserves or of net foreign assets. The idea of buffer stocks is not altogether new. Back in 1923 Keynes, when explaining the quantity theory, noted that moderate changes in base money may for a time fail to work out in higher prices, because the recipients of additional cash may initially prefer not to spend it (Keynes 1971a p. 66).

As has been hinted above, it could be objected that transaction and information costs in the financial markets are relatively low and can hardly explain the holding of buffer stocks. Economic agents should in principle be able quickly to rearrange their portfolios of financial assets, and in the process interest rate changes should bring money demand back to the level of money supply. First, however, interest rates may after all, as we have seen, not be so very flexible in the short run. Secondly, with portfolios made up of a wider range of assets, including goods and real estate, a monetary disturbance will directly influence the (stock) demand for goods as agents try to restore portfolio balance (Patinkin 1972a). In so far as money is net wealth, the demand for other assets will increase even at unchanged prices, by dint of the real-balance effect. But even if money is inside money and a real-balance effect does not occur, people will attempt to rearrange their portfolios. If prices are flexible, these adjustments can take place at a rapid pace through price adjustments that in their turn provoke quantity adjustments. If prices are sticky, these substitution effects cannot occur, but there may be nonprice quantity adjustments instead through what Knoester calls *spill-over effects*. (Laidler 1982 p. 46, and 1985 p. 247, rather confusingly tends to comprise these effects under the heading of 'wealth effects', though they may happen with inside money as well, that is, with money that does not represent net wealth.) Such adjustments may well be spread over a number of months or even quarters. The excess balances (which may be negative) over the long-term desired money stock, that is the buffer stocks, are willingly held, in a sense, because economic agents plan a gradual adjustment. This could serve as an explanation of the apparent instability resulting from money supply shocks and the lags found in empirical money-demand functions (see Cuthbertson and Taylor 1987 p. 103).

It has been noted by several authors (such as Davidson and Ireland 1987) that individual economic agents hold money precisely because it acts as a buffer. Receipts and expenditures cannot be exactly planned or forecast or such forecasts are very difficult, time-consuming and therefore expensive to do, and money holdings serve to accommodate discrepancies between the two. Agents do not strive for a certain exact value of their money holdings, as presupposed in the deterministic money demand models such as the Baumol-Tobin inventory theoretic models. Instead, they wish to keep their money holdings within a band and will monitor these only at intervals, not continuously (see for a model incorporating stochastic cash flows and upper and lower levels of cash balances the pioneering work of Miller and Orr, for instance Miller and Orr 1968). Of course, temporarily low money holdings by one agent will normally be balanced to a large extent by temporarily high holdings by another agent, and the conventional aggregate money-demand function may be quite stable. A shock, either real or monetary, may however lead to relatively low or high balances for the majority of agents. Only when the upper or lower limits of their individual money holding functions are reached will agents adjust their spending and portfolio allocation plans. This provides for a lag in money demand conceptually different from the one discussed in the preceding paragraph, because it concerns the time needed for adjusting plans rather than the time needed for executing them (in this vein Goodhart 1984 p. 257). All this means that on an aggregate level a money supply shock or a real shock will first affect income velocity before action is taken to adjust spending and portfolio allocation. The idea of upper and lower thresholds is in fact a variant of a transactions cost approach. Monitoring inflows and outflows of cash costs time and the results are not worth the effort of continuous monitoring.

A point in favour of this approach is that it can explain the empirical finding that the short-term income elasticity of money is quite low, say around 0.2 for the US, whilst long-term elasticities tend to be rather nearer unity (Akerlof and Milbourne 1980). Baumol-Tobin-type deterministic inventory-theoretic models predict income elasticities in the 0.5-1 range (see Visser 1974 pp. 75-9). In the context of such models, numerical examples show that the gains to be reaped by following strictly the optimization rule are negligible, at least for households (Akerlof and Milbourne 1980). Cheaper methods of cash management may diminish or already have diminished the importance of buffer stocks as explained in this approach, though.

The idea of a temporary quasi-equilibrium in the monetary sphere is also used by Hines to resolve the conflict between the liquidity preference and loanable fund theories of interest rate determination (Hines 1971). In Hines's analysis goods suppliers who sell an unexpectedly high number of goods during a period, may use the concomitant unexpectedly high volume of incoming cash either to reduce outstanding debt or hoard it in anticipation of increased expenditure (such as restoring inventories) during the next period. Instead of labelling this situation a quasi-equilibrium, one may also see it as an equilibrium situation, with planned expenditure one of the arguments in the money-demand function, that is, an incorporation of Keynes's *finance motive* in the money-demand function (Keynes 1937). In this solution there are no discrepancies between short-term and long-term money-demand functions and no buffer stocks proper. Instead, money demand is related to the planned rather than the current values of the arguments in the demand function (which is akin to some of the interpretations of the money-demand functions discussed in the section on the inclusion of the lagged dependent variable above).

A related idea is Cuthbertson and Taylor's notion of a *forward-looking buffer stock* model (1987 p. 118). They note that a change in the money supply may lead to a revision of expected income and price levels. If then expected values of these variables determine the demand for money, demand is swiftly adjusted to supply, at least to a great extent. Again, there are no buffer stocks proper, because there is no significant difference between money supply and money demand to be explained.

Another way of introducing buffer stocks, suggested by Kohli (1987 p. 194), is to make the demand for money a function of wealth. This will of course have more relevance for broad money than for narrow money. Wealth may fluctuate and a distinction between permanent and transitory wealth can be made. If transitory wealth is held to a large degree in the form of (broad) money, then a money-demand function which does not include transitory wealth may well be unstable. Money acts as a buffer because it absorbs transitory wealth. No statistical support has been found for this idea, though (Kohli 1987 p. 195).

The relevance of the idea of buffer stocks, or quasi-equilibrium, or temporary equilibrium, for the money-demand function is that it need not be unstable, even if empirical research gives the impression that it is (Mahajan 1980). If adjustment processes take time, the volume of money measured at any moment need not be the equilibrium volume at the given values of the explanatory variables, that is the volume that would be thrown up by the 'true' money-demand function. In this case, the parameters found in empirical research will shift over time after a shock. What is in fact measured is not money demand, but money supply. This may be taken to mean that single-equation models cannot satisfactorily capture the transmission process of monetary impulses (Laidler 1984 p. 29). The empirical evidence is inconclusive. Bordo, Choudri and Schwartz (1987) found results for Canada that were not inconsistent with the idea of narrow money acting as a buffer stock, but Kohli's extensive research, using several forms of the money-demand function, failed to find any support for a buffer function of money (Kohli 1987).

CURRENCY SUBSTITUTION

Another explanation of the apparent instability of the money-demand function is currency substitution. This idea, preached with unremitting zeal by R.I. McKinnon, implies instability in the demand for domestic currency, as foreign currency may act as a substitute for domestic currency in economic agents' portfolios (McKinnon 1979 ch. 10, 1982, 1984). Currency substitution may in

McKinnon's view either be direct or indirect. Direct currency substitution occurs when economic agents expect, for instance, a depreciation of their home currency and shift into foreign currency. McKinnon does not think this kind of currency substitution to be dominant, and empirical research does indeed give no reason to attach too much weight to it for developed nations (see the last section of Chapter 7). In countries suffering from rampant inflation, foreign currencies may of course replace domestic currency to an appreciable extent. It should be noted that direct currency substitution could hardly create instability in the money-demand function if the definition of the money stock included foreign-currency-denominated deposits held in resident banks, as in the Dutch definition of broad money.

McKinnon's argument hinges on indirect currency substitution. This takes place through the capital market. His reasoning is as follows. Assume that at a certain moment in time economic agents revise their expectations of the return on foreign bonds upward, for instance because they expect the home currency to depreciate. They wish to sell domestic bonds and to buy foreign bonds, which causes an upward pressure on the domestic interest rate and, perhaps, a downward one on the foreign interest rates. With a given money-demand function and, in a floating-rate system, a given money supply, interest rates cannot move. The increased demand for foreign bonds then works out in a rise in the exchange rate, to a level where an expected future fall in the exchange rate balances the relative fall in the attractiveness of domestic bonds. In the case of fixed exchange rates, capital exports will occur. The domestic money supply falls and the foreign money supply increases, until foreign and domestic interest rates differ by an amount reflecting the relative attractiveness of foreign and domestic bonds to investors (again, money demand is a stable function of the rate of interest in McKinnon's story).

McKinnon's message is that exchange rates should be held constant, because with flexible exchange rates a depreciation of a country's currency is likely to provoke inflation. He further assumes that the world money-demand function is stable in the sense that a stabilization of the world money supply growth results in a stabilization of the world rate of inflation. In order to stabilize world money growth, the leading industrial nations, the United States, Japan and the Federal Republic of Germany, should coordinate their monetary policies. They should, in particular, coordinate their domestic credit expansion. Liquidity inflows or outflows through the balance of payments should, moreover, not be sterilized. If one country sterilized, the world money supply would be affected. This is what happens in a key-currency system where international reserves are held in the form of interest-bearing debt of the key-currency country. US private sector balance-of-payments deficits for instance first lead to dollar payments by American residents into accounts held by nonresidents or their banks. Subsequently, those dollars are often used to buy American debt from American residents, resulting in return payments into the bank accounts held by those American residents. The net result is an unchanged American money supply, whilst the non-American money supply has risen (because the non-American private sector will have sold the dollars it received to domestic banks against domestic currency; it is those banks which buy American debt). If both countries sterilize, portfolio balance within a country may be precluded at the given rate of exchange, resulting in a continuous capital flow (see on sterilization and the money supply in a two-country model De Grauwe 1983). Depletion of foreign-exchange reserves and exhaustion of international credit may then put an end to stable exchange rates and to a stable price level.

Dornbusch (1984 p. 9, 1987 p. 16) argues that, if investors increase their preference for foreign bonds, it is the supply of foreign bonds that should be adjusted, not the supply of money. Sterilized intervention means that the monetary authorities sell foreign exchange and buy domestic debt. Investors fulfil their wish to substitute foreign for domestic debt and the domestic money supply remains unchanged. If money demand is a function of the rate of interest but not of the composition of the portfolio and furthermore independent of exchange rate expectations, the rate of interest will remain unchanged as well. Against this, McKinnon (1984 p. 33) maintains that a wish on the part of investors to create or change an interest differential between countries should not be frustrated. With free capital movements there would be no end to intervention and sterilization. Attempts to stabilize the domestic money supply are bound to fail in the face of massive capital movements and serve no useful purpose, in McKinnon's eyes. Better let domestic money supplies change, so that the interest rate differentials sought by investors can materialize. There is no reason to prevent exchange rate expectations or (other) risk differentials being expressed in interest rates. It appears that one important difference between the approaches of McKinnon and Dornbusch is that Dornbusch implicitly assumes a small interest elasticity of capital flows while McKinnon's ideas are predicated on the assumption of a very high interest elasticity of capital flows (see on the interest elasticity of capital flows Chapter 7). A comparatively modest capital flow suffices in Dornbusch's case to adjust portfolios such that the original interest rate is restored after a shift in preferences as to portfolio composition. McKinnon and Dornbusch in fact study different cases and neither can claim general validity for his approach, it seems.

McKinnon's proposal is intriguing, but one wonders if the relationships stressed by him are crucial enough to make the system work in practice in the way envisaged by him. For one thing, it is doubtful if one can meaningfully speak of a world money-demand function and, if so, whether it is as stable (in particular as a function of interest rates) as McKinnon asserts (Spinelli 1983). Also, capital movements need not be as elastic as McKinnon supposes them to be. Furthermore, McKinnon somewhat off-handedly assumes that capital flows will accommodate any trade or current account imbalance in a fixed-rate system without any problem. Finally, empirical research suggests that not only direct currency substitution, but foreign influences in general, so far have only had a minor influence on domestic money-demand functions (see the literature cited in the section on financial innovations and institutional changes above). Be that as it may, the empirical evidence so far does not corroborate McKinnon's explanation of money demand instability. But his attempt to spell out the preconditions for exchange-rate stability must be applauded. The contribution of the idea of currency substitution to the explanation of exchange-rate instability is discussed in the next chapter.

7. Exchange Rate Theories I

INTRODUCTION

The collapse of the Bretton Woods system of fixed but adjustable exchange rates in 1973 marked the end of a comparative calm not only in exchange-rate practice but in exchange-rate theory as well. In the typical textbook of the time, the balance of payments for a fixed-exchange-rate system was explained by income and expenditure on the current account as a function of the rate of exchange among other things, plus net capital imports as a function of the rate of interest or of both the rate of interest and national income. For a flexible-rate system it was the rate of exchange that was explained, by putting the balance identically equal to zero (see for instance Branson 1972 ch. 15). With infinitely interest-elastic capital flows this became the Mundell-Fleming model (see for instance Mundell 1963b). A slightly more elaborate portfolio model of capital movements could be grafted onto the basic (IS/LM type) model, such that account could be taken of stock adjustments (Grubel 1968). After a change in the data of the system, there will be a short-term impact following from a readjustment of existing portfolios, apart from a permanent influence on net capital flows. Short-term elasticities of capital flows are consequently higher than long-term elasticities in this approach. The current account was the centrepiece in most explanations of exchange rate movements and consideration of capital flows by and large only served to explain deviations from the norm implicit in current-account balance. It was thought, for instance, that exchange-rate movements in a flexible-rate system would first of all reflect differences in inflation rates between countries. A system of flexible exchange rates would also enable governments to exploit the Phillips-curve trade-off between unemployment and inflation (Artus and Young 1979). Capital movements were not expected to throw a spanner in the works and flexible rates would insulate countries from external disturbances.

Things turned out differently when the Bretton Woods system of fixed-but-adjustable exchange rates finally foundered in 1973, after having tottered and been patched up in 1971. Exchange rates apparently went their own merry way, unrelated to differences in inflation rates between countries or to the balance on the current account. Capital movements now take place on such a scale that they seem totally to swamp international payments on account of trade in goods and services. In the experience of one banker, international payments originate for only about one-tenth in the current account of the balance of payments (Oort 1987 p. 65). It has even been estimated by the BIS (Bank for International Settlements) that the volume of foreign exchange traded daily in 1990 was nearly $750 billion, which amounts to some 1/4th of the annual value of total world exports. It is not clear, however, to what extent conversions of one currency into another are involved. Part of the transactions volume relates to interbank movements of Eurodollars, Euroyen and so on. Anyhow, the experience since 1973 has been characterized by a dominance of capital movements over payments on the current account. Consequently, international economists were sent back to their studies to rethink exchange-rate theory. The result has been a spate of models that venture to explain the erratic behaviour of exchange rates after 1973. The variety of models is quite bewildering and even a treatise of monographic length could hardly do justice to most of them (see Krueger 1983). In a shorter survey there is not much else one can do than paint with a broad brush.

In order to discern some method in the model madness, or to impose some method on it, we will follow de Roos (1985) and group the various theories according to the period for which their explanation of the exchange rate is relevant. First, we discern a *very short period*, during which exchange-rate movements are explained by capital flows. In the *short period* the movements of the rate of exchange are explained by both capital flows and payments and receipts on the current account. The same goes for the *long period*, but there is an additional equilibrium condition in this case, namely that the current account and the capital account separately be in equilibrium. Finally, in the *very long period*, *purchasing power parity* (PPP) is assumed to prevail and factor prices are internationally equalized (a similar approach was followed by Sauernheimer 1981 in an attempt to capture the effects of monetary policy over successively the very short period, a Keynesian short period and the very long period in one model; one of the restrictions of his model was the assumption of uncovered interest parity which left no room for portfolio models, see below). The rates of exchange that follow from the longer-term models can be regarded as trends around which movements take place that are explained by shorter-term models. One idea is dealt with separately, as it is not a model in its own right but an approach that cuts across the boundaries of the periods in our classification, namely the idea of cash in advance. In this chapter we deal with the very short period whereas the other periods are tackled in the next one.

ASSET MODELS

In the very short period, only capital movements explain exchange rate changes. It can be imagined that changes in the data of the system that bear on capital flows influence the rate of exchange within hours or even minutes or seconds, whilst the current account needs more time to react. The rate of exchange then is determined by the demand for and supply of financial assets, not by flows of commodities. We deal with two sets of *asset models*: one in which domestic and foreign titles are perfect substitutes and one in which they are imperfect substitutes. The former are known as *monetary models* and the latter as *portfolio models*.

A common point of departure of asset models is the assumption that the foreign exchange market is an *efficient market*. A market is efficient if asset prices fully reflect all available information. Consequently, no profits can be made by trading on the basis of the available information and new information is immediately reflected in prices (Begg 1982 p. 206, Heri 1984, Sijben 1986 pp. 25-6). In finance literature three forms of efficiency are usually distinguished:

1. weak efficiency, with the information set made up of past prices;
2. semistrong efficiency, with the information set including all publicly available information;
3. strong efficiency, with the information set including all information, both public and private.

The difference between semistrong and strong efficiency does not seem very important in the case of exchange rates. Private information or insider information could only play a role in the case of secret plans to change parities or to influence a floating exchange rate. Efficiency in exchange rate theory is generally of the (semi)strong variety. Present information on, for instance, future monetary growth is seen as essential in expectations formation.

Two elements are involved in the concept of market efficiency. Firstly, rational expectations are assumed, which means that economic agents make no systematic mistakes when making forecasts on the basis of the available information or, in other words, that they apply the correct model, and secondly, that any discrepancies in (risk-adjusted) net returns on different assets are swiftly eliminated by arbitrage, that is, capital mobility is high.

Two comments are in order. Firstly, it does not always seem possible to separate imperfect substitutability and less-than-infinitely-high capital mobility. A case in point is the higher yield demanded by investors on long-term Dutch government debt relative to German government debt, despite default and exchange-rate risks that can hardly be higher on Dutch than on German debt. One possible explanation is that the German capital market is more *liquid* (that is, prices are less sensitive to the volume of any single transaction) than the Dutch one. Apparently investors fear that any appreciable unloading of Dutch government debt on the market would depress prices, if only for a short period of time, and saddle them with a loss. This means that arbitrage is not expected by investors to be quick enough to ensure equal returns over national capital markets.

Secondly, attempts to view exchange-rate behaviour as a special case of the Capital Asset Pricing Model (CAPM) seem misdirected, pace Sijben (1986 pp. 30-1). CAPM has at least three defects when deployed as a model to explain exchange-rate behaviour. Firstly, assets are assumed to be in fixed supply. Secondly, the supply of each asset is assumed to be relatively small and there are many assets. Shocks on the market for a particular asset, in particular changes in perceived risk and return, then do not cause feedback effects on the prices of other securities. Neither of these assumptions is valid for the foreign-exchange market (Levich 1985 p. 81). Lastly, CAPM in an international setting presupposes that purchasing power parity holds at all times. Only in that case will the real return on any asset be identical for all investors. With deviations from purchasing power parity, foreign and domestic demand for an asset will differ (Koedijk 1989 pp. 82, 109). CAPM however presupposes homogeneous expectations on the part of investors with regard to expected returns and risk of assets (see any good finance text, such as Alexander and Sharpe 1989 ch. 10).

MONETARY MODELS

Interest parity

In monetary models it is assumed that domestic and foreign interest-bearing titles are perfect substitutes. Economic agents are indifferent as to the shares of domestic and foreign titles in their portfolios, provided they yield the same return. The return on foreign titles is made up of the foreign interest rate plus any profit or loss on exchange-rate movements. Given either exchange-rate expectations that are held with certainty or risk-neutral investors, competitive markets with negligible transaction costs (that is, swift arbitrage), the foreign interest rate plus the expected profit from exchange rate movements equals the domestic interest rate and *uncovered interest parity* prevails. This idea dates back at least to an 1896 article by Irving Fisher (Levich 1978 p. 131) and is sometimes dubbed the *Fisher Open* theory or condition (McKinnon 1981 p. 548). There will also be *covered interest parity*; any difference between domestic and foreign interest rates is balanced by a premium or discount on the forward rate. An amount H invested at the domestic interest rate i will have grown after one period to $(1 + i)H$. An amount H exchanged into foreign currency at the spot rate e results in an amount H/e of foreign currency, which, if invested at the foreign interest rate i^f, will have grown after one period to $(1 + i^f)H/e$. Under covered interest parity, the forward rate F will make this amount equal to $(1 + i)H$:

$$(1 + i)H = (1 + i^f)H.F/e$$

or

$$(1 + i)/(1 + i^f) = F/e$$

$$(1 + i)/(1 + i^f) - 1 = F/e - 1$$

$$(F - e)/e = (i - i^f)/(1 + i^f) \tag{7.1}$$

If i^f is small and $(i - i^f)/(1 + i^f) \approx i - i^f$, equation 7.1 simplifies to

$$(F - e)/e = i - i^f \tag{7.2}$$

which says that the forward premium is equal to the difference between domestic and foreign interest rates.

Given foreign and domestic assets that are identical as to default risk and time to maturity, deviations from covered interest parity point to transaction costs (including information costs), (fear of) capital controls (political risk) or a finite elasticity of the supply of arbitrage funds. Not surprisingly, the covered interest parity assumption fares quite well in empirical tests involving Eurocurrency markets, where assets are comparable in all respects except currency of denomination, trade volume is high and information and other transaction costs are low (from an extensive literature we mention Dufey and Giddy 1978, who provide a survey of empirical studies on pp. 86-96, Cosandier and Lang 1981, Maennig and Tease 1987, Clinton 1988, and D.L. Thornton 1989). It may be noted that covered interest parity does not seem to hold for transactions covering several years. Apparently banks do not have an elastic supply of arbitrage funds for comparatively long periods (see on inelastic supply of arbitrage funds McKinnon 1979 ch. 5). Possible reasons mentioned by Levich (1985 p. 1027) are the loss of liquidity involved in supplying funds for such long periods, credit risks and an adverse impact on balance sheet ratios. What deviations there are for shorter periods, say up to one year, can to a great extent be explained by transaction costs, at least for the leading currencies (see Clinton 1988 and Maasoumi and Pippenger 1989).

With uncovered interest parity, the forward exchange rate will be made equal to the expected future exchange rate through the activities of speculators. If, for instance, speculators expect a future rise in the rate of exchange above the current forward rate, they will demand forward exchange with a view to selling it upon delivery at a profit. The arbitrageurs who offer forward exchange demand foreign exchange in the spot market in order to hedge their positions and push up the spot rate. Given domestic and foreign interest rates and therefore given the forward premium, the activities of the speculators see to it that the spot rate adjusts to the expected future rate, such that the forward rate that goes with the given interest differentials equals the expected future spot rate. The expected future rate of exchange determines the spot rate, given domestic and foreign interest rates. It should be noted that adjustments to changes in exogenous variables are assumed to take little time. It is, however, possible to think of situations in which the adjustments to reach the equilibrium situation where the returns on domestic and foreign investments are equal do take time.

In actual practice, outright speculation through the forward market may be insignificant relative to speculation via the spot market. Goodhart (1988b) learned from discussions with London bankers that, if corporate treasurers or pension fund managers or indeed bankers themselves expect currency A to appreciate relative to currency B to a greater extent than consistent with covered interest parity, they contract debt in currency B and buy currency A on the spot market. The effects are of course not different from when they buy currency A forward and the bank that sells currency A forward against currency B hedges its position by borrowing B and buying A. The advantage of the spot market over the forward market is higher liquidity. Besides, on the forward market dealings are restricted to, mostly, periods of 1, 3, 6 and 12 months. Another factor is that spot market transactions seem somehow to be less burdened with the social stigma of speculation than taking a position in the forward market. But beneath the fur they are really the same dog.

If we regress the spot rate of exchange on the lagged forward rate:

$$\ln e_t = a + b \ln F_{t-1} + u_t \tag{7.3}$$

subscripts denote points of time, u is a residual;

the error term u should be serially uncorrelated and E u_t = 0 (E = expected value) if the foreign exchange market is efficient. Under risk neutrality, the condition for the monetary approach, the constant a should not differ significantly from 0 nor should coefficient b differ much from 1. This implies that the expectation of excess profits of investing in one currency rather than another is zero. Exchange-rate fluctuations may, however, be quite substantial. They are, if markets are efficient, attributable to *news*, that is, developments that could not be foreseen when expectations were formed and that make economic agents revise their expectations. This may be one cause of the poor performance of the forward rate as a predictor of the future spot rate in empirical research (see Edwards 1983 and Goodhart 1988b; for research focusing on unexpected variations in interest rate differentials between countries Frenkel 1981(b), for the impact of news about money supply growth MacDonald 1983, and for an extensive discussion of news, including econometric aspects MacDonald 1988a ch. 12). In case of a *systematic* divergence between spot rates and lagged forward rates (as, for instance, found by Taylor 1987), other explanations must be tried too (see below).

Note that if wealth is an argument in the money-demand function, the analysis gets more complicated. A rise in the spot rate of exchange, for instance, increases the value of the foreign titles held by domestic agents expressed in the domestic currency. With wealth an argument in the money-demand function and the money supply given, this will exert upward pressure on the domestic interest rate and therefore downward pressure on the spot rate of exchange.

The basic flexprice monetary model

The basic monetary model of exchange-rate determination is made up of more building blocks than the mere uncovered interest parity assumption. Firstly, prices are, in quantity-theory fashion, assumed to be determined by the (exogenous) nominal money supply and a real money demand which is a function of (exogenous) real national income and the rate of interest:

$$Ms = Md = kPy^{\alpha}i^{-\beta} \tag{7.4}$$

Ms = money supply, Md = money demand, P = price level, y = real income.

Taking logs and solving for the price level:

$$\ln P = -\ln k - \alpha \ln y + \beta \ln i + \ln Ms \tag{7.5}$$

Assume, for the sake of simplicity, that k, α and β have the same value abroad as at home:

$$\ln P^f = -\ln k - \alpha \ln y^f + \beta \ln i^f + \ln Ms^f \tag{7.6}$$

The superscript f denotes foreign countries.

In order to close the system, purchasing power parity is invoked; the domestic price level is assumed to equal the foreign price level at the going rate of exchange:

$$e.P^f = P$$

or

$$\ln e = \ln P - \ln P^f \tag{7.7}$$

The rate of exchange now turns out to be determined by the stock demand for and supply of money at home and abroad:

$$\ln e = \alpha(\ln y^f - \ln y) - \beta(\ln i^f - \ln i) + (\ln Ms - \ln Ms^f) \tag{7.8}$$

One of the initially surprising upshots of this approach was that economic growth causes a fall in the rate of exchange (an appreciation of the domestic currency). The economic reasoning behind this result is that a growth in y increases the real volume of money demanded, which, given the nominal money supply, makes the price level fall. Given PPP, that will cause the rate of exchange to fall too. Note that the *real exchange rate*, that is the nominal exchange rate corrected for relative price level movements, is constant under PPP. Nominal exchange rate movements exactly offset diverging price level movements under PPP, so that the relative price of a bundle of domestic goods and a bundle of foreign goods at the going nominal rate of exchange does not change. (See for a thorough discussion of real exchange rates and PPP, interpreted as an equilibrium relationship, De Grauwe 1989. The IMF calculates various real exchange indices, based on relative value-added deflators, relative wholesale prices, relative export unit values, relative consumer prices and, in order to best capture changes in international competitiveness, unit labour costs; see *World Economic Outlook*, October 1990, pp. 10-11.)

The distinguishing feature of the monetary approach is the uncovered interest parity assumption. The value of $(i^f - i)$ reflects the expected fall in the rate of exchange, which in its turn equals the expected divergence in relative price changes or inflation rates. With perfect capital markets and consequently a uniform expected real rate of interest this implies that the (other) Fisher relationship, which says that the nominal rate of interest equals the real rate plus the expected inflation rate, holds. The real rate of interest is assumed exogenous, it can be thought to be determined by the marginal efficiency of capital. Real interest rates therefore are equal across countries in this model, a result which requires that both uncovered interest rate parity and PPP hold.

For $(\ln i^f - \ln i)$ we may now write $(\ln \pi^{f*} - \ln \pi^*)$, where the asterisk denotes expected values and π = the rate of inflation. The forward premium reflects the difference in expected inflation rates. The difference between expected inflation rates is itself determined by expected rates of real growth and of money growth. Differentiating equation 7.5 with respect to time and bearing in mind that in steady-state inflation i = constant yields

$$\pi^* = -\alpha g_y^* + g_{Ms}^* \tag{7.9}$$

where g = growth rate.

Current and expected future spot and forward rates all hinge on expected future real income and expected future money growth.

The first monetary models, notably the model developed by Johnson (1972) as a kind of afterthought in his pioneer study on the monetary approach to the balance of payments in a fixed-rate system, did not further explore those expectations. Nominal interest rates simply reflected inflation expectations and that was it. Expected real and money growth need not, however, be constant for all future periods. This can be taken account of in the following way. We have seen that $(i^f - i)$ reflects the expected fall in the rate of exchange, $(e_t - E_t\, e_{t+1})$. For equation 7.8 we then may write

$$\ln e = \alpha(\ln y^f - \ln y) - \beta(\ln e_t - \ln E_t\, e_{t+1}) + (\ln Ms - \ln Ms^f) \tag{7.10}$$

Economic agents are assumed to have rational expectations, that is, to know the relevant economic model and use all available information. E_t is the expectational operator conditional on the available information at date t.

For the sake of convenience, denote $[\alpha(\ln y^f - \ln y) + (\ln Ms - \ln Ms^f)]$ by ln z and drop the ln's. Equation 7.10 can then be rewritten as

$$e_t = z_t - ß(e_t - E_t\, e_{t+1})$$

or

$$e_t = [1/(1 + ß)](z_t + ßE_t\, e_{t+1}) \quad (7.11)$$

From equation 7.11 it follows that

$$E_t\, e_{t+1} = [1/(1 + ß)](E_t\, z_{t+1} + ßE_t\, e_{t+2}) \quad (7.12)$$

Substitute equation 7.12 in equation 7.11:

$$e_t = [1/(1 + ß)][z_t + ß/(1 + ß).E_t\, z_{t+1} + ß^2/(1 + ß).E_t\, e_{t+2}].$$

Repeat this procedure for the next date:

$$E_t\, e_{t+2} = (1/1 + ß)(E_t\, z_{t+2} + ßE_t\, e_{t+3})$$

so that

$$e_t = [1/(1 + ß)].[z_t + ß/(1 + ß).E_t\, z_{t+1} + ß^2/(1 + ß)^2.E_t\, z_{t+2} + ß^3/(1 + ß)^2.E_t\, e_{t+3}]$$

and so on *ad infinitum*:

$$e_t = [1/(1 + ß)][z_t + ß/(1 + ß).\, E_t\, z_{t+1} + ß^2/(1 + ß)^2.E_t\, z_{t+2} + ß^3/(1 + ß)^3.\, E_t\, z_{t+3} + ..]$$

$$= [1/(1 + ß)]\sum_{j=0}^{\infty} [(ß/(1 + ß)]^j E_t\, z_{t+j} \quad (7.13)$$

The current exchange rate in this *Equilibrium Exchange Rate Model* or monetary model with rational expectations hinges on the expected values of the exogenous variables at all future dates (Bilson 1978, 1979, Hoffman and Schlagenhauf 1983, Vander Kraats and Booth 1983). A change in expectations as to future monetary policy, for instance, immediately feeds back into the current spot rate. An increase in the expected future growth of money (higher values for $E_t\, z_{t+j}$) raises the expected rate of inflation and hence also the rate of interest. A higher rate of interest decreases money demand. Given the money supply this leads to a higher current price level and, given PPP, a higher rate of exchange. Real growth increases the demand for real balances, depresses the price level and causes the rate of exchange to fall.

The price of foreign exchange is formed in very much the same way as the prices of other financial assets in this model and may therefore be highly volatile. Research conducted by Obstfeld (1985 p. 431), who calculated standard deviations of monthly percentage changes over the February 1976-February 1985 period for the United States, Japan and Germany, shows that the variability of the *effective* (that is, trade-weighted) nominal exchange rate lies between the variability of the wholesale price index and the variability of the stock market price index. The assumption that the price level immediately adjusts is, of course, far removed from reality. As will be argued in Chapter 8, PPP is questionable even in the long run. Only for periods of hyperinflation, when monetary disturbances swamp any other influences on prices and exchange rates, does PPP not seem to be at variance with the facts (Frenkel 1978). Uncovered interest parity can, however, be combined with prices that are sticky in the short run. This is the subject of the next section.

Dornbusch's sticky price monetary model

In Dornbusch's *Exchange Rate Dynamics Model* (Dornbusch 1980 ch. 11, Bilson 1979) we can discern three elements. First, uncovered interest parity prevails at all times, as in all monetary models. Next, prices are determined by the quantity theory relationship, but they take time to adjust after a change in the money supply. Finally, the long-term equilibrium rate of exchange depends on PPP.

Assume that, starting from an equilibrium with full employment in an economy with a given and constant production capacity, the money supply increases (in the form of a discrete jump, so that there is no ongoing inflation and consequently no Fisherian inflation compensation in nominal interest rates). Prices adjust slowly. The real money supply therefore increases at first, depressing the rate of interest. Given interest parity, a discount on the forward exchange rate will appear. With uncovered interest rate parity, a discount on the forward rate corresponds with an expected future fall in the rate of exchange. However, the increased money supply implies a higher future domestic price level and, consequently, a future rise in the rate of exchange. These two movements are only compatible if the rate of exchange first rises above its new long-term equilibrium level and gradually falls back to it later. This phenomenon is known as *overshooting*. Economic agents know the new long-term equilibrium rate of exchange and will, at the original rate of exchange, demand foreign assets. If the domestic interest rate has fallen, it pays to continue to demand foreign assets even when the new equilibrium rate has been reached, because foreign assets yield a higher return than domestic assets. The exchange rate is pushed still further upwards, until its expected future fall (to its new long-term equilibrium value) just offsets the higher interest rate. This mechanism can only explain mild exchange-rate fluctuations. If adjustments are expected to take one year and monetary policy makes the 12-month interest rate in a country initially change by, say, 4 per cent, this would only make for an initial amount of overshooting of also 4 per cent that would gradually be reduced to zero in the course of the year (Homburg 1989). Other cases of overshooting will be dealt with in the section on currency substitution below and in Chapter 8.

It is worth noting that overshooting in the present model hinges on the combination of slow price adjustment and high substitutability of foreign and domestic assets, with a high speed of adjustment. The lower the degree of substitutability, the smaller the increase in the rate of exchange brought about by a fall in the domestic rate of interest. Below some degree of substitutability, or some speed of adjustment, overshooting will not occur. But a situation like that is of course not within the compass of the monetary model. Also, it is assumed that a monetary impulse first results in a liquidity effect on the rate of interest. It can be imagined, though, that rational agents who understand that prices will rise, take advantage of the opportunity to borrow at interest rates that for a while are low in real terms. The demand for credit rises temporarily and with it the demand for money (Lüdiger 1989). This works against the fall in nominal rates that overshooting in the Dornbusch models rests upon.

Empirical tests of Dornbusch's sticky price model have not been very successful, but Papell (1988) argues that this is because researchers have applied single-equation methods. The outcome of estimates with his own structural-equation model for the US, UK, Germany and Japan for the 1973-1984 period were consistent with overshooting for Germany.

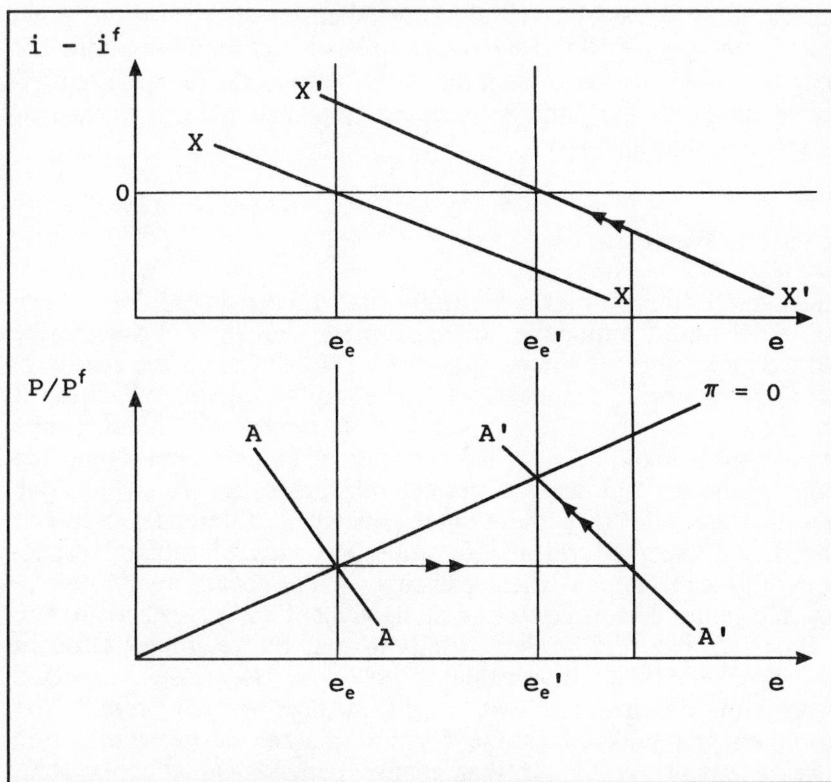

Figure 7.1. *Overshooting in the Dornbusch model (derived from Bilson 1979 p. 214).*

Commentary on Figure 7.1: In the upper half of the diagram, XX represents the locus of exchange rates and interest rate differentials compatible with equilibrium in the money market, given the equilibrium exchange rate e_e. X'X' and e_e' are the locus and the equilibrium exchange rate respectively after the money supply has increased. In the lower half, AA and A'A' represent the corresponding locus of relative price levels and exchange rates. $\pi = 0$ depicts the PPP condition, when all price adjustments after a unique shock have taken place. After an increase in the domestic money supply, the equilibrium exchange rate increases. Domestic prices stay put initially and the economy moves to a point on the A'A' curve to the right of the new equilibrium exchange rate. The domestic interest rate has temporarily fallen, as shown by the point reached on the X'X'-curve. As domestic prices rise and the economy moves upward along the A'A'-curve, the domestic interest rate increases too and the exchange rate moves back to its new long-term equilibrium level.

The peso problem

If uncovered interest parity prevails and agents in addition form their expectations rationally, forward rates should in principle be unbiased predictors of future spot rates. With rational expectations, agents use a correct model and make no systematic mistakes. If then there are persistent *ex post* excess returns on holding one currency over another, and risk premiums (which imply that the various assets are not seen as perfect substitutes) are ruled out, one is led to conclude that there were sustained differences between realized and expected values. Retaining the idea of rational expectations, this can happen when a change in the government's macroeconomic policy and a concomitant movement in the exchange rate are expected, but such a change fails to materialize for a period of time (Krasker 1980, Borenszstein 1987 pp. 34-7). An expected depreciation, for instance, will result in high *ex post* returns on investments not covered in the forward market during the period before it actually occurs. If that change depends on a policy shift, we have a *peso problem*. This expression refers to the situation in Mexico in the 1970s, when an expected devaluation of the peso was reflected in high domestic interest rates and a discount on the forward peso, long before the devaluation in fact took place in August 1976.

Speculative bubbles

In the preceding cases the exchange rate was firmly anchored in what are known as *market fundamentals*, including such variables as money supplies, interest rates, real incomes, price levels and inflation rates. In portfolio models, to be discussed below, fundamentals include relative asset supplies and in models not restricted to the very short run, trade balances can also be counted among the fundamentals. It has been argued by several authors that the rate of exchange may be influenced by other variables as well, even when retaining the efficiency condition that the expected excess return of holding foreign assets over the return on domestic assets is nil. The rate of exchange may be determined by rational expectations of (other market participants') whims, that is, my expectation of what other people's expectations will be. Those expectations may be governed by other factors than 'fundamentals'. We are back with Keynes's gloomy view of (in his case, stock) market valuation as a game of musical chairs (Keynes 1961 p. 156).

A *rational bubble* occurs when market participants weigh some expected chance of a continuing rise of a currency, for instance the dollar, against the probability of a crash. The expected rise may be totally unconnected with fundamentals. Assume that people know that in the long run fundamentals determine the rate of exchange, but that they expect the rate of exchange for some period of time to deviate from its fundamentals-compatible value (see Blanchard 1979). The expected rise in the rate of exchange is $E_t\ e_{t+1} - e_t$. Denote the rate of increase for any period t a_t. Speculators expect the increase to continue for a period at the rate a_t with a probability $(1 - p)$. Expected profits from speculation are $(1 - p)a_t$. The probability of a return of the exchange rate to its equilibrium value e_e is p and the associated loss amounts to $p(e_e - e_{t+1})$. Under (*ex ante*) uncovered interest parity (remember we are still within the compass of the monetary model), it follows that

$$i - i^f = (1 - p)a_t + p(e_e - e_{t+1}) \qquad (7.14)$$

G.W. Evans (1986) found evidence of a speculative bubble in the US dollar-pound sterling rate over the period 1981-1984. In this case, with the US dollar seen as the foreign currency, $i^f > i$ and there was a discount on the forward dollar. Still, it happened that the variable $a > 0$. The dollar continued appreciating even though American interest rates were higher than European and Japanese interest rates and a depreciation was expected in the end. In 1984 it was generally admitted that the dollar was overvalued; still, people invested in dollar assets. This may have been because of the expectation of individual investors to be able to pull out of the dollar just before its inevitable crash.

A curious corollary of the analysis which led to equation 7.14 is that, if a currency is overvalued and still appreciating, the rate of appreciation must be increasing over time. This is because the loss per unit of currency which the crash in the end will entail also increases over time, as the rate of exchange removes itself further and further from the equilibrium exchange rate (as perceived by the market participants). In terms of equation 7.14,

$$a = (i - i^f)/(1 - p) + (e_{t+1} - e_e).p/(1 - p) \qquad (7.15)$$

As long as the spot rate increases, given the interest rates and p, the value of the variable a must rise faster and faster. This result is conditional on a generally shared idea of what the equilibrium rate of exchange should be.

In the speculative bubble model, investors weigh the probability of a continued rise in the rate of exchange against the probability of a crash. There is *ex ante* uncovered interest rate parity. The interest rate differential between home and abroad reflects the expected exchange-rate change, that is, the mathematical expectation of the change in the rate of exchange. As long as the bubble does not burst, however, uncovered interest parity does not hold *ex post* and estimates of equation 7.3 seem to reject the monetary model, falsely, if there was indeed a bubble. Evans notes that there seems to be no satisfactory way to distinguish empirically between rational bubbles and two other explanations of exchange rate movements, apart from the possibility of unforeseeable 'news' making for a dollar appreciation (which makes for unforeseeable and unforeseen autocorrelation of the error term in equation 7.3). The first of these is that there may have been a peso problem, which resembles the rational bubble case in that *ex post* deviations from uncovered interest parity are quite compatible with the *ex ante* validity of uncovered interest parity. The other one is that expectations may not have been rational, either because a change in the fundamentals was not immediately perceived or because individually rational actors did not believe that other actors were rational. Portfolio models, of course, offer additional explanations.

It seems somewhat far-fetched to assume that the dollar was driven by a speculative bubble over a four-year-plus period. Speculative bubbles may explain short-term exchange-rate movements, but it is hard to believe that they could occur over periods spanning more than a few months. Perhaps economic agents had adjusted their expectations of the long-term equilibrium rate of the dollar upwards (Frankel 1985b pp. 201-2, Koromzay, Llewellyn and Potter 1987 pp. 29-30). As so often when competing theories or models are involved, a choice between them is made difficult because of observational equivalence, the phenomenon that the empirical evidence is compatible with several competing models. In the case of exchange rates, the fundamental problem is that it seems well-nigh impossible in the real world (as distinct from a model world) to pinpoint 'the' equilibrium exchange rate.

It should be emphasized that bubbles do not hinge on zero expected excess returns. They can also occur when a risk premium applies. In that case they properly fall under the next heading, that of portfolio analysis (a case in point is Woo 1987).

PORTFOLIO ANALYSIS

Risk premiums and exchange rates

In portfolio analysis domestic and foreign titles are not perfect substitutes. Covered interest parity holds but (*ex ante*) uncovered interest parity does not. Expected exchange-rate movements no longer correspond with interest differentials across countries. Portfolio analysis in a very-short-term setting studies the effects on the rate of exchange of decisions on the allocation of a given amount of wealth. In the very short term, changes in accumulated wealth can be taken as negligible in comparison to the stock of wealth. Again, the current account of the balance of payment is neglected.

When domestic and foreign titles are imperfect substitutes, the composition of portfolios, the rate of interest and the rate of exchange interact. The basic idea of portfolio analysis is that economic agents are risk averters, who demand a higher expected return if they are to add some risky asset to their portfolios. The relevant risk in the case of exchange-rate theory is exchange-rate risk. Assets are assumed to be identical as to maturity, taxability and default risk. The usual assumption is that the risk premium or required excess return increases with the share of the asset in question in the portfolio. Uncovered interest parity does not prevail in this case, but there is no reason why covered interest parity should not exist. Covered interest parity simply results from risk-avoiding behaviour by agents. The risk premium can be measured by the difference between required returns on assets denominated in different currencies or by the difference between the expected future spot rate and the forward rate: $r_t = E_t\, e_{t+1} - F^t$, where r = the risk premium. If, for instance, American investors demand a risk premium on sterling investments, the expected future rate of exchange of sterling in terms of dollars must be above the current forward rate. The American investors then expect to receive more dollars from unhedged sterling investments than from sterling positions that are hedged on the forward market. Given covered interest parity, this implies a higher expected return from unhedged investments in Britain than from investments in the US. The risk premium can also be seen as the expected profit from buying forward foreign exchange now and selling it in the future spot market (definitions of the risk premium vary, even within one publication: Koedijk 1989 defines the risk premium on p. 112 in the same way as we do here, but on p. 62 it is defined as the forward rate minus the expected future spot rate, as does Fama; so one should always be careful to ascertain which definition of the risk premium is used).

Variations in risk premiums can be a cause of exchange-rate fluctuations. Given domestic and foreign interest rates and the expected future spot rate, an increase in the risk premium r will depress both the forward rate and the current spot rate. This is because investors will demand less of the foreign currency at the original rate of exchange and in that way cause the rate of exchange to fall. Given covered interest parity, the forward rate moves in step with the current spot rate if interest rates are constant.

A simple representation of the portfolio model is the following:

$$Ms = Md = a_1 (i, i^f + x) W \tag{7.16}$$

$$Bs = Bd = a_2 (i, i^f + x) W \tag{7.17}$$

$$eQs = eQd = a_3 (i, i^f + x) W \tag{7.18}$$

$$a_1 + a_2 + a_3 = 1 \tag{7.19}$$

with x = expected change in the exchange rate; W = nominal wealth; Bs = supply of domestic bonds; Bd = demand for domestic bonds; Qs = domestic supply of foreign bonds, expressed in the number of bonds; Qd = domestic demand for foreign bonds. In order to avoid complications resulting from the impact of interest rate changes on bond prices, it seems best to define both domestic and foreign bonds as floating rate notes, the prices of which for all practical purposes are fixed. An alternative, suggested by de Jong (1983 p. 227), is to assume a very short time to maturity of the titles.

Given total wealth, domestic and foreign interest rates, exchange rate expectations, perceived risk on domestic and foreign titles and preferences as to combinations of risk and expected return, domestic economic agents want to invest a certain fraction a_3 of their wealth in foreign bonds. Given a_3.W, any combination of e and Qs that has the value a_3.W will fulfil the wishes of the economic agents. The product of the rate of exchange and the number of bonds is a constant. In a diagram with the number of bonds Q on the abscissa and the rate of exchange on the ordinate, the demand for foreign bonds as a function of the rate of exchange is represented by an orthogonal hyperbola (see Figure 7.2). The demand schedule and the given number of foreign bonds determine the rate of exchange.

The number of foreign bonds can be taken as given. In this model the current account is neglected and the central bank does not intervene in the foreign exchange market; nor do commercial banks, for that matter. Neglecting the current account and with the official settlements account in equilibrium, the capital account cannot but be in equilibrium as well. Hence, the number of foreign bonds cannot change. Now imagine that some change in the data of the system takes place, for instance, the domestic money supply increases. An excess supply of domestic money and an excess demand for domestic bonds and foreign bonds ensues. The rate of interest on domestic bonds is driven down, but the foreign rate of interest and foreign bond prices are given for domestic economic agents. The only variable they can influence is the rate of exchange. An increase in the demand for foreign bonds drives up the rate of exchange. The demand curve for foreign bonds shifts upwards (for any given volume of foreign bonds a higher rate of exchange is offered) and to the right (at any rate of exchange more foreign bonds are demanded). A fall in the perceived risk of investment in foreign bonds (in portfolio analysis commonly defined as the perceived standard deviation of possible future returns) will have similar results for the demand for foreign bonds. They will become more attractive to the normal risk averse investor.

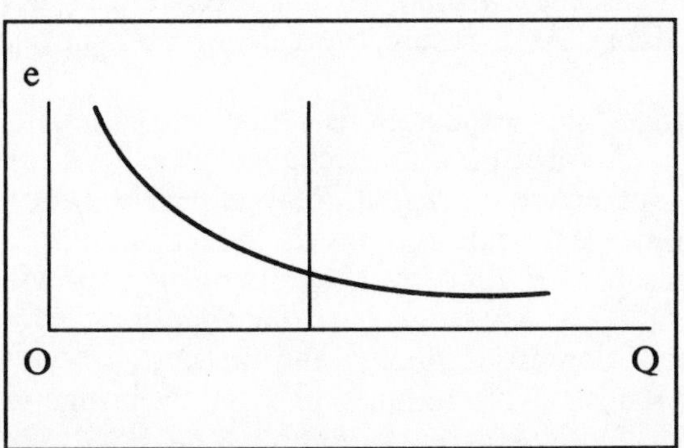

Figure 7.2. *Rate of exchange and number of foreign bonds.*

The basic specification of the model admits of variants. One simplifying specification is to model the demand for money as a demand for transactions purposes only (see Branson 1985 p. 145). In that case, portfolio considerations are absent in money demand and wealth is not an argument in the money demand function. An interesting case presents itself when net holdings of foreign bonds are negative, as Masson (1981) has shown (see also de Jong 1983 and Branson 1985 p. 152). Domestic economic agents then have a foreign-currency-denominated net debt *vis-à-vis* non-residents. Unlike the situation with positive net holdings, equilibrium situations may now be unstable. Let us first look at what happens after a random shock when net holdings are positive. Assume that the rate of exchange temporarily increases for some reason. The value of e, and therefore of eQs, will rise above its equilibrium value. The excess supply of foreign bonds will make the rate of exchange return to its equilibrium value. In the case where Qs < 0, however, an increase in e will increase the value of foreign-currency-denominated net debt vis-à-vis non-residents. Economic agents want to reduce the share of this net debt in their portfolios and exert a demand for foreign-currency-denominated bonds (to offset foreign-currency debt with foreign-currency assets) or for foreign currency (in order to pay off their debt). As a result, the rate of exchange is pushed further upward.

Under nonstatic exchange-rate expectations such destabilizing processes need not occur. A rise of the exchange rate will be intensified when Qs < 0, but economic agents may expect a return to the original level or some level not too much higher in future. After the exchange rate has passed that level, economic agents will therefore expect a future fall. The value of x in the equations 7.16-7.18 will turn negative and domestic money and domestic bonds become relatively more attractive. This reduces and finally brings to an end the net demand for foreign-currency-denominated bonds, or may even lead to an excess supply as investors wish to increase foreign-currency-denominated debt *vis-à-vis* nonresidents. The rate of exchange stops rising or may fall again (see for a more formal analysis Branson and Henderson 1985 pp. 777ff.).

The risk premiums involved in systematic differences between forward rates and expected future spot rates need not be constant, as has already been observed. They will in principle vary with the proportion of the different assets in wealthholders' portfolios, but they may also, given that proportion, vary over time. One cause may be that the covariance of the exchange rate with the return on other assets, which is the measure for the degree in which portfolio diversification can contribute to risk diminution, varies over time. Attempts to construct and estimate an empirical version of this kind of model are reported by Koedijk and Luttmer (1987), Bomhoff and Koedijk (1988), and Koedijk (1989). It may be noted that changes in the asset composition as such do not seem able to explain a great deal of the actual fluctuations in real-returns differences, such as the high excess returns on dollar holdings during 1980-1984 (that is, higher returns than compatible with uncovered interest parity), given plausible risk-aversion coefficients. Frankel found that an increase in the volume of foreign assets of 1 per cent of world wealth would require a risk premium of no more than about 0.02 per cent per annum (Frankel 1986 p. S54, see also Frankel 1985b p. 211, and 1985a, as discussed in Chapter 2 in the section on *ex post* crowding out). In order to explain exchange-rate fluctuations in a portfolio framework one then has to rely on variations over time of the risk premium. Frankel (1986 p. S63) is not hopeful about the explanatory power of this approach and Froot and Frankel (1989) found a substantial average level of the risk premium but no connection between the varying part of the risk premium and expected exchange-rate movements (which incidentally were generated by survey data). Instead they found substantial systematic expectational errors. Diebold and Pauly (1988) found evidence of a varying risk premium in the DMark-dollar rate, but noted that this is empirically hard to separate from market irrationality or rational bubbles. Fama (1984) and Hodrick and Srivastava (1986) found for a number of currencies that the risk premium r as they defined it covaried negatively with the expected rate of change of the rate of exchange, or covaried positively in our definition. This is puzzling, because it implies that the premium r becomes larger when the rate of exchange is expected to rise and smaller when the rate of exchange is expected to fall. As Fama (1988 p. 327) puts it, a good story for this phenomenon is difficult to tell, for it means that if, for instance, the German expected inflation rate is lower than the British one and the DMark is therefore expected to appreciate in terms of sterling, Mark-denominated bonds carry a higher risk premium than when the Mark is expected to fall. Now it seems reasonable to assume that higher inflation rates increase uncertainty (about inflation rates, and thus about real returns), so one would expect, if anything, investors to demand higher risk premiums in inflation-prone countries. Fama's and Hodrick and Srivastava's findings are compatible with a situation where interest rates do not fully reflect future exchange-rate changes, or, put differently, the Fisher open condition does not hold. Unhedged investments in appreciating countries then yield a higher real return than unhedged investments in depreciating countries. The expected future spot rate for appreciating currencies thus is higher than the interest-rate determined current forward rate, and the converse for depreciating countries. If no good reason is found why risk premiums should be higher for appreciating currencies, one is tempted to conclude that in such cases there is either irrationality or unevenly distributed 'news'. Aivazian, Callen, Krinsky and Kwan (1986) found that changes in variances of exchange-rate changes have a larger impact on asset demand than changes in expected returns. This means that increasing variance leads to higher risk premiums, which is intuitively acceptable. Koedijk (1989 pp. 252-3) reports generally satisfactory results of his approach, but is unable to explain the ongoing appreciation of the US dollar between March 1984 and February 1985. So one may arrive at the admittedly somewhat lame conclusion that there are interesting, but not conclusive, results from applying the risk approach to exchange-rate determination.

A problem with these portfolio models for the very short term is that the rate of exchange is a rate at which no exchange need take place at all. In the case of a free float, exchange-rate movements see to it that the existing volumes of domestic and foreign debt are willingly held by investors. As there are no net capital movements and the current account, including payments of capital income, is neglected, no international payments have to be made. The rate of exchange is not the price at which foreign currency is bought and sold; it is nothing but a numeraire linking the domestic and foreign currency prices of foreign bonds. This problem disappears if we not only allow domestic agents to hold foreign debt but also foreign agents to hold domestic debt. The volume of foreign debt held by domestic agents need no longer be constant in that case, even if there are no net capital inflows or outflows: the volume of foreign debt held by domestic agents can increase if they succeed in selling domestic debt (bonds) to foreign agents and decrease if they buy back domestic debt. Another possibility is that domestic agents hold both foreign debt and foreign currency. In that case it is again possible to change the volume of foreign debt held by domestic agents even in the very short term, this time not against domestic debt but against foreign money (see the section on currency substitution below).

Safe haven effects

A special kind of portfolio effect on exchange rates is the *safe haven effect*. In the case of the safe haven effect, domestic and foreign titles differ as to political risk. Residents of a country may fear high taxes or high future taxes. Also, they may hedge against future changes of government that might bring with it confiscation of their property. Or they may prefer to hold funds abroad not only to evade taxes but also to keep out of the hands of the police. In general, the safe haven effect does not so much concern a comparison between rates of return that induces people to invest abroad as a wish to keep the principal safely out of the hands of the domestic authorities (of course confiscation can be seen as a negative return). Under this heading come the profits from drug trafficking, but also investments in real estate abroad by Hong Kong residents who want to have a place to flee to after China takes over in 1997. Not all so-called capital flight can be seen as being motivated by safe haven considerations. Much of it, in particular from Latin America, resulted from a fear of negative real returns on domestic investments in a situation of double- or triple-digit inflation and can be explained by standard risk-return analysis.

The safe haven effect might provide an explanation of the puzzling rise of the dollar during the last three quarters of a year or so before its reached its zenith in February 1985, when most market participants considered the dollar overvalued. It is, though, hard to find a yardstick for this effect. An attempt has been made by Ayanian (1989), who regressed real dollar exchange rates for eleven countries over the 1973-1986 period on, firstly, US defence efforts and, secondly, on their capitals' distance from Washington and Moscow respectively. The idea behind this is that capital flight that is motivated by a fear of political turmoil is likely to be directed toward countries with a stable political climate that, moreover, are not under serious military threat from a foreign power.

Currency substitution

Another special case of portfolio diversification is the holding of both domestic and foreign currencies by a country's economic agents, which was already touched upon in Chapters 5 and 6. If we include foreign money in domestic agents' portfolios, we have to add an equation to system 7.16-7.19. Also, the expected rate of change of the exchange rate is included as an argument in the various demand functions. This is because the demand for foreign money is first of all a function of expected exchange-rate changes (see de Jong 1990 p. 14). The system now becomes as follows:

$$Ms = Md = a_1 (i, if + x, x) W \quad (7.20)$$

$$Bs = Bd = a_2 (i, i^f + x, x) W \quad (7.21)$$

$$eQs = eQd = a_3 (i, i^f + x, x) W \quad (7.22)$$

$$eMfs = eMfd = a_4 (i, i^f + x, x) W \quad (7.23)$$

$a_1 + a_2 + a_3 + a_4 = 1$; Mf = foreign exchange held by residents.

Apart from the aim of portfolio diversification, a reduction in transaction costs may be an important motive for firms engaged in foreign trade to hold foreign exchange (see on transactions costs and their importance for currency substitution Handa and Bana 1990). Obviously, other scale variables than wealth would be relevant in this case (see the section on the arguments in the money-demand function in Chapter 6).

Shifts from domestic into foreign currency and vice versa are an independent source of exchange-rate instability. Little can be said, though, on the degree to which exchange rates move as a result of currency substitution. Much-cited is the reasoning by Calvo and Rodriguez (1977), which runs as follows. Assume that the domestic money supply growth increases. Expected domestic inflation increases, too. This makes domestic currency less attractive to hold relative to foreign currency. Real balances in domestic currency fall, which gives a one-time boost to goods prices, over and above the new (higher) rate of inflation. The rate of exchange is not only affected by these goods price developments. Domestic agents wish to increase their real balances of foreign currency (and, one might add, foreign agents wish to decrease their holdings of the home country's currency). With a given supply of foreign exchange at any moment, this extra demand for foreign exchange first translates into a higher price of foreign exchange, that is, a higher rate of exchange. The rate of exchange increases by more than the domestic price level, which means that the real exchange rate increases (the domestic price level falls relative to the foreign price level at the going rate of exchange). It may be expected that after some time the real rate of exchange falls, as the higher real rate improves the current account of the balance of payments and enables economic agents to add foreign exchange to their portfolios, but that mechanism springs the limits of the very short term. There will have been exchange-rate overshooting: the exchange rate first reacted very strongly before returning to its long-term equilibrium value. The equilibrium value will be higher than without currency substitution, though, for in a growing economy or a world where foreign countries also are subject to inflation, albeit at a lower rate, domestic agents continuously wish to add to their holdings of foreign currency. In a growing economy this is because they wish to increase their real cash balances; in the case of foreign inflation it follows from a wish to keep real balances intact.

In the above reasoning, economic agents only shifted between domestic and foreign monies. If portfolios also contain other assets the analysis becomes less clear-cut. An increased demand for real foreign cash balances can also be met, at least partly, from selling other foreign assets. Shifts between foreign non-monetary assets (bonds) and foreign money leave the rate of exchange unaffected (Engel 1989; see also Zervoyianni 1988 for an analysis with a similar model which also includes the real sector of the economy and distinguishes between various degrees of substitutability between the assets in the portfolios). The difference with the portfolio model discussed in the section on risk premiums and exchange rates is that in the very short run it is not the volume of foreign bonds that is given, but rather the foreign-exchange value of the sum of foreign bonds and foreign money.

Currency substitution has been extensively subjected to empirical research. Problems abound. Foreign interest rates are at times used as arguments in the domestic money-demand function, in order to measure the degree of substitutability. But it is not clear how this effect can be distinguished from the substitution between money and bonds in a portfolio model, where capital mobility is involved. Melvin (1985), following the lead provided by B. Klein, therefore adds the 'quality' of money as an argument to the money-demand function. This 'quality' is measured by inflation uncertainty. Melvin reports evidence of currency substitution, with the DMark as the most popular substitute for other currencies. With increasing inflation uncertainty in a country, the demand for Marks rises. This causes additional volatility in exchange rates, over and above the volatility from other sources. Cuddington (1983 p. 115) notes that currency substitution is not usually studied within a general-equilibrium portfolio framework. The common procedure is to assume a sequential portfolio choice process where investors first decide how to divide their wealth over money and non-monetary financial assets, and next, how to divide their money balances over domestic and foreign money. For the latter decision, interest rates are taken as given and are interpreted as opportunity costs, together with expected exchange-rate changes. This is a dubious procedure. An increase in the foreign rate of interest, for instance, may increase the demand for foreign non-monetary assets. Both domestic and foreign money is held. If we abstract from the current account, there may not be much that could change the domestic money supply, but foreign currency balances fall. This is not a case of currency substitution but of capital flows. It is, in addition, not at first sight clear why uncovered interest rates should be seen as the opportunity cost of holding foreign currency. Bergstrand and Bundt (1990) see interest rates as representing the marginal productivities of monetary inputs in the production of money services, which could be a solution to this problem.

Empirical research suggests that currency substitution is not a significant factor in exchange-rate movements between the currencies of the industrialized rich countries (Cuddington 1983, Laney, Radcliffe and Willett 1984, Batten and Hafer 1984). In economically less-developed countries, though, rampant inflation could induce people to replace domestic by foreign currency, which can hardly fail to put upward pressure on exchange rates (or, in a fixed-but-adjustable-peg setting, hasten the decision to devalue). A few examples are Egypt, where foreign exchange held with banks increased from about 25 per cent of the broad money supply in 1980 to around 40 per cent in 1985, and Yugoslavia, where foreign exchange held with banks increased from 26 per cent to 45 per cent of the broad money supply in the same period (El-Erian 1987). These figures only cover bank deposits. No reliable figures on notes and coin are available. To cite another case, Dornbusch (1988 pp. 244-5) reports that in Mexico dollar-denominated deposits with resident banks rose from a level of 4-5 per cent of total bank deposits during the early 1970s to around 20 per cent from 1977 to 1981 and again to some 40 per cent in 1982 (after which they fell steeply). In addition, considerable capital exports occurred. Obviously, currency substitution to the degree found in these countries poses additional problems apart from increasing the variability of exchange rates. Firstly, *seigniorage*, that is, the revenue accruing to the government from the creation of base money, falls and secondly, monetary policy becomes more difficult to plan and execute (see Ramírez-Rojas 1986, who gives figures for seigniorage for some countries running as high as 10 per cent or more of GNP). This is because the demand for domestic money becomes less stable, so that the impact of monetary policy measures is harder to forecast. If the authorities then allow people to hold foreign-currency deposits at domestic banks, they at least gain some idea of the seriousness of the problem and, in addition, they could try to conduct monetary policy by influencing the rate of interest paid on foreign currency deposits. Legal opportunities to hold foreign exchange at domestic banks, moreover, may serve as alternatives to capital flight and in that way prevent foreign exchange crises from occurring. Nonetheless, if banks are only allowed to offer foreign-currency-denominated deposits if they hold foreign exchange to the same amount themselves, wild fluctuations in the exchange rate are still a distinct possibility. Bank customers' demand for foreign exchange to be held at that bank results in a demand for foreign exchange on the part of the banks. The best one can hope for is that the bank customers already possess foreign exchange which they sell to the bank in exchange for foreign-currency-denominated deposits.

8. Exchange Rate Theories II

THE SHORT PERIOD

In the analysis of exchange-rate determination for the very short period the current account of the balance of payments was neglected. Beyond the very short period the current account joins the capital account in the explanation of the rate of exchange. We first deal with the short period. Given nonintervention by the central bank and the commercial banks, the balance of payments of the nonbank sector is in equilibrium, but the current account and the capital account separately may show a surplus or a deficit. A surplus on one account is the mirror image of a deficit on the other. An equilibrium on the foreign-exchange market cannot but be temporary if the current account is in disequilibrium. A disequilibrium on the current account means that claims by residents on nonresidents or claims by nonresidents on residents are being built up, which lead to future receipts or payments on the current account. Besides, national wealth will increase in the case of an accumulation of claims or decrease in the case of an accumulation of liabilities, which may influence the rate of interest and will both directly and indirectly, via the rate of interest, affect domestic spending. In short-period analysis these consequences of a disequilibrium in the current account are neglected. They are taken up in the analysis of the long period.

The IS/LM model

The standard IS/LM model can easily be expanded for an open economy. The current account depends on national income and the rate of exchange, and capital flows are a function of the rate of interest and possibly of national income. The rate of exchange follows from the following identity:

$$X(e) - Im(Y, e) + K(i,Y) \equiv 0 \quad (8.1)$$

X = exports, Im = imports, Y = nominal national income, K = net capital inflow.

As Sinn (1983 p. 36) observes, this model specifies the speed with which portfolios are adjusted, leaving the portfolio structure itself indeterminate. A portfolio model may be grafted onto the IS/LM model in order to capture the stock adjustments consequent upon a change in the data of the system (see Argy 1981 pp. 128-9; for an analysis of a variety of disturbances and policy measures in an IS/LM model with a portfolio see Branson 1985; for a flexible-price IS/LM model for an open economy see Bladen Hovell and Green 1989; and for a model that includes money-financed and bond-financed government budget deficits but does not spell out the current account see Baltensperger and Böhm 1982). Assume for the sake of simplicity that there is no inflation, so that real interest rates do not differ from nominal interest rates, and that domestic residents hold foreign assets but foreign residents only hold their home country assets. Let the proportion of foreign titles in domestic portfolios depend on the difference between foreign and domestic interest rates:

$$eQ/W = b(i^f - i) \quad (8.2)$$

b is a parameter, not a function.

Note that this formulation does not allow of perfect substitutability of domestic and foreign assets as in monetary models. With $i^f = i$, no foreign assets would be held in the present formulation, whilst in monetary models any proportion of domestic portfolios could be held in foreign assets.

Net capital inflow, K, equals minus the increase in the volume of foreign titles times the rate of exchange. Total differentiation of equation 8.2 yields

$$e.dQ + Q.de = bW.d(i^f - i) + b(i^f - i).dW$$

and net capital inflow is

$$K = - e.dQ = Q.de - bW.d(i^f - i) - b(i^f - i).dW \quad (8.3)$$

Now assume that the domestic interest rate increases and economic agents wish to reduce the share of foreign titles in their portfolios. It is to be expected that the rate of exchange falls, as more foreign exchange is supplied at the original rate, following from the sale of foreign titles, and a deficit on the current account has to develop in

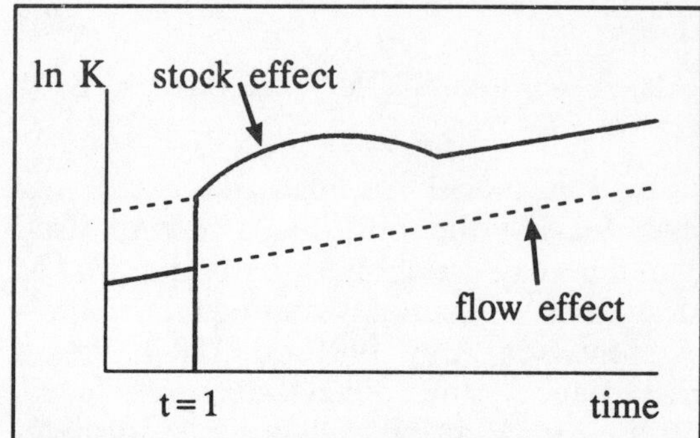

Figure 8.1. *Capital flows in a portfolio setting.*

ln K = natural logarithm net capital inflow, t=1 is point in time at which domestic interest rate rises.

order to accommodate the net capital inflow. A fall in the rate of exchange in and by itself goes some way to fulfil a wish to reduce the share of foreign titles in the portfolio. This effect is captured by the term Q.de (note that in this case de is negative). The *stock effect* following from the wish to restructure existing portfolios is captured by the term $bW.d(i^f - i)$. This is a short-term effect, as in subsequent periods $d(i^f - i)$ will be zero again. The stock effect is neglected in models in which capital flows are a function of differences in interest rates. There is also a continuing *flow effect* following from the fact that a larger or smaller fraction of wealth increases will be invested abroad after a change in interest rate differences (or other changes for that matter, such as a change in relative riskiness). This effect is found by subtracting $- b(i^f - i).dW$ at the original rates of interest from $- b(i^f - i).dW$ at the new rates of interest. The resulting inflow (which may of course be negative, that is, an outflow) is a continuing flow depending on the growth of wealth (see Figure 8.1).

Volatility of the rate of exchange may be caused not only by the capital account, as we discussed in the last chapter, but also by the current account. In particular, lagged adjustment of the current account after exchange-rate changes may cause *overshooting*. Overshooting is a result of some lagged adjustment. Various lags may be responsible. Apart from the cases dealt with in this section and the next one, we have seen that overshooting may result from lagged adjustment of the price level (the Dornbusch case covered in Chapter 7) and we will see that it may also be brought about by lagged adjustment in portfolio composition (see below).

After an exchange-rate change, import and export volumes need some time to adjust, given the relative price changes brought about by the appreciation or depreciation. Assume that a depreciation is called for in order to prevent a deficit on the current account (we abstract from the capital account). If volumes react slowly at first, a relatively large depreciation will occur. As time goes by, imports decrease and exports continue to grow, so that the depreciation has to be partly reversed in order to maintain a balanced current account. This process may be protracted if, as seems to have been the case in the United States during the first half of the 1980s, whole industries have disappeared because of a high value of the currency and a depreciation is slow in wooing back those industries (Dornbusch 1987 p. 9). This *hysteresis effect* may necessitate a long period of undervaluation of the currency relative to its long-term equilibrium rate.

If the Marshall-Lerner condition is not immediately fulfilled, the foreign-exchange market would be unstable if left to its current-account devices. Stabilizing capital flows must come to the rescue in that case. A depreciation that would, if only temporarily, increase a current-account deficit (that is, produce a J-curve effect), would raise the rate of exchange until speculators felt that after some period of time the rate of exchange would fall again to some degree. They then sell (owned or borrowed) foreign exchange, expecting to be able to buy it back later at a lower price. They may also sell foreign exchange on the forward market. The arbitrageurs who act as buyers of forward foreign exchange will hedge their positions by borrowing foreign exchange and selling the proceeds on the spot market. In both cases the spot rate falls.

One may wonder if speculation via currency options would also help to stabilize the foreign-exchange market. Speculators who expect a future fall of the rate of exchange (that is a future appreciation of the domestic currency) may buy put options. Increased demand for put options drives their prices up. Some speculators will then find the forward market more attractive and in this way speculation through put options will indirectly help to raise the spot rate.

With rational expectations (and no interest rate changes, see Chapter 7 on the Dornbusch model) capital movements may even prevent any overshooting. Economic agents know the relevant economic model, they know how the data of the model have changed and therefore they know the new equilibrium value of the rate of exchange. Any tendency to overshoot will immediately be counteracted by stabilizing speculation.

As we saw in Chapter 7 in the section on the Dornbusch model, a monetary shock that in the first instance influences the rate of interest will cause overshooting, provided asset substitutability and the speed of adjustment are high. If a rise in the rate of exchange improves the current account and asset substitutability or the speed of adjustment is low, no overshooting need occur. A J-curve effect in its turn will, as we have just seen, increase the degree of overshooting if asset substitutability is low. This is because the capital imports needed to tide over the temporary deterioration of the current account will only be induced if the lower interest rate consequent on a positive money-supply shock is offset by a (much) higher expected appreciation (exchange-rate fall). If assets are very poor substitutes, or adjustment is very slow, instability may occur (as in the case without capital movements). The rate of interest falls, capital exports push up the rate of exchange, the current account deteriorates, pushing the exchange further up and so on. The expectation of a future exchange-rate fall (appreciation of the domestic currency) may induce capital imports, but not in sufficient volume to counteract the rise in the exchange rate caused by the deterioration of the current account (Frenkel and Rodriguez 1982, Witzel 1984).

Dependent-economy models

In *dependent-economy models* or *Australian models* there are two goods, as in the IS/LM model. The dichotomy in this case is not between home goods and foreign goods, but between tradeables and nontradeables. Tradeables are produced, consumed and exported or imported; nontradeables are exclusively produced for domestic consumption. For tradeables the *law of one price* (LOP) holds. This says that similar goods carry the same price in each and every market, expressed in one currency at the going exchange rates. Expositions of the model usually start with the assumption of no capital flows (Argy 1981 ch. 13, Frenkel and Mussa 1985 pp. 716-23). Capital flows then are added, in consonance with the assumption of LOP made for the tradeable goods sector, under the assumption of perfectly integrated capital markets. In other words, uncovered interest parity prevails (see Argy 1981 ch. 13). As in the Equilibrium Exchange Rate Model, exchange-rate expectations can be introduced via the forward rate (see Frenkel and Mussa 1985 p. 718). The proportions in which tradeables and nontradeables are produced and consumed depend on relative prices. The price mechanism ensures full employment. The market for nontradeables is cleared by price movements. The price of tradeables is determined by the world market price and the rate of exchange; excess supply or excess demand does not make the price move but causes a surplus, respectively a deficit, on the current account. Exchange-rate changes do not affect the foreign-currency price of tradeables.

The terms of trade in the sense of the relative price of export goods in terms of import goods are fixed, at unity, as exportables and importables are lumped together under the heading of tradeables. Nominal rates of exchange can change, of course, and so can real rates, because the relative prices of tradeables and nontradeables can shift. The average price level in a country therefore need not move in step with the exchange rate. In other words, PPP need not obtain.

As in the standard monetary model, real growth increases the demand for real balances and causes an appreciation of the currency. One perhaps counterintuitive result from two-sector reasoning is that an autonomous increase in nominal spending may lead to an appreciation of the currency. This may occur when most or all of the additional spending is on nontradeables. The relative price of nontradeables will rise, drawing resources away from the tradeables sector. Nominal money demand increases which, with a given money supply, brings about a higher average price level and a higher rate of interest. The higher rate of interest in its turn chokes off the increase in demand (remember that productive capacity was already fully utilized at the start, no slack existed to absorb an increase in real demand). Now a higher average price level with a lower relative price of tradeables is compatible with a higher absolute price of tradeables, an unchanging one and a lower one. A lower absolute domestic price of tradeables implies a fall in the rate of exchange, that is an appreciation of the domestic currency, given the world market prices of tradeables.

If we in addition introduce fully interest-elastic capital flows, an appreciation is unavoidable, even in case the increase in demand is only partly directed to nontradeables. The domestic rate of interest cannot diverge from the foreign rate in that situation, given static exchange-rate expectations. With a given money supply, constant full employment and a stable money demand function, an unchanged interest rate implies an unchanged average price level. This will immediately be obvious from the equation of exchange $MV = Py$, with M = money supply, V = velocity of circulation, P = price level and y = real production or income. With a stable money demand function V will be constant if the rate of interest is constant. Given M and y it follows that P remains unchanged. A lower relative price of tradeables can only come about through a lower absolute price of tradeables, that is, an appreciation of the domestic currency. Obviously, if the rate of interest remains unchanged the increase in demand is not choked off. The increase in demand for nontradeables is met by a higher production of nontradeables, through a shift in relative prices. The fall in the relative price of tradeables, combined with a possible initial rise in the demand for tradeables, yields an excess demand that is met through imports and paid for through capital imports.

Though the Law of One Price is not empirically valid (see below), it may serve as a useful first approximation. The history of the stabilization attempts in Latin America's Southern Cone during the late 1970s can be interpreted in terms of the dependent economy model (Corbo and de Melo 1987, Corbo, de Melo and Tybout 1986). Attempts to curb price increases by liberalizing international trade were based on the idea that domestic producers of tradeables would be compelled to conform to foreign prices. In the case of Argentina, the model was not relevant because protection remained high, but the Chilean attempt was better thought through and relatively successful. Of course the success of such a strategy hinges on a number of additional conditions, the most important one probably being that fiscal policy keep aggregate demand growth within limits. The model admits of causation both running from exchange rates to prices and from prices to exchange rates. Unplanned devaluation does not invalidate the model, therefore. If, for instance, capital imports depress the nominal exchange rate (that is, make for an appreciation), the prices of tradeables, which are constrained by foreign competition, will fall relative to the prices of nontradeables. Production will shift to nontradeables whilst the demand for tradeables, which have become relatively cheaper, increases. If net capital imports stop, a devaluation or depreciation is imperative in order to increase the relative price of tradeables and eliminate the excess demand for tradeables (which is equal to the current account deficit in this model). Obviously, the condition of prudent fiscal policy comes into play at this point.

As in the IS/LM model, overshooting of the rate of exchange may occur because of adjustments that take time. Starting again with capital imports, in this case continuing over the years, first the domestic currency will appreciate and the rate of exchange falls. As time goes by, however, it gets easier to transfer factors of production from the tradeables sector to the nontradeables sector. Put differently, the elasticity of supply in a sector is greater in the long run than in the short run. The relative price of nontradeables moves back in the direction of the original situation and the currency starts to depreciate again. Hoffmann and Homburg (1990) use this mechanism to explain the puzzling movements of the dollar over the 1980-1987 period.

Dependent-economy models derive their importance not only from their inherent qualities in explaining real-life developments, but also from the fact that they underlie much of IMF and World Bank economic analysis (see IMF *Annual Report 1989* p. 16, World Bank *Report 1989* p. 127).

THE LONG PERIOD

The Dornbusch-Fischer model

In the long period the rate of exchange will move until both the current account and the capital account are separately in equilibrium. The study of long-term adjustment processes is still in its infancy. A milestone is the article by Dornbusch and Fischer (1980), which if anything made it clear that even with quite simple assumptions the analysis tends to get rather complicated. Production is given and constant, prices are flexible and the means of production are fully employed. The home country is small, which means that the prices of imports are given and constant in terms of the foreign currency and the world interest rate is given, too. Economic agents hold two assets: domestic money and foreign bonds. Foreign bonds are defined as yielding one unit of foreign produce per time unit. The price level moves to equilibrate the money market and the rate of exchange moves to make the terms of trade equilibrate the market for domestic goods, exports and domestic demand for home goods being a function of the terms of trade. Short-term equilibrium may leave the current account in disequilibrium. The volume of foreign assets expands or contracts, affecting domestic spending until the current account is in equilibrium and full equilibrium is reached.

Money demand is a function of the (foreign) rate of interest and of income. Income is defined as the value of domestic production plus net capital income from abroad. Equilibrium in the domestic money market is represented by

$$M = k[i^f, (Py + eP^f.Q)] \qquad (8.4)$$

$eP^f.Q$ is the domestic value of the foreign goods earned as capital income on the foreign bonds.

For equation 8.4 we may write

$$m = k[i^f, (y + e.P^f/P.Q)] \qquad (8.5)$$

m is the real money supply, M/P.

If the foreign rate of interest and domestic real production are constant, and we define the terms of trade R as $R = P/eP^f$, equation 8.5 can be written as

$$m = k(1/R, Q) \tag{8.6}$$

In the market for domestic goods equilibrium obtains when

$$y = D(R, w) + X(R) \tag{8.7}$$

D = domestic demand for home goods, w = real wealth = $m + e.P^f.1/P.1/i^f.Q = m + Q.1/i^f.1/R$ (the nominal foreign price of foreign bonds is one unit of foreign produce divided by the foreign rate of interest).

With equilibrium in the market for domestic goods (brought about by movements in the terms of trade), a current account imbalance may exist. Neglecting investment and government income and expenditure, the surplus on the current account is equal to savings. Dornbusch and Fischer assume savings to be a function of wealth:

$$S = S(w) \qquad S_w < 0 \tag{8.8}$$

S = real savings, S_w is the partial derivative of S with respect to w.

Let us now trace how a current account surplus makes the system move to full equilibrium. Q increases, and with it total wealth w. Real money demand rises. The domestic price level falls as a result. Total real wealth rises even further. Domestic spending receives a boost and equilibrium in the market for domestic goods can only be preserved if the relative price of domestic goods increases, that is, if R rises. With P falling, this requires an appreciation of the domestic currency, that is a fall in the exchange rate. This process will continue until real wealth has risen far enough to reduce savings to nil.

Though this model was presented as an exchange-rate model, it is debatable if it is really such a thing. In this case, the rate of exchange is not even needed as a numeraire linking foreign and domestic currencies, as the yield on foreign bonds is paid in foreign goods. The value of foreign bonds can therefore be expressed in terms of foreign goods. The model is in fact a barter model and solves for the terms of trade, which is a real, not a nominal, magnitude.

The portfolio model once again

In the Dornbusch-Fischer model, economic agents held rudimentary portfolios, made up of domestic money and foreign bonds only. If we return to our earlier portfolio model, we can deduce a few results for the development of the exchange rate from a richer menu of assets in agents' portfolios, even if the reasoning is somewhat intuitive rather than formal (see for a formal analysis Branson 1984).

Let us assume that the domestic money supply increases, as a result of open market purchases. The volume of domestic bonds falls and wealth remains constant initially. The rate of interest falls (bond prices are driven up) and investors wish to increase their holdings of foreign titles. The rate of exchange is pushed up. We now extend our earlier analysis of portfolio adjustments by taking the current account into account. A higher exchange rate will cause a surplus on the current account (provided the Marshall-Lerner condition is fulfilled). Given nonintervention by the central bank and the commercial banks, there is a deficit on the capital account. In other words, economic agents increase their holdings of foreign bonds. As their wish for more foreign bonds is getting fulfilled, the rate of exchange will fall again. We here see another case of exchange-rate overshooting. The initial upward movement will be dampened if rational investors foresee the eventual fall in the exchange rate. Not all models incorporate capital earnings from abroad. A higher volume of foreign bonds will increase those capital earnings, which adds to the receipts on the current account. In order to balance the current account, the rate of exchange will have to fall even further. It will be clear that even in a world where capital movements dominate the foreign-exchange market, the current account still is pertinent to the exchange rate, because current-account imbalances bear on the net volume of foreign titles.

Current-account imbalances will make the system also move via wealth effects. A current-account surplus increases wealth. This will exert upward pressure on both the rate of interest (if wealth figures as an argument in the money demand function and hence the LM-curve shifts to left) and consumption expenditure. A higher rate of interest will tend to depress the exchange rate through capital imports but to raise it through a depressing effect on national income and thus on imports. More consumption in its turn leads to a higher national income and thus to higher imports and exerts upward pressure on the rate of exchange. The outcome is uncertain.

Things can also start moving by other causes than open market policies of course. It can be imagined, for instance, that fear of protectionist measures in the EC induces North American and Asian producers to set up production facilities in Europe. This translates into a temporary capital inflow into Europe that makes the European currencies appreciate. In the course of time this leads to permanently higher dividend payments to non-European countries, which may necessitate a perhaps even higher rate of exchange of non-European currencies or lower external value of the European currencies than in the point of departure (neglecting the effects of the direct foreign investment on the external trade of the Community). The portfolio stock effect that caused a temporary appreciation is followed by a flow effect that if anything causes a depreciation. A similar effect results from a diminished preference of a country's residents for foreign assets: the rate of exchange falls (the country's currency appreciates) as portfolios are reshuffled, but the flow effect will eventually cause a rise in the rate of exchange. The rest of the world will have to pay a lower amount of interest and dividends and therefore has to run a lower trade surplus.

It was implicitly assumed that goods prices were constant or sticky. If they move with the money supply, overshooting need not occur. The domestic rate of interest need not change and the rate of exchange may simply adjust to balance the current account at the higher domestic price level, maintaining current account equilibrium and keeping the real value of foreign bond holdings constant at an unchanged volume. Or if the domestic interest rate is set to remain at a lower level as a result of the open market purchases, an initial rise in the exchange rate which increases the volume of foreign bonds through a current-account surplus need not be followed by a fall. Goods prices may rise gradually and a higher rate of exchange, first needed to create a surplus on the current account in order to buy foreign bonds, subsequently only serves to equilibrate the current account.

The portfolio model can be coupled not only to an IS/LM model, but also to a dependent-economy model (see for an example with analyses of the path to long-term equilibrium after a shock Hallwood and MacDonald 1986 pp. 112-26). In this model the Law of One Price is assumed to hold in goods markets, whilst the corresponding perfect capital elasticity is assumed not to hold. This may seem a bit odd at first sight, as transaction costs (including information costs) are much lower in capital markets than in goods markets. Quick arbitrage, however, cannot remedy foreign exchange risk. Put differently, high capital mobility does not imply perfect elasticity.

In the usual portfolio models real capital is conspicuous by its absence. In the case of current account imbalances, the portfolio composition changes and relative yields will change as well. Both the rate of investment and the market value of real capital will vary with those yields (see for an empirical model with equity assets Sarantis 1987, and for a theoretical model with endogenous investment and production and money as a means of transaction Stockman and Svensson 1987). Depending on wealth effects, that value will in its turn affect spending and money demand. No neat conclusions are possible any more, anything may happen (see Dornbusch 1987 pp. 8-9).

THE VERY LONG PERIOD

In the basic version of the monetary model of exchange-rate determination as described in Chapter 7, money supplies in the various countries in the world, or rather the model, determine price levels via stable money demand functions and those price levels in their turn determine the rate of exchange via the purchasing power parity assumption. The rate of exchange here is determined by the stock supply of and stock demand for the various currencies. Adherents of the monetary model are inclined to view it as a useful tool to explain or predict exchange-rate changes over the not-so-long term (years rather than decades). One of the implications of the PPP assumption is 'that exchange-rate movements reflect diverging inflation rates between countries. This corollary is borne out in practice, in a loose way, over decades rather than years (Lee 1974; see, however, for more negative findings Adler and Lehmann 1983). There is, however, overwhelming evidence that PPP is not valid in any strict sense, except perhaps during hyperinflations, when monetary disturbances and inflation tend to swamp all other influences on the rate of exchange (Frenkel 1978). Indeed, one of the main problems of the post-1973 period has been the extreme variability of real exchange rates (Frenkel 1981a and De Grauwe 1989 pp. 61-4; though MacDonald 1988b finds that PPP cannot be rejected for the post-1973 period when wholesale prices rather than consumer proces are used), whilst PPP would imply constant real rates. Nominal exchange-rate changes would only reflect diverging inflation rates in that case. For the early 1920s more positive outcomes have been found, though, not only for exchange rates involving the German mark, but also for the sterling-French franc rate, the dollar-franc rate and the dollar-sterling rate (provided we exclude the year 1924, when speculators probably acted in anticipation of a return of sterling to the prewar rate, see Taylor and McMahon 1988).

A necessary, but not sufficient, condition for validity of PPP is that the Law of One Price holds. Apart from the absence of transportation costs, validity of the LOP demands perfect markets, pure competition and free entry. This is manifestly not the case in practice, even if there are always forces working in that direction. Empirical research indicates that prices of similar goods in various countries tend to move in the same direction, but are not identical. Arbitrage is not perfect (de Roos 1981, Lächler 1985) and the weak version of the LOP which says that exchange-rate changes offset divergent inflation rates between countries' tradeables does not stand up either (Obstfeld 1985 p. 376). Nominal exchange-rate changes do not immediately lead to compensating export price adjustments (Genberg 1978, Spitäller 1980). The corollary that real exchange-rate changes are closely correlated with nominal exchange-rate changes is borne out in practice (Obstfeld 1985 p. 377). Even in commodity markets, with a lower degree of product differentiation than industrial goods markets, the LOP is not valid in the short term, though it tends to be so in the longer term (see Protopapadakis and Stoll 1986, who find that 90 per cent of a deviation from the LOP is on average eliminated within 10 weeks, the adjustment period varying from one week to 120 weeks, depending on the commodity).

Even if the LOP were valid, PPP would not necessarily be so. A purely statistical artefact is that, if the weights given to various goods in the computation of the price index differ among countries, divergent price developments of different goods result in divergent price index movements even if LOP holds for all goods. This does not, however, seem to seriously distort the picture in practice (Davutyan and Pippenger 1985). Of more importance is that, in terms of the dependent-economy model, different relative prices between tradeables and nontradeables in different countries may undermine PPP. These relative prices may diverge between countries because of differences in consumer preferences (Heitger 1987) and because of different relative labour productivities between sectors, apart from the impact of international capital flows on exchange rates and consequently on the relative price of tradeables and nontradeables in a country. In rich countries whose export industries are characterized by high labour productivity and high wages, at least in some service sectors productivity cannot be that much higher than in poorer countries with on average lower labour productivity and lower wages (this argument goes back to Balassa 1964). Examples are education, haircuts and care for the sick and elderly. The relative price of such services will be higher in rich countries than in poor countries and PPP does not obtain, even if the LOP does.

It can be argued that in the very long run the same technology is available all over the globe and production functions will be identical for similar goods in all countries. We then live in a Heckscher-Ohlin-Samuelson world where goods (including services) trade serves to equalize factor prices over the various trading countries. As de Roos (1985 pp. 28-9) emphasizes, PPP obtains in that case. It might be objected that not all goods will be traded, even in the long run, and that different factor proportions in the nontradeables sectors in the various countries may prevent PPP being established. Factor prices will, however, be equalized, if not by goods trade then by factor migration. Factor proportions in the nontradeables sectors will then be the same everywhere and PPP obtains. It remains possible, though, that PPP not even then obtains, if measured by producer prices or wholesale prices, in case some specialization in production between countries is retained. In that case the goods bundles produced in different countries differ and price indexes may show divergent behaviour. Specialization that persists in the very long run presupposes factors of production that are not free to migrate, to wit natural resources, or scale economies, which make it advantageous even for countries with identical factor proportions and tastes to specialize.

In the monetary approach to the rate of exchange it was the exogenous money supply in the trading countries that determined price levels and through these the rate of exchange. PPP *per se* does not imply this direction of causality. It can be interpreted as an equilibrium relationship between the exchange rate and the relation of two price levels (Zis 1988 p. 70). Causality can as well be the other way round, as when the money supply in one country is endogenous and the rate of exchange determines the price level. The authorities could in such a case choose any exchange rate. Given the price level in a dominant country, the price level in a dependent economy would adjust so that PPP is fulfilled and the money supply would adjust as well, either through an elastic domestic money supply or through capital imports (this is in effect the fixed-but-adjustable peg version of the basic flexprice monetary model from Chapter 7; see Johnson 1972).

CASH-IN-ADVANCE MODELS

Some exchange-rate models do not contain a rate of exchange, strictly speaking, and money is often in fact inessential, that is, money does not really affect the exchange of goods. A few attempts have been made to remedy this defect by stipulating that goods and nonmonetary financial assets can only be bought after the required cash balances have been obtained. The idea is to take the transactions demand for money seriously, but it appears well-nigh impossible to model this demand without imposing a very rigid transactions structure. Stockman (1980), for instance, portrays a representative individual who enters each period with certain amounts of domestic money and foreign exchange. First the individual harvests his or her output and sells it. Next (s)he purchases consumption goods (including foreign goods) with the initial cash balances. After that, payment for the goods just sold is received and finally (s)he buys (or sells) foreign exchange to be carried to the next period. Trade credit is excluded. In a model developed more recently by Stockman and Svensson (1987), asset markets again open only after goods market close. Foreign goods can only be bought with foreign currency first bought on asset markets. These restrictions are later relaxed, to some extent. The analysis (which focuses on capital flows resulting from an increase in world wealth in a stochastic model with savings and investment) does not lead to clear-cut conclusions (see also Obstfeld and Stockman 1985 pp. 967-8). Finally, Helpman and Razin (1984) find, in a model that includes investments, that it matters for exchange-rate movements whether international payments are made in the seller's currency or in the buyer's currency. Again, various outcomes are possible, depending on savings (time preference) and investment behaviour.

Though difficult to model satisfactorily, the idea that foreign payments can only be made after foreign exchange has been obtained is intuitively appealing (for that part of imports that is not invoiced in the importer's currency) and has at times been deployed to explain actual exchange-rate movements, though in a rather loose way (see for instance Friedman and Schwartz 1963 p. 78 on the US dollar during the greenback period in the nineteenth century). Even so, it remains to be seen whether important new insights on exchange-rate movements can be gained from the idea that foreign exchange may be demanded before the date that foreign payments are made rather than on that date.

CONCLUDING COMMENTS

In view of the bewildering variety of exchange-rate models, it is not surprising that econometric testing has yielded disappointing results. Indeed, had those results been more satisfactory, no such proliferation of models would have occurred in the first place. We must reconcile ourselves to the fact that human behaviour can only be imperfectly modelled, let alone satisfactorily predicted. In particular, expectations will probably always remain difficult to capture in an econometric specification. The whole concept of rational expectations in an exchange-rate context is suspect because, with the demise of PPP, it is difficult to imagine a 'true' model throwing up an equilibrium exchange rate to which the system should converge within an investor's time horizon. Of course, portfolio models suggest that the system can only be in long-term equilibrium if the current account is in equilibrium, but there is no reason why this kind of long-term equilibrium should be relevant to real-world behaviour. Experience shows that countries can live with prolonged current-account imbalances. Net capital imports or exports need not signify a situation that cannot be sustained for some period of time. In this sense there is, for instance, no reason to call a situation of net capital imports, employed to finance investments which will enable the country in question to service its debt in the future, a disequilibrium situation. As the use that is made of capital imports may thus be decisive, it does not looks possible to attach notions of equilibrium or disequilibrium to any particular balance-of-payments situation simply on the strength of balance-of-payments figures. Lacking an empirically useful definition of the equilibrium exchange rate, modelling international capital flows needs must be difficult, because exchange-rate expectations lack an anchor. It is no surprise then that investors' demand and supply of funds and with it international capital flows at times seem to be subject to fashions. During one period it is the relative 'strength' (real growth or perceived real growth potential) of an economy that investors base their decisions upon, during another period relative inflation rates, and during yet other periods current account imbalances.

When discussing the various models in this chapter and the previous one, we mentioned some of the econometric evidence. We conclude this chapter with a roundup of some additional recent econometric research (see for more complete reviews, including discussions of the econometric issues involved, Levich 1985 and

MacDonald 1988a). Wasserfallen and Kyburz (1985) found few traces of any impact of fundamentals on Swiss franc exchange rates for the 1974-1980 period. Leventakis (1987) did not fare much better in attempts to make a number of models trace the movements of the German mark against the US dollar over the period 1974I-1984IV. Backus (1984 pp. 842-3) was led to conclude that the US dollar-Canadian dollar exchange rate was close to a random walk during the 1970s. Mussa (1984 p. 18, 1986 pp. 132, 199) also found that exchange rates followed a random walk, which in his view points to the dominance of randomly distributed 'news' affecting exchange-rate changes. Meese and Rogoff (1983) compare out-of-sample forecasts using a flexprice monetary model, a Dornbusch-type sticky-price monetary model and a Dornbusch-type model that allows for changes in the long-term real exchange rate. Despite using realized values of fundamentals, the models did not improve on random-walk models for horizons varying from one to twelve months. Frankel (1984) could find no support for the flexprice monetary model, the sticky-price (Dornbusch) monetary model or the portfolio balance model in a test of the dollar rate of five currencies over the 1974-mid-1981 period. Contrary to Meese and Rogoff, Isard (1987 p. 6) finds the evidence of a random walk of real exchange rates less than convincing. Lagged dependent variables are significant in empirical estimations of real exchange rates. This is not incompatible with, but need not imply, some idea of a long-term equilibrium PPP level. He is led to state that 'the existing models of systematic behavior explain little of the observed variances of exchange rates during the 1970s and 1980s' (1987 p. 3). Similarly, Gros (1989) found that the variability of various DMark rates over the 1973-1985 period could not be explained by the variability of the underlying fundamentals, applying both flexible-price and fixed-price monetary models and the portfolio model. Uncovered interest parity does not perform too badly in Backus's runs, which would be consistent with the random walk of the underlying variables (the money supply and real national income) found by him. However, much of the exchange rate variation was not explained. For a possible explanation, Backus points to large changes in relative prices of natural resources and endogeneity of the money supply, both of which were neglected in the models. He did not find evidence of overshooting after a monetary shock either. Cumby and Obstfeld (1984) in their turn could find little confirmation of uncovered interest parity. It will be remembered from Chapter 7 that if either uncovered interest parity or PPP is violated, interest rate differentials do not reflect inflation differentials and real interest rates differ across countries.

Tests of uncovered interest rate parity are hindered by the possibility of rational bubbles and the peso problem occurring and of a skewed *ex post* distribution of innovations or 'news'. These all result in autocorrelation in the error term in equation 7.3, or a systematic divergence between expected and realized exchange rates, without invalidating the combined hypotheses of rational expectations and perfect asset substitutability. Besides, systematic divergences (including a positive value of a in equation 7.3, or a b-coefficient diverging from unity) may result both from a possibly varying risk factor, that is, imperfect substitutability, or from irrationality (Horne 1983 p. 102), not to mention learning processes on the part of investors. Another factor, mentioned by Frankel (1984), Leventakis (1987 p. 373) and Gerlach (1987 p. 140), is instability in money demand functions (see also Khan and Willett 1984, who provide a survey of empirical studies of the monetary model). This does not necessarily invalidate any theory but certainly hinders empirical testing. Frankel (1984 pp. 245-6) argues that a downward shift in United States money demand and an upward shift in German money demand can explain the fall of the dollar *vis-à-vis* the Mark in the late 1970s (note that a downward shift in money demand is tantamount to an increase in the money supply). More generally, parameter instability may have occurred. However that may be, students of the behaviour of the American dollar over the first half of the 1980s are led to the conclusion that the market disregarded fundamentals and simply got it wrong (Krugman 1985 p. 458, Koromzay, Llewellyn and Potter 1987 p. 32). But, to repeat our argument, even if the market took account of fundamentals, it would lack a solid model that could serve as a guide to form expectations on exchange rate behaviour, given expectations concerning such fundamentals as real growth, money growth, inflation rates and interest rates, and relative asset supplies in the case of portfolio models and the balance on the current account in models that are not restricted to the very short term.

There is even, in the words of Gros (1989 p. 274), no general agreement about the fundamentals that ought to determine exchange rates. What, one is inclined to ask, is the use of invoking 'the correct model' if unanimity among economists is far to seek on fundamental relationships such as the connection between US government deficits and the rate of interest. Such a connection is denied, among others, by P. Evans (1985), by virtue of Ricardian equivalence. In this situation, 'one economist's bubble is another economist's fundamentals-driven appreciation', as Islam (1988 p. 23) puts it. Paying more attention to the credibility of government policies may go some way to solve the problem. But even if economic agents receive the correct signals on future money growth, government deficits and so on, they lack a suitable model to predict the future exchange rate. They may therefore be swayed in their decisions by considerations that are hard to track after the event, let alone to forecast. Only if governments succeed in convincing agents that they are willing, and able, to harness monetary and fiscal policy for the defence of the rate of exchange, can more or less homogeneous expectations be expected.

Perhaps we should after all reject the idea that the market for foreign exchange is governed by rational expectations. Goodhart (1988b) dismisses the rational expectations idea that all agents use a single 'correct' model of the economy. In particular, on the basis of interviews with London foreign-exchange traders he tends to ascribe the gyrations of exchange rates to the varying weight which portfolio managers attach to the advice of respectively *fundamentalists* who expect exchange rates to move to some fundamentals-driven equilibrium and of *chartists* who subscribe to 'technical' analysis of exchange rate fluctuations. Things could have been worse than they actually are, in his view. If 'fundamentalists' had their way, exchange rates would show more Dornbusch-like overshooting (though we have seen that such overshooting would be very moderate), but fortunately others may dampen such movements. Then, people need time to assimilate new information and on top of that the authorities step in from time to time. This is not to say that fundamentals are unimportant, but certainly exchange rates can be out of line with fundamentals for considerable periods of time and capital flows allow exchange rates to be in some sort of equilibrium within a more or less wide range rather than at one unique value, given those fundamentals.

Bibliography

Acx, R., and M. Quintyn (1982) 'Tarifering als remedie tegen de dalende rentabiliteit in de Belgische financiële sector', *Bank- en Effectenbedrijf*, vol. 31 no. 3.

Adler, M., and B. Lehmann (1983) 'Deviations from PPP in the Long Run', *Journal of Finance*, vol. 38 no. 5.

Aivazian, V.A., J.L. Callen, I. Krinsky and C.C.Y. Kwan (1986) 'International Exchange Risk and Asset Substitutability', *Journal of International Money and Finance*, vol. 5 no. 4.

Akerlof, G.A., and R.D. Milbourne (1980) 'The Short Run Demand for Money', *Economic Journal*, vol. 90 no. 361, December.

Akhtar, M.A. (1983) *Financial Innovations and their Implications for Monetary Policy: An International Perspective*, BIS Economic Papers no. 9.

Alchian, A.A. (1977) 'Why Money?', *Journal of Money, Credit, and Banking*, vol. 9 no. 1 part 2.

Alexander, G.J., and W.F. Sharpe (1989) *Fundamentals of Investments*, Englewood Cliffs, Prentice-Hall.

Andersen, L.C., and J.L. Jordan (1968) 'Monetary and Fiscal Actions: A Test of their Relative Importance in Economic Stabilization', *Review*, Federal Reserve Bank of St Louis, vol. 50 no. 1.

Andersen, P.S. (1985) *The Stability of Money Demand Functions: An Alternative Approach*, BIS Economic Papers no. 14.

Arango, S., and M.I. Nadiri (1981) 'Demand for Money in Open Economies', *Journal of Monetary Economics*, vol. 7 no. 1.

Arestis, P. (1985) 'Is There Any Crowding-out of Private Expenditure by Fiscal Actions?', in P. Arestis and T. Skouras (eds) 1985.

Arestis, P. (ed.) (1988) *Post-Keynesian Monetary Economics: New Approaches to Financial Modelling*, Aldershot, Edward Elgar.

Arestis, P., and Th. Skouras (eds) (1985) *Post Keynesian Economic Theory*, Brighton, Wheatsheaf.

Argy, V. (1981) *The Postwar International Money Crisis*, London, George Allen & Unwin.

Arrow, K.J. (1982) 'Risk Perception in Psychology and Economics', *Economic Inquiry*, vol. 20 no. 1.

Artus, J.R., and J.H. Young (1979) 'Fixed and Flexible Exchange Rates: A Renewal of the Debate', *IMF Staff Papers*, vol. 26 no. 4.

Asako, K. (1982) 'Rational Expectations and the Effectiveness of Monetary Policy with Special Reference to the Barro-Fischer Model', *Journal of Monetary Economics*, vol. 9 no. 1.

Atkinson, P., A. Blundell-Wignall, M. Randoni and H. Ziegelschmidt (1984) 'The Efficacy of Monetary Targeting: The Stability of Demand for Money in Major OECD Countries', *OECD Economic Studies*, no. 3.

Attfield, C.L.F., D. Demery and N.W. Duck (1981) 'A Quarterly Model of Unanticipated Monetary Growth, Output and the Price Level in the U.K. 1963-1978', *Journal of Monetary Economics*, vol. 8 no. 3.

Attfield, C.L.F., D. Demery and N.W. Duck (1985), *Rational Expectations in Macroeconomics*, Oxford, Basil Blackwell.

Ayanian, R. (1989) 'Geopolitics and the dollar', *Journal of International Money and Finance*, vol. 8 no. 3.

Baade, R.A., and N. Nazmi (1989) 'Currency Substitution and Money Demand in the United States, West Germany and Japan', *Kredit und Kapital*, vol. 22 no. 3.

Backus, D. (1984) 'Empirical models of the exchange rate: separating the wheat from the chaff', *Canadian Journal of Economics*, vol. 17 no. 4.

Bagehot, W. (1920) *Lombard Street*, London, John Murray (4th printing of the 14th ed.; first ed. London, Kegan, Paul & Co., 1873).

Balassa, B. (1964) 'The Purchasing-Power Parity Doctrine: A Reappraisal', *Journal of Political Economy*, vol. 72 no. 6.

Baltensperger, E., and P. Böhm (1982) 'Stand und Entwicklungstendenzen der Wechselkurstheorie - ein Überblick', *Aussenwirtschaft*, vol. 37 no. 2-3.

Bank of England (1972) 'The Demand for Money: The Evidence of Empirical Investigations', in H.G. Johnson *et al.* (eds), *Readings in British Monetary Economics*, Oxford, Oxford University Press. Extracts from 'The importance of money (Appendix I)', *Bank of England Quarterly Bulletin*, vol. 10 no. 3, 1970.

Bank for International Settlements (1986), *Recent Innovations in International Banking*, Basle.

Barnett, W.A., E.K. Offenbacher and P.A. Spindt (1984) 'The New Divisia Monetary Aggregates', *Journal of Political Economy*, vol. 92 no. 6.

Barro, R.J. (1974) 'Are Government Bonds Net Wealth?', *Journal of Political Economy*, vol. 82 no. 6.

Barro, R.J. (1976) 'Reply to Feldstein and Buchanan', *Journal of Political Economy*, vol. 84 no. 2.

Barro, R.J. (1977) 'Unanticipated Money Growth and Unemployment in the United States', *American Economic Review*, vol. 67 no. 2. Reprinted in R.E. Lucas, Jr and Th.J. Sargent (eds), 1981.

Barro, R.J. (1978) 'Unanticipated Money, Output, and the Price Level in the United States', *Journal of Political Economy*, vol. 86 no. 4. Reprinted in R.E. Lucas, Jr and Th.J. Sargent (eds), 1981.

Barro, R.J., and S. Fischer (1976) 'Recent developments in monetary theory', *Journal of Monetary Economics*, vol. 2 no. 2.

Barro, R.J., and M. Rush (1980) 'Unanticipated Money and Economic Activity', in S. Fischer (ed.), *Rational Expectations and Economic Activity*, Chicago, University of Chicago Press.

Barro, R.J., and A.M. Santomero (1972) 'Household Money Holdings and The Demand Deposit Rate', *Journal of Money, Credit, and Banking*, vol. 4 no. 2.

Batchelor, R.A., and A.B. Orr (1988) 'Inflation Expectations Revisited', *Economica*, vol. 55 no. 219.

Batten, D.S., and R.W. Hafer (1984) 'Currency Substitution: A Test of Its Importance', *Review*, Federal Reserve Bank of St Louis, vol. 66 no. 7.

Batten, D.S., and R.W. Hafer (1986) 'The Impact of International Factors on U.S. Inflation: An Empirical Test of the Currency Substitution Hypothesis', *Southern Economic Journal*, vol. 53 no. 2.

Begg, D.K.H. (1982) *The Rational Expectations Revolution in Macroeconomics*, Oxford, Philip Allan.

Benassy, J.-P. (1975) 'Disequilibrium Exchange in Barter and Monetary Economies', *Economic Inquiry*, vol. 13 no. 2.

Benjamin, D.K., and L.A. Kochin (1979a) 'Voluntary Unemployment in Interwar Britain', *The Banker*, vol. 129 no. 636.

Benjamin, D.K., and L.A. Kochin (1979b) 'Searching for an Explanation of Unemployment in Interwar Britain', *Journal of Political Economy*, vol. 87 no. 3.

Benjamin, D.K., and L.A. Kochin (1982) 'Unemployment and Unemployment Benefits in Twentieth-Century Britain: A Reply to Our Critics', *Journal of Political Economy*, vol. 90 no. 2.

Benston, G.J. (1972) 'Economies of Scale of Financial Institutions', *Journal of Money, Credit, and Banking*, vol. 4 no. 2.

Bergstrand, J.H., and T.P. Bundt (1990) 'Currency substitution and monetary autonomy: the foreign demand for US demand deposits', *Journal of International Money and Finance*, vol. 9 no. 3.

Bilson, J.F.O. (1978) 'Rational Expectations and the Exchange Rate', in J.A. Frenkel and H.G. Johnson (eds), *The Economics of Exchange Rates: Selected Studies*, Reading, Mass., Addison-Wesley.

Bilson, J.F.O. (1979) 'Recent Developments in Monetary Models of Exchange Rate Determination', *IMF Staff Papers*, vol. 26 no. 2.

Black, F. (1970) 'Banking and Interest Rates in a World Without Money', *Journal of Bank Research*, vol. 1, Autumn.

Bladen Hovell, R., and C. Green (1989) 'Crowding-out and Pulling-in of Fiscal Policy under Fixed and Flexible Exchange Rates', in R. MacDonald and M.P. Taylor (eds), *Exchange Rates and Open Economy Macroeconomics*, Oxford, Basil Blackwell.

Blanchard, O.J. (1979) 'Speculative Bubbles, Crashes and Rational Expectations', *Economics Letters*, vol. 3.

Blinder, A.S., and S. Fischer (1981) 'Inventories, Rational Expectations, and the Business Cycle', *Journal of Monetary Economics*, vol. 8 no. 3.

Blinder, A.S., and R.M. Solow (1973) 'Does Fiscal Policy Matter?', *Journal of Public Economics*, vol. 2.

Blinder. A.S., and R.M. Solow (1974) 'Analytical Foundations of Fiscal Policy', in A.S. Blinder, R.M. Solow *et al.*, *The Economics of Public Finance*, Washington, D.C., Brookings Institution.

Boland, L.A. (1982) *The Foundations of Economic Method*, London, George Allen & Unwin.

Bomberger, W.A., and G.E. Makinen (1980) 'Money Demand in Open Economies: Alternative Specifications', *Southern Economic Journal*, vol. 47 no. 1.

Bomhoff, E.J. (1980) *Inflation, the Quantity Theory and Rational Expectations*, North Holland, Amsterdam.

Bomhoff, E.J., and C.G. Koedijk (1988) 'Bilateral Exchange Rates and Risk Premiums', *Journal of International Money and Finance*, vol. 7 no. 2.

Boorman, J.T. (1972) 'The Evidence on the Demand for Money: Theoretical Formulations and Empirical Results', in J.T. Boorman and Th.M. Havrilesky, *Money Supply, Money Demand, and Macroeconomic Models*, Boston, Allyn & Bacon.

Bordo, M.D., E.V. Choudri and A.J. Schwartz (1987) 'The Behavior of Money Stock under Interest Rate Control: Some Evidence for Canada', *Journal of Money, Credit, and Banking*, vol. 19 no. 2.

Bordo, M.D., and L. Jonung (1981) 'The Long Run Behavior of the Income Velocity of Money in Five Advanced Countries, 1870 - 1975: An Institutional Approach', *Economic Inquiry*, vol. 19 no. 1.

Borenszstein, E.R. (1987) 'Alternative Hypotheses About the Excess Return on Dollar Assets, 1980-84', *IMF Staff Papers*, vol. 34 no. 1.

Boughton, J.M. (1981) 'Recent Instability of the Demand for Money: An International Perspective', *Southern Economic Journal*, vol. 47 no. 3.

Branson, W.H. (1972) *Macroeconomic Theory and Policy*, New York, Harper & Row.

Branson, W.H. (1976) 'The Dual Roles of the Government Budget and the Balance of Payments in the Movement from Short-Run to Long-Run Equilibrium', *Quarterly Journal of Economics*, vol. 90 no. 3.

Branson, W.H. (1984) 'Exchange Rate Policy after a Decade of "Floating" ', in J.F.O. Bilson and R.C. Marston (eds), *Exchange Rate Theory and Practice*, Chicago, University of Chicago Press.

Branson, W.H. (1985) 'The Dynamic Interaction of Exchange Rates and Trade Flows', in T. Peeters, P. Praet and P. Reding (eds), *International Trade and Exchange Rates in the Late Eighties*, Amsterdam, North-Holland, and Brussels, Editions de l'Université de Bruxelles.

Branson, W.H., and D.W. Henderson (1985) 'The Specification and Influence of Asset Markets', in R.W. Jones and P.B. Kenen (eds), *Handbook of International Economics* vol. II, Amsterdam, North-Holland.

Bray, M. (1985) 'Rational Expectations, Information and Asset Markets: An Introduction', *Oxford Economic Papers*, vol. 37 no. 2.

Broadberry, S.N. (1983) 'Unemployment in Interwar Britain: A Disequilibrium Approach', *Oxford Economic Papers*, vol. 35 no. 3.

Brunner, K. (1970) 'The "Monetarist Revolution in Monetary Theory" ', *Weltwirtschaftliches Archiv*, vol. 105 no. 1.

Brunner, K. (1971) 'A survey of selected issues in monetary theory', *Schweizerische Zeitschrift für Volkswirtschaft und Statistik*, vol. 107 no. 1.

Brunner, K., A. Cukierman and A.H. Meltzer (1983) 'Money and Economic Activity, Inventories and Business Cycles', *Journal of Monetary Economics*, vol. 11 no. 3.

Brunner, K., and A.H. Meltzer (1971) 'The Uses of Money: Money in the Theory of an Exchange Economy', *American Economic Review*, vol. 61 no. 5.

Buchanan, J. (1976) 'Barro on the Ricardian Equivalence Theorem', *Journal of Political Economy*, vol. 84 no. 2.

Buiter, W. (1985) 'A Guide to Public Sector Debts and Deficits', *Economic Policy*, no. 1.

Butkiewicz, J.L. (1979) 'Outside Wealth, the Demand for Money and the Crowding Out Effect', *Journal of Monetary Economics*, vol. 5 no. 2.

Calvo, G.A., and C.A. Rodriguez (1977) 'A Model of Exchange Rate Determination under Currency Substitution and Rational Expectations', *Journal of Political Economy*, vol. 85 no. 3.

Cameron, R. (1967) 'Scotland, 1750-1845', in R. Cameron *et al.*, *Banking in the Early Stages of Industrialization*, London, Oxford University Press.

Cannan, E. (ed.) (1969) *The Paper Pound of 1797-1821; A Reprint of the Bullion Report*, 2nd ed., New York, Kelley. Originally published London, P.S. King, 1925.

Carlson, J.A., and M. Parkin (1975) 'Inflation Expectations', *Economica*, vol. 42 no. 166.

Carlton, D.W. (1986) 'The Rigidity of Prices', *American Economic Review*, vol. 76 no. 4.

Cebula, R.J. (1978) 'An Empirical Analysis of the "Crowding Out" Effect of Fiscal Policy in the United States and Canada', *Kyklos*, vol. 31 no. 3.

Centraal Planbureau (1987) *The Central Planning Bureau Monetary Model of the Dutch Economy*, The Hague.

Chan, L.K.C. (1983) 'Uncertainty and the Neutrality of Government Financing Policy', *Journal of Monetary Economics*, vol. 11 no. 3.

Chan-Lee, J.H., and H. Kato (1984) 'A Comparison of Simulation Properties of National Econometric Models,' *OECD Economic Studies*, no. 2.

Ciccolo, J., and G. Fromm (1980) ' 'q', Corporate Investment, and Balance Sheet Behavior', *Journal of Money, Credit, and Banking*, vol. 12 no. 2.

Claassen, E.M. (1984) 'Monetary Integration and Monetary Stability: the Economic Criteria of the Monetary Constitution', in P. Salin (ed.).

Clinton, K. (1988) 'Transactions Costs and Covered Interest Arbitrage: Theory and Evidence', *Journal of Political Economy*, vol. 96 no. 2.

Clower, R.W. (1965) 'The Keynesian Counterrevolution: A Theoretical Appraisal', in F.H. Hahn and F.P.R. Brechling (eds), *The Theory of Interest Rates*, London, Macmillan.

Clower, R.W. (1969a) 'Introduction', in R.W. Clower (ed.), *Monetary Theory*, Harmondsworth, Penguin.

Clower, R.W. (1969b), 'Foundations of Monetary Theory', in R.W. Clower (ed.), *Monetary theory*, Harmondsworth, Penguin. First published as 'A reconsideration of the microfoundations of monetary theory', *Western Economic Journal*, vol. 6, 1967.

Clower, R.W. (1975) 'Reflections on the Keynesian Perplex', *Zeitschrift für Nationalökonomie*, vol. 35 no. 1/2.

Clower, R.W. (1977) 'The Anatomy of Monetary Theory', *American Economic Review*, vol. 67 no. 1.

Clower, R.W., and P.W. Howitt (1984) 'The Transactions Theory of the Demand for Money; A Reconsideration', ch. 13 in D.A. Walker (ed.), *Money and Markets, Essays by R.W. Clower*, Cambridge, Cambridge University Press. First published in *Journal of Political Economy*, vol. 86, 1978.

Clower, R.W., and A. Leijonhufvud (1984) 'The Coordination of Economic Activities', ch. 15 in D.A. Walker (ed.), *Money and Markets; Essays by R.W. Clower*, Cambridge, Cambridge University Press. First published in *American Economic Review*, vol. 65, 1975.

Collins, M. (1982) 'Unemployment in Interwar Britain: Still Searching for an Explanation', *Journal of Political Economy*, vol. 90 no. 2.

Corbo, V., and J. de Melo (1987) 'Lessons from the Southern Cone Policy Reforms', *The World Bank Research Observer*, vol. 2 no. 2.

Corbo, V., J. de Melo and J. Tybout (1986), 'What Went Wrong with the Recent Reforms in the Southern Cone', *Economic Development and Cultural Change*, vol. 34 no. 3.

Corden, M.W. (1987) 'The Relevance for Developing Countries of Recent Developments in Macroeconomic Theory', *World Bank Research Observer*, vol. 2 no. 2.

Cosandier, P.A., and B.R. Lang (1981) 'Interest Rate Parity Tests', *Journal of Banking and Finance*, vol. 5 no. 2.

Cotis, J.-Ph. (1988) 'Unemployment Breeds Unemployment', *IMF Survey*, 15 August.

Cowen, T., and R. Kroszner (1987) 'The Development of the New Monetary Economics', *Journal of Political Economy*, vol. 95 no. 3.

Cowen, T., and R. Kroszner (1989) 'Scottish Banking before 1845: A Model for Laissez-Faire?', *Journal of Money, Credit, and Banking*, vol. 21 no. 2.

Cross, R. (ed.) (1988) *Unemployment, Hysteresis, and the Natural Rate Hypothesis*, Oxford, Basil Blackwell.

Cuddington, J.T. (1983) 'Currency Substitution, Capital Mobility and Money Demand', *Journal of International Money and Finance*, vol. 2 no. 2.

Cumby, R.E., and M. Obstfeld (1984) 'International Interest Rates and Price Level Linkages under Flexible Exchange Rates: A Review of Recent Evidence', in J.F.O. Bilson and R.C. Marston (eds), *Exchange Rate Theory and Practice*, Chicago, University of Chicago Press.

Cuthbertson, K., and M.P. Taylor (1987) 'Buffer-Stock Money: An Appraisal', in C. Goodhart, D. Currie and D.T. Llewellyn (eds), *The Operation and Regulation of Financial Markets*, London, Macmillan.

Darby, M.R. (1976) 'Three-and-a-Half Million U.S. Employees Have Been Mislaid; Or, an Explanation of Unemployment, 1934-1941', *Journal of Political Economy*, vol. 84 no. 1.

Darby, M.R., A.R. Mascaro and M.L. Marlow (1989) 'The Empirical Reliability of Monetary Aggregates as Indicators: 1983-1987', *Economic Inquiry*, vol. 27 no. 4.

Darrat, A.F. (1989) 'Fiscal Deficits and Long-Term Interest Rates: Further Evidence from Annual Data', *Southern Economic Journal*, vol. 56 no. 2.

David, P.A., and J.L. Scadding (1974) 'Private Savings, Ultrarationality, Aggregation, and "Denison's Law" ', *Journal of Political Economy*, vol. 82 no. 2.

Davidson, J., and J. Ireland (1987) 'Buffer Stock Models of the Monetary Sector', *National Institute Economic Review*, vol. 121, August.

Davutyan, N., and J. Pippenger (1985) 'Purchasing Power Parity Did Not Collapse During the 1970's', *American Economic Review*, vol. 75 no. 5.

De Grauwe, P. (1983) 'What Are the Scope and Limits of Fruitful International Monetary Cooperation in the 1980s?', in G.M. von Furstenberg (ed.), *International Money and Credit: The Policy Roles*, Washington, D.C., International Monetary Fund.

De Grauwe, P. (1989) *International Money; Post-War Trends and Theories*, Oxford, Oxford University Press.

de Haan, J. (1989) *Public Debt: Pestiferous or Propitious?*, PhD thesis, Groningen State University, Groningen.

de Haan, J., and D. Zelhorst (1988) 'The Empirical Evidence on the Ricardian Equivalence Hypothesis', *Kredit und Kapital*, vol. 21 no. 2.

de Haan, J., and D. Zelhorst (1989) 'Particuliere besparingen en overheidsschuld: de analyses van Boskin e.a., een Nederlandse invalshoek', *Maandschrift economie*, vol. 53 no. 1.

de Jong, E. (1983) 'Wisselkoersfluctuaties op korte termijn en recente wisselkoerstheorieën; een beknopt overzicht', *Maandschrift Economie*, vol. 47 no. 5.

de Jong, E. (1990) *Exchange Rate Determination and Optimal Economic Policy Under Alternative Exchange Rate Regimes*, PhD thesis, University of Amsterdam.

De Nederlandsche Bank (1990) *Jaarverslag 1989* (Report over 1989).

de Roos, F. (1981) 'Purchasing Power Parity Theory and the Monetary Approach to the Balance of Payments', *De Economist*, vol. 129 no. 1.

de Roos, F. (1985) *De vorming van de wisselkoers*, Amsterdam, Noord-Hollandsche Uitgevers Mij. (Mededelingen der Koninklijke Nederlandse Akademie van Wetenschappen, afd. Letterkunde, Nieuwe reeks, deel 48 no. 2).

de Roos, F. (1989) 'Gewijzigd inzicht: opmerkingen over wisselkoerssystemen', in J. Zijlstra and F. de Roos, *De les van veertig jaar en nog iets and Gewijzigd inzicht: opmerkingen over wisselkoerssystemen*, Alphen aan den Rijn, Samsom.

Debreu, G. (1959) *Theory of Value*, New Haven, Yale University Press.

den Butter, F.A.G. (1984), 'Macro-economische modellenbouw: een terugblik en enige recente ontwikkelingen', *Economisch Statistische Berichten*, vol. 69 no. 3484, 5 December.

den Butter, F.A.G. (1986) *Macro-economische modellenbouw en monetaire transmissie*, PhD thesis, Rotterdam; published as *Model en theorie in de macro-economie*, Leiden, Stenfert Kroese.

den Butter, F.A.G. (1988) 'The DNB Econometric Model of the Netherlands Economy (Morkmon)', in W. Driehuis, M.M.G. Fase and H. den Hartog (eds), *Challenges for Macroeconomic Modelling*, Amsterdam. North-Holland.

den Butter, F.A.G., and M.M.G. Fase (1981) 'The Demand for Money in EEC Countries', *Journal of Monetary Economics*, vol. 8 no. 2.

den Butter, F.A.G., and J.B. Kuné (1976) 'De functionele vorm van de geldvraagvergelijking', *Tijdschrift voor Economie en Management*, vol. 21 no. 2.

den Butter, F.A.G., and H.A.A. Verbon (1982) 'The Specification Problem in Regression Analysis', *International Statistical Review*, vol. 50.

Dennis, G.E.J. (1981) *Monetary Economics*, London, Longman.

Diamond, D.W. (1984) 'Financial Intermediation and Delegated Monitoring', *Review of Economic Studies*, vol. 51.

Diamond, D.W., and P.H. Dybvig (1983), 'Bank Runs, Deposit Insurance, and Liquidity', *Journal of Political Economy*, vol. 91 no. 3.

Diamond, P., and D. Fudenberg (1989) 'Rational Expectations Business Cycles in Search Equilibrium', *Journal of Political Economy*, vol. 97 no. 3.

Diebold, F.X., and P. Pauly (1988) 'Endogenous risk in a portfolio-balance rational-expectations model of the deutschemark-dollar rate', *European Economic Review*, vol. 32 no. 1.

Dornbusch, R. (1980) *Open Economy Macroeconomics*, New York, Basic Books.

Dornbusch, R. (1984) 'The Overvalued Dollar', *Lloyds Bank Review*, no. 152, April.

Dornbusch, R. (1987) 'Exchange Rate Economics: 1986', *Economic Journal*, vol. 97 no. 385, March.

Dornbusch, R. (1988) 'Mexico: stabilization, debt and growth', *Economic Policy*, no. 7.

Dornbusch, R., and S. Fischer (1980) 'Exchange Rates and the Current Account', *American Economic Review*, vol. 70 no. 5.

Dotsey, M. (1984) 'An Investigation of Cash Management Practices and Their Effects on the Demand for Money', *Economic Review*, Federal Reserve Bank of Richmond, vol. 70 no. 5.

Dotsey, M. (1985) 'Controversy Over the Federal Budget Deficit: A Theoretical Perspective', *Economic Review*, Federal Reserve Bank of Richmond, vol. 71 no. 5.

Dotsey, M., and R.G. King (1988) 'Rational Expectations Business Cycle Models: A Survey', *Economic Review*, Federal Reserve Bank of Richmond, vol. 74 no. 2.

Driehuis, W., M.M.G. Fase and H. den Hartog (eds) (1988) *Challenges for Macroeconomic Modelling*, Amsterdam, North-Holland.

Driscoll, M.J., J.L. Ford, A.W. Mullineux and S. Sen (1983) 'Money, Output, Rational Expectations and Neutrality: Some Econometric Results for the UK', *Economica*, vol. 50 no. 199.

Dufey, G., and I.H. Giddy (1978) *The International Money Market*, Englewood Cliffs, N.J., Prentice-Hall.

Dwyer Jr., G.P., and R.A. Gilbert (1989) 'Bank Runs and Private Remedies', *Review*, Federal Reserve Bank of St Louis. vol. 71 no. 3.

Eckstein, O. (1981) *Core Inflation*, Englewood Cliffs, Prentice-Hall.

Eden, B. (1986) 'Trading Uncertainty and the Cash-in-Advance Constraint', *Journal of Monetary Economics*, vol. 18.

Edwards, S. (1983) 'Floating Exchange Rates, Expectations and New Information', *Journal of Monetary Economics*, vol. 11 no. 4.

Eizenga, W. (1972) *Banken en het betalingsverkeer van gezinshuishoudingen*, Alphen aan den Rijn, Samsom.

El-Erian, M.A. (1987) 'Depósitos en divisas en PMD', *Finanzas y Desarrollo*, vol. 24 no. 4 (also in English in *Finance and Development*).

Engel, C. (1989) 'The trade balance and real exchange rate under currency substitution', *Journal of International Money and Finance*, vol. 8 no. 1.

Evans, G.W. (1986) 'A Test for Speculative Bubbles in the Sterling-Dollar Exchange Rate', *American Economic Review*, vol. 76 no. 4.

Evans, P. (1985) 'Do Large Deficits Produce High Interest Rates?', *American Economic Review*, vol. 75 no. 1.

Evans, P. (1986) 'Is the Dollar High Because of Large Budget Deficits?', *Journal of Monetary Economics*, vol. 18.

Fama, E.F. (1980) 'Banking in the Theory of Finance', *Journal of Monetary Economics*, vol. 6 no. 1.

Fama, E.F. (1983) 'Financial Intermediation and Price Level Control', *Journal of Monetary Economics*, vol. 12.

Fama, E.F. (1984) 'Forward and Spot Exchange Rates', *Journal of Monetary Economics*, vol. 14.

Fase, M.M.G. (1985) 'Monetary Control: the Dutch Experience: Some Reflections on the Liquidity Ratio', in C. van Ewijk and J.J. Klants (eds), *Monetary Conditions for Economic Recovery*, Dordrecht, Martinus Nijhoff.

Fase, M.M.G., and C.C.A. Winder (1990) 'The Demand for Money in the Netherlands Revisited', *De Economist*, vol. 138 no. 3.

Feldstein, M. (1982) 'Government Deficits and Aggregate Demand', *Journal of Monetary Economics*, vol. 9 no. 1.

Fetter, R.W. (1953) 'The Bullion Report Re-examined', in T.S. Ashton and R.S. Sayers (eds), *Papers in English Monetary History*, London, Oxford University Press. First published in *Quarterly Journal of Economics*, August 1942.

Fields, T.W., and W.R. Hart (1990) 'On Integrating the Ricardian Equivalence Theorem and the IS-LM Framework', *Economic Inquiry*, vol. 28 no. 1.

Fischer, S. (1975) 'Recent Developments in Monetary Theory', *American Economic Review*, vol. 65 no. 2 (Papers and Proceedings).

Fischer, S. (1977) 'Long-Term Contracts, Rational Expectations, and the Optimal Money Supply Rule', *Journal of Political Economy*, vol. 85 no. 1.

Fischer, S. (1979) 'Anticipations and the Nonneutrality of Money', *Journal of Political Economy*, vol. 87 no. 2.

Fischer, S. (1986) 'Friedman versus Hayek on private money', *Journal of Monetary Economics*, vol. 17.

Fischer, S. (1988) 'Recent developments in macroeconomics', *Economic Journal*, vol. 98 no. 391, June.

Fischer, S. (ed.) (1980) *Rational Expectations and Economic Policy*, Chicago, University of Chicago Press.

Fisher, I. (1930) *The Theory of Interest*, New York, Macmillan.

Fisher, I. (1963) *The Purchasing Power of Money*, New York, Kelley, 1963. Reprint of the 2nd ed. of 1922.

Forman, L. (1980) 'Rational Expectations and the Real World', *Challenge*, vol. 23 no. 5.

Frankel, J.A. (1984) 'Tests of Monetary and Portfolio Balance Models of Exchange Rate Determination', in J.F.O. Bilson and R.C. Marston (eds), *Exchange Rate Theory and Practice*, Chicago, University of Chicago Press.

Frankel, J.A. (1985a) 'Portfolio Crowding-Out, Empirically Estimated', *Quarterly Journal of Economics*, vol. 100, Supplement.

Frankel, J.A. (1985b) 'The Dazzling Dollar', *Brookings Papers on Economic Activity*, 1985 no. 1.

Frankel, J.A. (1986) 'The Implications of Mean-Variance Optimization for Four Questions in International Macroeconomics', *Journal of International Money and Finance*, vol. 5 no. 1, Supplement.

Frenkel, J.A. (1978) 'A Monetary Approach to the Exchange Rate: Doctrinal Aspects and Empirical Evidence', in J.A. Frenkel and H.G. Johnson (eds), *The Economics of Exchange Rates: Selected Studies*, Reading, Mass., Addison-Wesley. First published in *Scandinavian Journal of Economics*, vol. 78 no. 2, 1976.

Frenkel, J.A. (1981a) 'The Collapse of Purchasing Power Parities during the 1970's', *European Economic Review*, vol. 16 no. 1.

Frenkel, J.A. (1981b) 'Flexible Exchange Rates, Prices, and the Role of "News": Lessons from the 1970s', *Journal of Political Economy*, vol. 89 no. 4.

Frenkel, J.A., and M.L. Mussa (1985) 'Asset Markets, Exchange Rates and the Balance of Payments', in R.W. Jones and P.B. Kenen (eds), *Handbook of International Economics*, vol. II, Amsterdam, North-Holland.

Frenkel, J.A., and C.A. Rodriguez (1982) 'Exchange Rate Dynamics and the Overshooting Hypothesis', *IMF Staff Papers*, vol. 29 no. 1.

Friedman, B.M. (1979) 'Optimal expectations and the extreme information assumption of 'rational expectations' macromodels', *Journal of Monetary Economics*, vol. 5 no. 1.

Friedman, B.M (1980), 'Survey Evidence on the 'Rationality' of

Interest Rate Expectations', *Journal of Monetary Economics*, vol. 6 no. 4.

Friedman, M. (1953) 'The Methodology of Positive Economics', in M. Friedman, *Essays in Positive Economics*, Chicago, University of Chicago Press.

Friedman, M. (1956) 'The Quantity Theory of Money: A Restatement', in M. Friedman (ed.), *Studies in the Quantity Theoy of Money*, Chicago, University of Chicago Press.

Friedman, M. (1962) *Capitalism and Freedom*, Chicago, University of Chicago Press.

Friedman, M. (1969a) 'The Role of Monetary Policy', in M. Friedman, *The Optimum Quantity of Money and Other Essays*, London, Macmillan. Presidential address to the American Economic Association, first published in *American Economic Review*, vol. 58 no. 1, 1968.

Friedman, M. (1969b) 'The Optimum Quantity of Money', in M. Friedman, *The Optimum Quantity of Money and Other Essays*, London, Macmillan.

Friedman, M. (1970) 'A Theoretical Framework for Monetary Analysis', *Journal of Political Economy*, vol. 78 no. 2.

Friedman, M. (1971a) 'A Monetary Theory of Nominal Income', *Journal of Political Economy*, vol. 79 no. 2.

Friedman, M. (1971b) 'A Note on U.S. and U.K. Velocity of Circulation', in G. Clayton, J.C. Gilbert and R. Sedgwick (eds), *Monetary Theory and Monetary Policy in the 1970s*, London, Oxford University Press.

Friedman, M. (1976) *Price Theory*, Chicago, Aldine.

Friedman, M. (1984) 'Currency competition: A sceptical view', in P. Salin (ed.).

Friedman, M. (1986) 'Death of Monetarism Greatly Exaggerated', *Wall Street Journal*, 25 September.

Friedman, M., and W.W. Heller (1968) *Monetary vs. Fiscal Policy*, New York, Norton.

Friedman, M., and D. Meiselman (1963) 'The Relative Stability of Monetary Velocity and the Investment Multiplier in the United States, 1897-1958', in Commission on Money and Credit, *Stabilization Policies*, Englewood Cliffs, N.J., Prentice-Hall.

Friedman, M., and A.J. Schwartz (1963) *A Monetary History of the United States, 1867-1960*, Princeton, N.J., Princeton University Press.

Friedman, M., and A.J. Schwartz (1969) 'Money and Business Cycles', in M. Friedman, *The Optimum Quantity of Money and*

Other Essays, London, Macmillan. First published in *Review of Economics and Statistics*, vol. 45 no. l, part 2, 1963.

Friedman, M., and A.J. Schwartz (1986) 'Has government any role in money?', *Journal of Monetary Economics*, vol. 17 no. 1.

Fromm, G., and L.R. Klein (1973) 'A Comparison of Eleven Econometric Models of the United States', *American Economic Review*, vol. 63 no. 2 (Papers and Proceedings).

Froot, K.A., and J.A. Frankel (1989) 'Forward Discount Bias: Is It An Exchange Rate Premium?', *Quarterly Journal of Economics*, vol. 104 no. 1.

Gale, D. (1982) *Money: in equilibrium*, Welwyn, Nisbet, and Cambridge, Cambridge University Press.

Gale, D. (1983) *Money: in disequilibrium*, Welwyn, Nisbet, and Cambridge, Cambridge University Press.

Geanakoplos, J. (1989) 'Arrow-Debreu Model of General Equilibrium', in J. Eatwell, M. Milgate and P. Newman (eds), *The New Palgrave: General Equilibrium*, London, Macmillan.

Genberg, H. (1978) 'Purchasing Power Parity Under Fixed and Flexible Exchange Rates', *Journal of International Economics*, vol. 8 no. 2.

Gerlach, S. (1987) 'Exchange Rates; A Review Essay', *Journal of Monetary Economics*, vol. 19 no. 1.

Gilbert, R.A. (1983) 'Economies of Scale in Correspondent Banking', *Journal of Money, Credit, and Banking*, vol. 15 no. 4.

Glasner, D. (1989) *Free Banking and Monetary Reform*, Cambridge, Cambridge University Press.

Goldfeld, S.M. (1989) 'Demand for Money: Empirical Studies', in J. Eatwell, M. Milgate and P. Newman (eds), *The New Palgrave: Money*, London, Macmillan.

Goodfriend, M. (1985) 'Reinterpreting Money Demand Regressions', in K. Brunner and A.H. Meltzer (eds), *Understanding Monetary Regimes*, Carnegie-Rochester Conference Series on Public Policy no. 22.

Goodhart, C.A.E. (1975) *Money, Information and Uncertainty*, London, Macmillan.

Goodhart, C.A.E. (1984) *Monetary Theory and Practice; The UK Experience*, London, Macmillan.

Goodhart, C.A.E. (1988a) *The Evolution of Central Banks*, Cambridge, Mass., MIT Press.

Goodhart, C.A.E. (1988b) 'The Foreign Exchange Market: A Random Walk with a Dragging Anchor', *Economica*, vol. 55 no. 220.

Gordon, R.J. (1981) 'Output Fluctuations and Gradual Price Adjustment', *Journal of Economic Literature*, vol. 19 no. 2.

Gordon, R.J. (1982) 'Price Inertia and Policy Ineffectiveness in the United States, 1890-1980', *Journal of Political Economy*, vol. 90 no. 6.

Gordon, R.J. (1983) 'A Century of Evidence on Wage and Price Stickiness in the United States, the United Kingdom, and Japan', in J. Tobin (ed.), *Macroeconomics, Prices, and Quantities; Essays in Memory of Arthur M. Okun*, Oxford, Basil Blackwell.

Gorton, G. (1985) 'Banking Theory and Free Banking History', *Journal of Monetary Economics*, vol. 16.

Greenfield, R.L., and L.B. Yeager (1983) 'A Laissez-Faire Approach to Monetary Theory', *Journal of Money, Credit, and Banking*, vol. 15 no. 3.

Greenfield, R.L., and L.B. Yeager (1986) 'Competitive Payments Systems: Comment', *American Economic Review*, vol. 76 no. 4.

Greenwald, B., and J.E. Stiglitz (1987) 'Keynesian, New Keynesian and New Classical Economics', *Oxford Economic Papers*, vol. 39.

Gros, D. (1989) 'On the Volatility of Exchange Rates: Tests of Monetary and Portfolio Balance Models of Exchange Rate Determination', *Weltwirtschaftliches Archiv*, vol. 125 no. 2.

Grossman, H.I. (1980) 'Rational Expectations, Business Cycles, and Government Behavior', in S. Fischer (ed.) 1980.

Grubel, H.G. (1968) 'Internationally Diversified Portfolios: Welfare Gains and Capital Flows', *American Economic Review*, vol. 58. Reprinted in J.H. Dunning (ed.), *International Investment*, Harmondsworth, Penguin.

Gurley, J.G., and E.S. Shaw (1960) *Money in a Theory of Finance*, Washington, D.C., Brookings Institution.

Haberler, G. (1963) *Prosperity and Depression*, 4th ed., New York, Atheneum.

Hafer, R.W. (1984) 'The Money-GNP Link: Assessing Alternative Transaction Measures', *Review*, Federal Reserve Bank of St Louis, vol. 66 no. 3.

Hafer, R.W. (1985) 'Monetary Stabilization Policy: Evidence from Money Demand Forecasts', *Review*, Federal Reserve Bank of St Louis, vol. 67 no. 5.

Hafer, R.W., and S.E. Hein (1979) 'Evidence on the Temporal Stability of the Demand for Money Relationship in the United States', *Review*, Federal Reserve Bank of St Louis, vol. 61 no. 12.

Hafer, R.W., and S.E. Hein (1982) 'The Shift in Money Demand: What Really Happened?', *Review*, Federal Reserve Bank of St Louis, vol. 64 no. 2.

Hahn, F.H. (1973) 'On the foundations of monetary theory', in M. Parkin and A.R. Nobay (eds), *Essays in Modern Economics*, London, Longman.

Hahn, F.H. (1980a) 'Monetarism and Economic Theory', *Economica*, vol. 47 no. 185.

Hahn, F.H. (1980b) 'Unemployment from a Theoretical Viewpoint', *Economica*, vol. 47 no. 187.

Hahn, F.H. (1982) *Money and Inflation*, Oxford, Basil Blackwell.

Hahn, F.H. (1985a) *Money, Growth and Stability*, Oxford, Basil Blackwell.

Hahn, F.H. (1985b) 'Equilibrium with Transaction Costs', ch. 4 in Hahn 1985b. First published in *Econometrica*, vol. 39, 1971.

Hahn, F.H. (1988) 'On Monetary Theory', *Economic Journal*, vol. 98 no. 393, December.

Hall R.E. (1982) 'Monetary Trends in the United States and the United Kingdom: A Review from the Perspective of New Developments in Monetary Economics', *Journal of Economic Literature*, vol. 20 no. 4.

Hallwood, P., and R. MacDonald (1986) *International Money; Theory, Evidence and Institutions*, Oxford, Basil Blackwell.

Haltiwanger, J.C., and M. Waldman (1989) 'Rational Expectations in the Aggregate', *Economic Inquiry*, vol. 27 no. 4.

Hammond, B. (1948) 'Banking in the Early West: Monopoly, Prohibition, and Laissez Faire', *Journal of Economic History*, vol. 8 no. 1.

Hancock, K.J. (1970) 'The Reduction of Unemployment as a Problem of Public Policy, 1920-1929', in S. Pollard (ed.), *The Gold Standard and Employment Policies between the Wars*, London, Methuen. First published in *Economic History Review*, 2nd series, vol. 15, December 1962.

Handa, J., and I.M. Bana (1990) 'Currency Substitution and Transactions Costs', *Empirical Economics*, vol. 15 no. 3.

Harberger, A.C. (1986) 'A Primer on the Chilean Economy, 1973-1983', in A.M. Choksi and D. Papageorgiou (eds), *Economic Liberalization in Developing Countries*, Oxford, Basil Blackwell.

Harris, L. (1985) *Monetary Theory*, New York, McGraw-Hill.

Hatton, T.J. (1983) 'Unemployment Benefits and the Macroeconomics of the Interwar Labour Market: A Further Analysis', *Oxford Economic Papers*, vol. 35 no. 3.

Hawtrey, R.G. (1925) 'Public Expenditure and the Demand for Labour', *Economica*, vol. 5 no. 13, March.

Hayek, F.A. (1937) *Monetary Nationalism and Institutional Stability*, London, Longmans, Green. Reprinted New York, A.M. Kelley, 1971.

Hayek, F.A. (1944) *The Road to Serfdom*, London, Routledge & Kegan Paul.

Hayek, F.A. (1978a) *New Studies in Philosophy, Politics, Economics and the History of Ideas*, London, Routledge & Kegan Paul.

Hayek, F.A. (1978b) *Denationalisation of Money*, 2nd ed., London, Institute of Economic Affairs.

Hayek, F.A. (1978c) 'Choice in currency: a way to stop inflation', in F.A. Hayek 1978a. First published as a separate brochure by the Institute of Economic Affairs, London, 1976.

Hayek, F.A. (1984a) 'The Future Monetary Unit of Value', in B.N. Siegel (ed.), *Money in Crisis*, Cambridge, Mass., Ballinger.

Hayek, F.A. (1984b) 'The Future Unit of Value', in P. Salin (ed.), 1984.

Heerkens, R.W.J. (1983) 'Een onderzoek naar het verband tussen investeringen en Tobin's Q', in A.C.C. Herst, J. van der Meulen and G.J. Ruizendaal (eds), *Financiering en belegging. Stand van zaken anno 1983*, Rotterdam, Erasmus University.

Heim, C.E., and P. Mirowski (1987) 'Interest Rates and Crowding-Out During Britain's Industrial Revolution', *Journal of Economic History*, vol. 47 no. 1.

Heitger, B. (1987) 'Purchasing Power Parity under Flexible Exchange Rates - The Impact of Structural Change', *Weltwirtschaftliches Archiv*, vol. 123 no. 1.

Hellwig, M.F. (1985) 'What do we know about Currency Competition?', *Zeitschrift für Wirtschafts- und Sozialwissenschaften*, vol. 105 no. 5.

Helpman, E. (1983) 'Comment on Fama 1983', *Journal of Monetary Economics*, vol. 12.

Helpman, E., and A. Razin (1984) 'The Role of Saving and Investment in Exchange Rate Determination under Alternative Monetary Mechanisms', *Journal of Monetary Economics*, vol. 13 no. 4.

Hentschel, N. (1976) 'The Microfoundations of Monetary Theory', *Kredit und Kapital*, vol. 9 no. 1.

Heri, E.W. (1984) 'Wechselkursbewegungen. Einige Ergebnisse einer Analyse der kurzen Frist', *Kredit und Kapital*, vol. 17 no. 2.

Hicks, J.R. (1967) 'The Two Triads - Lecture I', in *Critical Essays in Monetary Theory*, Oxford, Oxford University Press.

Hines, A.G. (1971) *On the Reappraisal of Keynesian Economics*, London, Martin Robertson.

Hodrick, R.J., and S. Srivistava (1986) 'The Covariation of Risk

Premiums and Expected Future Spot Exchange Rates', *Journal of International Money and Finance*, vol. 5 no. 1, Supplement.

Hoffman, D.L., and D.E. Schlagenhauf (1983) 'Rational Expectations and Monetary Models of Exchange Rate Determination', *Journal of Monetary Economics*, vol. 11 no. 3.

Hoffmann, J., and S. Homburg (1990) 'Explaining the Rise and Decline of the Dollar', *Kyklos*, vol. 43 no. 1.

Homburg, S. (1989) 'Some Notes on Overshooting', *Zeitschrift für Wirtschafts- und Sozialwissenschaften*, vol. 109 no. 3.

Hoover, K.D. (1984) 'Two Types of Monetarism', *Journal of Economic Literature*, vol. 22 no. 1.

Hoover, K.D. (1988a) 'Money, Prices and Finance in the New Monetary Economics', *Oxford Economic Papers*, vol. 40 no. 1.

Hoover, K.D. (1988b) *The New Classical Macroeconomics*, Oxford, Basil Blackwell.

Horne, J. (1983) 'The Asset Market Model of the Balance of Payments and the Exchange Rate: A Survey of Empirical Evidence', *Journal of International Money and Finance*, vol. 2 no. 2.

Hume, D. (1955) 'Of Money', in D. Hume, *Writings in Economics* (ed. E. Rotwein), Edinburgh, Nelson.

Humphrey, D.B. (1987) 'Cost Dispersion and the Measurement of Economies in Banking', *Economic Review*, Federal Reserve Bank of Richmond, vol. 73 no. 3.

Illing, G. (1985) *Geld und asymmetrische Information*, Berlin, Springer-Verlag.

Infante, E.F., and J.L. Stein (1976) 'Does Fiscal Policy Matter?', *Journal of Monetary Economics*, vol. 2 no. 4.

International Monetary Fund, *Annual Report 1989*.

Isard, P. (1987) 'Lessons from Empirical Models of Exchange Rates', *IMF Staff Papers*, vol. 34 no. 1.

Islam, S. (1988) *The Dollar and the Policy-Performance-Confidence Mix*, Essays in International Finance no. 170, Princeton, N.J., International Finance Section, Princeton University.

Johnson, H.G. (1962) 'Monetary Theory and Policy', *American Economic Review*, vol. 52 no. 3. Reprinted in H.G. Johnson, *Essays in Monetary Economics*, London, George Allen & Unwin, 1967.

Johnson, H.G. (1967) 'Recent Developments in Monetary Theory', in H.G. Johnson, *Essays in Monetary Economics*, London, George Allen & Unwin 1967.

Johnson, H.G. (1970) 'Recent Developments in Monetary Theory - A Commentary', in D.R. Croome and H.G. Johnson (eds), *Money in Britain 1959-1969*, London, Oxford University Press.

Johnson, H.G. (1972) 'The Monetary Approach to Balance-of-Payments Theory', in H.G. Johnson, *Further Essays in Monetary Economics*, London, George Allen & Unwin. Reprinted in J.A. Frenkel and H.G. Johnson (eds), *The Monetary Approach to the Balance of Payments*, London, George Allen & Unwin, 1976 and, with a number of annoying typographical errors in the formulas, in M.B. Connolly and A.K. Swoboda (eds), *International Trade and Money*, London, George Allen & Unwin, 1973.

Johnson, H.G. (1974) 'Major Issues in Monetary Economics', *Oxford Economic Papers*, n.s. vol. 26 no. 2.

Jones, R.A. (1976) 'The Origin and Development of Media of Exchange', *Journal of Political Economy*, vol. 84 no. 4 pt. 1.

Journal of Political Economy (1972) vol. 80 no. 5, special issue on Monetary Theory.

Judd, J.P., and J.L. Scadding (1982) 'The Search for a Stable Money Demand Function: A Survey of the Post-1973 Literature', *Journal of Economic Literature*, vol. 20 no. 3.

Kahn, J.A. (1985) 'Another Look at Free Banking in the United States', *American Economic Review*, vol. 75 no. 4.

Kaldor, N. (1982) *The Scourge of Monetarism*, Oxford, Oxford University Press.

Kareken, J.H., and N. Wallace (eds) (1980) *Models of Monetary Economics*, Minneapolis, Federal Reserve Bank of Minneapolis.

Kareken, J.H., and N. Wallace (1980) 'Introduction', in J.H. Kareken and N. Wallace (eds), 1980.

Keynes, J.M. (1937) 'The "Ex-Ante" Theory of the Rate of Interest', *Economic Journal*, vol. 47 no. 188.

Keynes, J.M. (1961) *The General Theory of Employment, Interest and Money*, 13th printing, London, Macmillan.

Keynes, J.M. (1971a) *A Tract on Monetary Reform*, London, Macmillan (first published 1923).

Keynes, J.M. (1971b) *A Treatise on Money*, London, Macmillan (first published 1930).

Khan, W., and T.D. Willett (1984) 'The Monetary Approach to Exchange Rates: A Review of Recent Empirical Studies', *Kredit und Kapital*, vol. 17 no. 2.

Kindleberger, C.P. (1978) *Manias, Panics, and Crashes*, London, Macmillan.

Kindleberger, C.P. (1987) *The World in Depression 1929-1939*, 2nd ed., Harmondsworth, Penguin.

King, R.G. (1983) 'On the Economics of Private Money', *Journal of Monetary Economics*, vol. 12.

King, R.G., and Ch.I. Plosser (1986) 'Money as the Mechanism of Exchange', *Journal of Monetary Economics*, vol. 17.

Klamer, A. (1984) *The New Classical Macroeconomics*, Brighton, Wheatsheaf.

Klein, B. (1974) 'The Competitive Supply of Money', *Journal of Money, Credit, and Banking*, vol. 6 no. 4.

Klein, B. (1976) 'Competing Monies (comment on Tullock 1975)', *Journal of Money, Credit, and Banking*, vol. 8 no. 4.

Knoester, A. (1980) *Over geld en economische politiek*, Leiden, Stenfert Kroese.

Knoester, A. (1984) 'Theoretical Principles of the Buffer Mechanism, Monetary Quasi-Equilibrium and its Spillover Effects', *Kredit und Kapital*, vol. 17 no. 2.

Kochin, L.A. (1974) 'Are Future Taxes Anticipated by Consumers?', *Journal of Money, Credit, and Banking*, vol. 6 no. 3.

Koedijk, C.G. (1989) *Studies in Empirical Exchange Rate Economics*, PhD thesis, Erasmus University, Rotterdam.

Koedijk, C.G., and E.G.J. Luttmer (1987) 'Exchange Rates and Risk', in W.G. Hallerbach *et al.* (eds), *Finance and Investment, State of the Art 1987*, Rotterdam, Erasmus University.

Koelewijn, J. (1989) 'De (im)perfecte vermogensmarkt, (in)efficiëntie, intermediatie en structuurveranderingen', in A.B. Dorsman, H.G. Eijgenhuijsen, J. Koelewijn and H. Visser (eds), *Het financieel systeem in ontwikkeling*, Leiden, Stenfert Kroese.

Kohli, U. (1987) 'Exogenous Money, Monetary (Dis)equilibrium and Expectational Lags', *Kredit und Kapital*, vol. 20 no. 2.

Kool, C.J.M. (1989) *Recursive Bayesian Forecasting in Economics: The Multistate Kalman Filter Method*, PhD thesis, Rotterdam, Erasmus University.

Koromzay, V., J. Llewellyn and S. Potter (1987) 'The Rise and Fall of the Dollar: Some Explanations, Consequences and Lessons', *Economic Journal*, vol. 97 no. 385.

Korteweg, P. (1976) 'Activisme of automatie in de monetaire politiek?', *Economisch Statistische Berichten*, vol. 61 no. 3054.

Kösters, W. (1973) 'Ergebnisse und Probleme empirischer Tests geldtheoretischer Hypothesen', in C. Köhler (ed.), *Geldpolitik - kontrovers*, Cologne, Bund-Verlag.

Krasker, W.S. (1980) 'The 'peso problem' in testing forward exchange markets', *Journal of Monetary Economics*, vol. 6 no. 2.

Krueger, A.O. (1983) *Exchange-Rate Determination*, Cambridge, Cambridge University Press.

Krugman, P.R. (1985), Comment on Obstfeld, 1985, *Brookings Papers on Economic Activity*, no. 2.

Lächler, U. (1985) 'The Elasticity of Substitution between Imported and Domestically Produced Goods in Germany', *Weltwirtschaftliches Archiv*, vol. 121 no. 1.

Laidler, D.E.W. (1969) *The Demand for Money: Theories and Evidence*, Scranton, International Textbook Company.

Laidler, D.E.W. (1981) 'Monetarism: An Interpretation and an Assessment', *Economic Journal*, vol. 81 no. 361.

Laidler, D.E.W. (1982) *Monetarist Perspectives*, Oxford, Philip Allan.

Laidler, D.E.W. (1984) 'The Buffer Stock Notion in Monetary Economics', *Economic Journal*, vol. 94, Supplement.

Laidler, D.E.W. (1985) 'Expectations and adjustment in the monetary sector revisited; a comment', in K. Brunner and A.H. Meltzer (eds), *Understanding Monetary Regimes*, Carnegie-Rochester Conference Series on Public Policy, vol. 22.

Laidler, D.E.W. (1990a) 'Fiscal Deficits and International Monetary Institutions', ch. 10 in D.E.W. Laidler, *Taking Money Seriously*, Hemel Hempstead, Philip Allan. First published in J. Buchanan, C.K. Rowley and R.D. Tollison (eds), *Deficits*, Oxford, Basil Blackwell, 1987.

Laidler, D.E.W. (1990b) 'The Legacy Of The Monetarist Controversy', *Review*, Federal Reserve Bank of St Louis, vol. 72 no. 2.

Laidler, D.E.W. (1990c) 'The New-Classical Contribution to Macroeconomics', ch. 4 in D.E.W. Laidler, *Taking Money Seriously*, op.cit. First published in *Banca Nazionale del Lavoro Quarterly Review*, 1986.

Laidler, D.E.W. (1990d) 'Monetarism, Microfoundations and the Theory of Monetary Policy', Ch. 6 in D.E.W. Laidler, Taking Money Seriously, op. cit.

Lal, D., and S. van Wijnbergen (1985) 'Government Deficits, the Real Interest Rate and LDC Debt; On Global Crowding Out', *European Economic Review*, vol. 29.

Lamfalussy, A. (1990) 'Monetary policy and financial market liberalisation', in A.H.E.M. Wellink, A. Lamfalussy, S.K. Kuipers and E. Sterken, *De mogelijkheden voor het monetaire beleid na de liberalisatie*, Amsterdam, NIBE.

Laney, L.O., C.D. Radcliffe and T.D. Willett (1984) 'Currency Substitution: Comment', *Southern Economic Journal*, vol. 50 no. 4.

Lee, M.A. (1974) *Excess Inflation and Currency Depreciation*, PhD thesis, University of Chicago, cited in A.B. Laffer 'The Phenomenon of Worldwide Inflation: A Study in International Market Integration', in D.I. Meiselman and A.B. Laffer (eds), *The Phenomenon of Worldwide Inflation*, Washington, D.C., American Enterprise Institute for Public Policy Research 1975.

Leiderman, L., and M.I. Blejer (1988) 'Modeling and Testing Ricardian Equivalence', *IMF Staff Papers*, vol. 35 no. 1.

Leijonhufvud, A. (1968) *On Keynesian Economics and the Economics of Keynes*, New York, Oxford University Press.

Leijonhufvud, A. (1969) *Keynes and the Classics*, London, Institute of Economic Affairs.

Leijonhufvud, A. (1973) 'Effective Demand Failures', *Swedish Journal of Economics*, vol. 75 no. 1.

Leventakis, J.A. (1987) 'Exchange Rate Models: Do They Work?', *Weltwirtschaftliches Archiv*, vol. 123 no. 2.

Levich, R.M. (1978) 'Tests of Forecasting Models and Market Efficiency in the International Money Market', in J.A. Frenkel and H.G. Johnson (eds), *The Economics of Exchange Rates: Selected Studies*, Reading, Mass., Addison-Wesley.

Levich, R.M. (1985) 'Empirical Studies of Exchange Rates: Price Behavior, Rate Determination and Market Efficiency', in R.W. Jones and P.B. Kenen (eds), *Handbook of International Economics*, vol. II, Amsterdam, North-Holland.

Lomax, D.F. (1983) 'International Moneys and Monetary Arrangements in Private Markets', in G.M. von Furstenberg (ed.), *International Money and Credit: The Policy Roles*, Washington, D.C., International Monetary Fund.

Long Jr, J.B., and Ch.I. Plosser (1983) 'Real Business Cycles', *Journal of Political Economy*, vol. 91 no. 1.

Lucas Jr, R.E. (1972) 'Expectations and the Neutrality of Money', *Journal of Economic Theory*, vol. 4 no. 2.

Lucas Jr, R.E. (1973) 'Some International Evidence on Output-Inflation Tradeoffs', *American Economic Review*, vol. 63 no. 3.

Lucas Jr, R.E. (1975) 'An Equilibrium Model of the Business Cycle', *Journal of Political Economy*, vol. 83 no. 6.

Lucas Jr, R.E. (1976) 'Econometric Policy Evaluation: A Critique', in K. Brunner and A.H. Meltzer (eds), *The Phillips Curve and Labor Markets*, Carnegie-Rochester Conference Series on Public Policy, vol. 1.

Lucas Jr, R.E. (1977) 'Understanding Business Cycles', in K. Brunner and A.H. Meltzer (eds), *Stabilization of the Domestic and International Economy*, Carnegie-Rochester Conference Series on Public Policy, vol. 5.

Lucas Jr, R.E. (1980) 'Equilibrium in a Pure Currency Economy', in Kareken and Wallace (eds).

Lucas Jr, R.E. (1987) *Models of Business Cycles*, Oxford, Basil Blackwell.

Lucas Jr, R.E., and Th.J. Sargent (eds), *Rational Expectations and Econometric Practice*, London, George Allen & Unwin.

Lüdiger, M. (1989) 'Wechselkursovershooting contra effiziente Devisenmärkte', *Kredit und Kapital*, vol. 22 no. 2.

Maasoumi, E., and J. Pippenger (1989) 'Transaction Costs and the Interest Parity Theorem: Comment', *Journal of Political Economy*, vol. 97 no. 1.

MacDonald, R. (1983) 'Some Tests of the Rational Expectations Hypothesis in the Foreign Exchange Market', *Scottish Journal of Political Economy*, vol. 30 no. 3.

MacDonald, R. (1988a) *Floating Exchange Rates; Theories and Evidence*, London, Unwin Hyman.

MacDonald, R. (1988b) 'Purchasing Power Parity: Some 'Long Run' Evidence from the Recent Float', *De Economist*, vol. 136 no. 2.

Maennig, W.G.C., and W.J. Tease (1987) 'Covered Interest Parity in Non-Dollar Euromarkets', *Weltwirtschaftliches Archiv*, vol. 123 no. 4.

Mahajan, Y. Lal (1980) 'Stability of the Demand for Money Functions: A Cross Country Analysis', *Indian Economic Journal*, vol. 28 no. l.

Malinvaud, E. (1977) *The Theory of Unemployment Reconsidered*, Oxford, Basil Blackwell.

Malkiel, B.G., G.M. von Furstenberg and H.S. Watson (1979) 'Expectations, Tobin's q, and Industry Investment', *Journal of Finance*, vol. 34 no. 2.

Mankiw, N.G. (1986) 'Issues in Keynesian Macroeconomics', *Journal of Monetary Economics*, vol. 18.

Marshall, A. (1965) *Money, Credit and Commerce*, New York, Kelley. Originally published 1923.

Masson, P.R. (1981) 'Dynamic stability of portfolio balance models of the exchange rate', *Journal of International Economics*, vol. 11 no. 4.

Mayer, T. (1975) 'The Structure of Monetarism', *Kredit und Kapital*, vol. 8 nos. 2 and 3.

Mayer, T. (1984) 'The government budget constraint and standard macrotheory', *Journal of Monetary Economics*, vol. 13.

McCafferty, S. (1982) 'Rational Expectations, Disequilibrium Quantities, and Policy Effectiveness in a Non-Market-Clearing Framework', *Weltwirtschaftliches Archiv*, vol. 118 no. 3.

McCallum, B.T. (1977) 'Price-Level Stickiness and the Feasibility of Monetary Stabilization Policy with Rational Expectations', *Journal of Political Economy*, vol. 85 no. 3.

McCallum, B.T. (1979) 'The Current State of the Policy-Ineffectiveness Debate', *American Economic Review*, vol. 69 no. 2.

McCallum, B.T. (1980a) 'The Significance of Rational Expectations Theory', *Challenge*, vol. 22 no. 6.

McCallum, B.T. (1980b) 'Rational Expectations and Macroeconomic Stabilization Policy', *Journal of Money, Credit, and Banking*, vol. 12 no. 4 part II.

McCallum, B.T. (1985) 'Bank Deregulation, Accounting Systems of Exchange, and the Unit of Account: A Critical Review', in K. Brunner and A.H. Meltzer (eds), *The 'New Monetary Economics', Fiscal Issues and Unemployment*, Carnegie-Rochester Conference Series on Public Policy, vol. 23.

McCallum, B.T. (1989) *Monetary Economics; Theory and Policy*, New York, Macmillan.

McKinnon, R.I. (1979) *Money in International Exchange*, New York, Oxford University Press.

McKinnon, R.I. (1981) 'The Exchange Rate and Macroeconomic Policy: Changing Postwar Perceptions', *Journal of Economic Literature*, vol. 19 no. 2.

McKinnon, R.I. (1982) 'Currency Substitution and Instability in the World Dollar Standard', *American Economic Review*, vol. 72 no. 3.

McKinnon, R.I. (1984) *An International Standard for Monetary Stabilization*, Washington, D.C., Institute for International Economics.

Meade, J.E. (1970) *The Theory of Indicative Planning*, Manchester, Manchester University Press.

Meese, R.A., and K. Rogoff (1983) 'Empirical Exchange Rate Models of the Seventies', *Journal of International Economics*, vol. 14 no. 1/2.

Mehra, Y.P. (1989) 'Some Further Results on the Source of Shift in M1 Demand in the 1980s', *Economic Review*, Federal Reserve Bank of Richmond, vol. 75 no. 5.

Meltzer, A.H. (1981) 'Keynes's General Theory: A Different Perspective', *Journal of Economic Literature*, vol. 19 no. 2.

Meltzer, A.H. (1988) *Keynes's monetary theory; A different interpretation*, Cambridge, Cambridge University Press.

Melvin, M. (1985) 'Currency Substitution and Western European Monetary Unification', *Economica*, vol. 52 no. 205.

Metcalf, D., S.J. Nickell and N. Floros (1982) 'Still Searching for an Explanation of Unemployment in Interwar Britain', *Journal of Political Economy*, vol. 90 no. 2.

Miller, M.H., and D. Orr (1968) 'The Demand for Money by Firms: Extensions of Analytic Results', *Journal of Finance*, vol. 23 no. 5.

Minford, P. (1986) 'Rational Expectations and Monetary Policy', *Scottish Journal of Political Economy*, vol. 33 no. 4.

Minford, P., and D. Peel (1981) 'The Role of Monetary Stabilization Policy under Rational Expectations', *Manchester School*, vol. 49 no. 1.

Minsky, H.P. (1982) *Can "It" Happen Again? Essays on Instability and Finance*, Armonk, N.Y., M.E. Sharpe.

Minsky, H.P. (1986) *Stabilizing an Unstable Economy*, New Haven, Yale University Press.

Minsky, H.P. (1988) 'Back from the Brink' (interview), *Challenge*, vol. 31 no. 1.

Mises, L. von (1966) *Human Action*, 3rd ed., n.p., Henry Regnery (reprint Chicago, Contemporary Books).

Monissen, H.G. (1973) 'Die relative Stabilität von Kreislaufgeschwindigkeit des Geldes und Investitionsmultiplikator: Eine Zusammenfassung der Diskussion', *Jahrbuch für Sozialwissenschaften*, vol. 24 no. 3.

Montiel, P.J. (1987) 'Output and Unanticipated Money in the Dependent Economy Model', *IMF Staff Papers*, vol. 34 no. 2.

Mundell, R.A. (1963a) 'Inflation and Real Interest', *Journal of Political Economy*, vol. 71 no. 3.

Mundell, R.A. (1963b) 'Capital Mobility and Stabilization Policy under Fixed and Flexible Exchange Rates', *Canadian Journal of Economics and Political Science*, vol. 29 no. 4. Reprinted in R.E. Caves and H.G. Johnson (eds), *Readings in International Economics*, London, George Allen & Unwin, 1968.

Mundell, R.A. (1971) *Monetary Theory*, Pacific Palisades, Goodyear.

Mussa, M. (1984) 'The Theory of Exchange Rate Determination', in J.F.O. Bilson and R.C. Marston (eds), *Exchange Rate Theory and Practice*, Chicago, University of Chicago Press.

Mussa, M. (1986) 'Nominal Exchange Rate Regimes and the Behavior of Real Exchange Rates: Evidence and Implications', in K. Brunner and A.H. Meltzer (eds), *Real Business Cycles, Real Exchange Rates and Actual Policies*, Carnegie-Rochester Conference Series on Public Policy vol. 25, Amsterdam, North-Holland.

Muth, J.F. (1961) 'Rational Expectations and the Theory of Price Movements', *Economica*, vol. 29 no. 3.

Neary, J.P., and J.E. Stiglitz (1983) 'Toward a Reconstruction of Keynesian Economics: Expectations and Constrained Equilibria', *Quarterly Journal of Economics*, vol. 98 supplement.

Nguyen, D.T., and S.J. Turnovsky (1983) 'The Dynamic Effects of Fiscal and Monetary Policies under Bond Financing', *Journal of Monetary Economics*, vol. 11 no. 1.

Nicoletti, G. (1988) 'A Cross-Country Analysis of Private Consumption, Inflation and the "Debt Neutrality Hypothesis" ', *OECD Economic Studies*, no. 11.

Niehans, J. (1969) 'Money in a Static Theory of Optimal Payment Arrangements', *Journal of Money, Credit, and Banking*, vol. 1 no. 4.

Niehans, J. (1971) 'Money and Barter in General Equilibrium with Transactions Costs', *American Economic Review*, vol. 61 no. 5.

Niehans, J. (1975) 'Interest and Credit in General Equilibrium with Transactions Costs', *American Economic Review*, vol. 65 no. 4.

Niehans, J. (1978) *The Theory of Money*, Baltimore, Johns Hopkins University Press.

Niehans, J. (1987) 'Classical Monetary Theory, New and Old', Journal of Money, Credit, and Banking, vol. 19 no. 4.

Nobay, R., and H.G. Johnson (1977) 'Monetarism: A Historic-Theoretic Perspective', *Journal of Economic Literature*, vol. 15 no. 2.

Obstfeld, M. (1985) 'Floating Exchange Rates: Experience and Prospects', *Brookings Papers on Economic Activity*, 1985 no. 2.

Obstfeld, M., and A.C. Stockman (1985) 'Exchange-Rate Dynamics' in R.W. Jones and P.B. Kenen (eds), *Handbook of International Economics,* vol. II, Amsterdam, North-Holland.

O'Driscoll Jr, G.P. (1977) 'The Ricardian Nonequivalence Theorem', *Journal of Political Economy*, vol. 85 no. 1.

Oh, S. (1989) 'A Theory of a Generally Acceptable Medium ofExchange and Barter', *Journal of Monetary Economics*, vol. 23 no. 1.

Okun, A.M. (1981) *Prices and Quantities: A Macroeconomic Approach*, Oxford, Basil Blackwell.

Oort, C.J. (1987) 'The influences of international capital flows on world trade', in H. Visser and E. Schoorl (eds), *Trade in Transit*, Dordrecht, Kluwer.

Ormerod, P.A., and G.D.N. Worswick (1982) 'Unemployment in Interwar Britain', *Journal of Political Economy*, vol. 90 no. 2.

Ostroy, J.M. (1973) 'The Informational Efficiency of Monetary Exchange', *American Economic Review*, vol. 63 no. 4.

Ostroy, J.M. (1989) 'Money and General Equilibrium Theory', in J. Eatwell, M. Milgate and P. Newman (eds), *General Equilibrium (The New Palgrave)*, London, Macmillan.

Ostroy, J.M., and R.M. Starr (1974) 'Money and the Decentralization of Exchange', *Econometrica*, vol. 42 no. 6.

Oxley, L.T. (1983) 'Rational Expectations and Macroeconomic Policy: A Review Article', *Scottish Journal of Political Economy*, vol. 30 no. 2.

Paleologos, J. (1986) 'Unanticipated Money, Output, and Inflation in Greece', *Public Finance*, vol. 41 no. 3.

Papell, D.H. (1988) 'Expectations and Exchange Rate Dynamics after a Decade of Floating', *Journal of International Economics*, vol. 25 no. 3/4.

Patinkin, D. (1952) 'Price Flexibility and Full Employment', in F.A. Lutz and L.W. Mints (eds), *Readings in Monetary Theory*, London, George Allen & Unwin, as a revised version of an article in *American Economic Review*, vol. 38, 1948. Also reprinted in D. Patinkin, *Studies in Monetary Economics*, New York, Harper & Row, 1972.

Patinkin, D. (1965) *Money, Interest, and Prices*, 2nd ed., New York, Harper & Row.

Patinkin, D. (1972a) 'On the Nature of the Monetary Mechanism', ch. 8 in *Studies in Monetary Economics*, New York, Harper & Row. First published as the 1967 Wicksell Lectures, Stockhol, Almqvist and Wiksell.

Patinkin, D. (1972b) 'Money and Wealth', ch. 9 in *Studies in Monetary Economics*, New York, Harper & Row, 1972.

Patinkin, D., and D. Levhari (1968) 'The Role of Money in a Simple Growth Model', *American Economic Review*, vol. 58. Reprinted as ch. 11 in D. Patinkin, *Studies in Monetary Economies*, New York, Harper & Row, 1972.

Perlman, M. (1987) 'Of a Controversial Passage in Hume', *Journal of Political Economy*, vol. 95 no. 2.

Pesando, J.E. (1975) 'A Note on the Rationality of the Livingston Price Expectations', *Journal of Political Economy*, vol. 83 no. 4.

Pesaran, M.H. (1989) *The Limits to Rational Expectations*, 2nd, slightly revised, printing, Oxford, Basil Blackwell.

Pesek, B.P. (1988) *Microeconomics of Money and Banking and Other Essays*, Hemel Hempstead, Harvester Wheatsheaf.

Pesek, B.P., and Th. R. Saving (1967), *Money, Wealth, and Economic Theory*, New York, Macmillan.

Phelps, E.S. (1971) 'Introduction', in E.S. Phelps *et al.*, *Microeconomic Foundations of Employment and Inflation Theory*, London, Macmillan.

Phelps, E.S., and J.B. Taylor (1977) 'Stabilizing Powers of Monetary Policy under Rational Expectations', *Journal of Political Economy*, vol. 85 no. 1.

Phillips, A.W. (1958) 'The Relationship between Unemployment and the Rate of Change of Money Wage Rates in the United Kingdom, 1861-1957', *Economica*, n.s. vol. 25. Reprinted as 'Unemployment and Wage Rates' in R.J. Ball and P. Doyle (eds), *Inflation*, Harmondsworth, Penguin, 1969.

Pierce, D.G., and D.M. Shaw (1974) *Monetary Economics*, London, Butterworth.

Pigou, A.C. (1943) 'The Classical Stationary State', *Economic Journal*, vol. 53 no. 212.

Porter, R.D., and E.K. Offenbacher (1984) 'Financial Innovations and Measurement of Monetary Aggregates', in Federal Reserve Bank of St Louis, *Financial Innovations*, Boston, Kluwer-Nijhoff.

Price, L.D.D. (1972) 'The demand for money in the United Kingdom: a further investigation', *Quarterly Bulletin*, Bank of England, vol. 12 no. 1.

Protopapadakis, A.A., and H.R. Stoll (1986) 'The Law of One Price in International Commodity Markets: A Reformulation and Some Formal Tests', *Journal of International Money and Finance*, vol. 5 no. 3.

Quintyn, M., (1986) *De uitvoerbaarheid van een geldgroeibeleid*, PhD thesis, Rijksuniversiteit, Ghent, 1986.

Radner, R. (1968) 'Competitive Equilibrium under Uncertainty', *Econometrica*, vol. 36 no. 1.

Ramakrishnan, R.T.S., and A.V. Thakor (1984) 'Information Reliability and a Theory of Financial Intermediation', *Review of Economic Studies*, vol. 51.

Ramírez-Rojas, C.L. (1986) 'La sustitución monetaria en países en desarrollo', *Finanzas y Desarrollo*, vol. 23 no. 2 (also in English in *Finance and Development*).

Rasche, R.H. (1987) 'M1-Velocity and Money-Demand Functions: Do Stable Relationships Exist?', in Carnegie-Rochester Conference Series on Public Policy, no. 27.

Reekie, W.D. (1984) *Markets, Entrepreneurs and Liberty; An Austrian View of Capitalism*, Brighton, Wheatsheaf Books.

Ricardo, D. (1965) *The Principles of Political Economy and Taxation*, London, Dent (Everyman's Library edition).

Ritter, L.S., and W.L. Silber (1970) *Money*, New York, Basic Books.

Rockoff, H. (1985) 'New Evidence on Free Banking in the United States', *American Economic Review*, vol. 75 no. 4.

Rogers, C. (1985) 'A Critique of Clower's Dual Decision Hypothesis', *South African Journal of Economics*, vol. 53 no. 1.

Rotemberg, J.J. (1982) 'Sticky Prices in the United States', *Journal of Political Economy*, vol. 90 no. 6.

Rousseas, S. (1986) *Post Keynesian Monetary Economics*, London, Macmillan.

Runde, J., and C. Torr (1985) 'Divergent Expectations and Rational Expectations', *South African Journal of Economics*, vol. 53 no. 3.

Salin, P. (1984) 'General introduction', in P. Salin (ed.).

Salin, P. ed. (1984) *Currency competition and monetary union*, The Hague, Martinus Nijhoff.

Sarantis, N. (1987) 'A Dynamic Asset Market Model for the Exchange Rate of Pound Sterling', *Weltwirtschaftliches Archiv*, vol. 123 no. 1.

Sargent, Th. J. (1976) 'Testing for Neutrality and Rationality', in *A Prescription for Monetary Policy: Proceedings from a Seminar Series*, Minneapolis, Federal Reserve Bank of Minneapolis.

Sargent, Th. J., and N. Wallace (1975) ' 'Rational' Expectations, the Optimal Monetary Instrument, and the Optimal Money Supply Rule', *Journal of Political Economy*, vol. 83 no. 2.

Sauernheimer, K. (1981) 'Wechselkurstheorien im Lichte jüngerer Erfahrungen', *Jahrbuch für Sozialwissenschaft*, vol. 32 no. 2.

Selgin, G.A., and L.H. White (1987) 'The Evolution of a Free Banking System', *Economic Inquiry*, vol. 25 no. 3.

Sheffrin, S.M. (1983) *Rational Expectations*, Cambridge, Cambridge University Press.

Shiller, R.J. (1978) 'Rational Expectations and the Dynamic Structure of Macroeconomic Models', *Journal of Monetary Economics*, vol. 4 no. 1.

Sijben, J.J. (1978) *Money and Economic Growth*, Leiden, Martinus Nijhoff.

Sijben, J.J. (1980) *Rational expectations and monetary policy*, Alphen aan den Rijn. Sijthoff & Noordhoff.

Sijben, J.J. (1986) *Geld en financiering: een toenemende vervlechting* (inaugural lecture), Tilburg, Tilburg University Press.

Silberston, A. (1973) 'Price Behaviour of Firms', in *Surveys of Applied Economics*, vol. I, London, Macmillan. First published in *Economic Journal*, vol. 80, 1970.

Sinn, H.W. (1983) 'International Capital Movements, Flexible Exchange Rates, and the IS-LM Model: A Comparison Between the Portfolio-Balance and the Flow Hypotheses', *Weltwirtschaftliches Archiv*, vol. 119 no. 1.

Smith, W.L. (1970) 'On Some Current Issues in Monetary Economics: An Interpretation', *Journal of Economic Literature*, vol. 8 no. 3.

Snower, D.J. (1984) 'Rational Expectations, Nonlinearities, and the Effectiveness of Monetary Policy', *Oxford Economic Papers*, vol. 36 no. 2.

Spinelli, F. (1983) 'Currency Substitution, Flexible Exchange Rates, and the Case for International Monetary Cooperation', *IMF Staff Papers*, vol. 30 no. 4.

Spitäller, E. (1980) 'Short-Run Effects of Exchange Rate Changes on Terms of Trade and Trade Balance', *IMF Staff Papers*, vol. 27 no. 2.

Sprinkel, B.W. (1971) *Money and Markets*, Homewood, Irwin.

Starbatty, J. (1982) 'Zur Umkehrung des Greshamschen Gesetzes bei Entnationalisierung des Geldes', *Kredit und Kapital*, vol. 15 no.3.

Starr, R.M. (1980) 'General Equilibrium Approaches to the Study of Monetary Economies: Comments on Recent Developments', in Kareken and Wallace (eds).

Stiglitz, J.E. (1988) 'Money, Credit, and Business Fluctuations', *Economic Record*, vol. 64 no. 187.

Stockman, A.C. (1980) 'A Theory of Exchange Rate Determination', *Journal of Political Economy*, vol. 88 no. 4.

Stockman, A.C. (1990) 'International Transmission and Real Business Cycle Models', *American Economic Review*, vol. 80 no. 2.

Stockman, A.C., and L.E.O. Svensson (1987) 'Capital Flows, Investment, and Exchange Rates', *Journal of Monetary Economics*, vol. 19 no. 2.

Stone, C.C., and D.L. Thornton (1987) 'Solving the 1980's Velocity Puzzle: A Progress Report', *Review*, Federal Reserve Bank of St Louis, vol. 69 no. 7.

Summers, L.H. (1983) 'Comments on the King paper', *Journal of Monetary Economics*, vol. 12.

Tanner, J.E. (1979) 'An Empirical Investigation of Tax Discounting', *Journal of Money, Credit, and Banking*, vol. 11 no. 2.

Tatom, J.A. (1990) 'The Effects of Financial Innovations on Checkable Deposits, M1 and M2', *Review*, Federal Reserve Bank of St Louis, vol. 72 no. 4.

Taylor, M.P. (1987) 'Risk Premia and Foreign Exchange: A Multiple Time Series Approach to Testing Uncovered Interest-Rate Parity', *Weltwirtschaftliches Archiv*, vol. 123 no. 4.

Taylor, M.P., and P.C. McMahon (1988) 'Purchasing power parity in the 1920s', *European Economic Review*, vol. 32 no. 1.

Thornton, D.L. (1989) 'Tests of Covered Interest Rate Parity', *Review*, Federal Reserve Bank of St. Louis, vol. 71 no. 4.

Thornton, H. (1978) *An Enquiry into the Nature and Effects of the Paper Credit of Great Britain* (ed. F.A. von Hayek), Fairfield, Kelley. Reprint of an edition published by George Allen & Unwin, London, 1939. First published 1802.

Thurow, L.C. (1983) *Dangerous Currents: The State of Economics*, Oxford, Oxford University Press.

Timberlake Jr, R.H. (1984) 'The Central Banking Role of Clearinghouse Associations', *Journal of Money, Credit, and Banking*, vol. 16 no. 1.

Tobin, J. (1965) 'Money and Economic Growth', *Econometrica*, vol. 33 no. 4.

Tobin, J. (1971a) *Essays in Economics*, vol. 1: *Macroeconomics*, Amsterdam, North-Holland.

Tobin, J. (1971b) 'The Monetary Interpretation of History (A Review Article)', in J. Tobin 1971(a). First published in *American Economic Review*, vol. 55 no. 3, 1965.

Tobin, J. (1971c) 'Money, Capital, and Other Stores of Value', in J. Tobin, 1971(a). First published in *American Economic Review*, vol. 51 no. 2 (Papers and Proceedings), 1961.

Tobin, J. (1978) 'Comment from an Academic Scribbler', *Journal of Monetary Economics*, vol. 4 no. 3.

Tobin, J., (1980a) *Asset Accumulation and Economic Activity*, Oxford, Basil Blackwell.

Tobin, J. (1980b) 'Discussion', in Kareken and Wallace (eds).

Tobin, J. (1981) 'The Monetarist Counter-Revolution Today - an Appraisal', *Economic Journal*, vol. 91 no. 361.

Tourani Rad, A. (1989) *The Interest-Free Banking and the Impact of Abolition of Interest on the Economic System*, PhD thesis, Brussels, Vrije Universiteit Brussel.

Tullock, G. (1975) 'Competing Monies', *Journal of Money, Credit, and Banking*, vol. 7 no. 4.

Tversky, A., and D. Kahneman (1986) 'Rational Choice and the Framing of Decisions', *Journal of Business*, vol. 59 no. 4 pt 2.

van Ewijk, C. (1986) 'Interest Payments and the Stability of the Government Budget Deficit in an Open and Growing Economy', *De Economist*, vol. 134 no. 2.

van Hulst, N. (1984) *De effectiviteit van geleide loonpolitiek in theorie en praktijk*, Groningen, Wolters-Noordhoff.

van Zijp, R.W. (1990) 'Hayek en Lucas: een vergelijking', *Maandschrift economie*, vol. 54 no. 2.

Vander Kraats, R.H., and L.D. Booth (1983) 'Empirical Tests of the Monetary Approach to Exchange-Rate Determination', *Journal of International Money and Finance*, vol. 2 no. 3.

Vaubel, R. (1978) *Strategies for Currency Unification*, Tübingen, J.C.B. Mohr (Paul Siebeck).

Vaubel, R. (1984) 'The Government's Money Monopoly: Externalities or Natural Monopoly?', *Kyklos*, vol. 37 no. 1.

Vaubel, R. (1985) 'Competing Currencies: The Case for Free Entry', *Zeitschrift für Wirtschafts- und Sozialwissenschaften*, vol. 105 no. 5.

Villanueva, D., and A. Mirakhor (1990) 'Strategies for Financial Reforms; Interest Rate Policies, Stabilization, and Bank Supervision in Developing Countries', *IMF Staff Papers*, vol. 37 no. 3.

Visser, H. (1974) *The Quantity of Money*, London, Martin Robertson.

Visser, H. (1980) *Monetaire theorie*, 2nd ed., Leiden, Stenfert Kroese.

Visser, H. (1983) 'De overheid en de vermogensmarkt', *Maandblad voor accountancy en bedrijfshuishoudkunde*, vol. 57 no. 7/8.

Visser, H. (1984) *New Classical Macroeconomics as Seen by an Impressed Non-believer or, Keynes and the Classics All Over Again*, Tilburg, SUERF.

Visser, H. (1988) 'Austrian Thinking on International Economics', *Journal of Economic Studies*, vol. 16 no. 3/4.

Visser, H. (1989a) 'Exchange rate theories', *De Economist*, vol. 137 no. 1.

Visser, H. (1989b) 'De monetaire orde', in A.B. Dorsman, H.G. Eijgenhuijsen, J. Koelewijn and H. Visser (eds), *Het financieel systeem in ontwikkeling*, Leiden, Stenfert Kroese.

Wagner, H. (1981) 'Wirtschaftspolitik im Lichte rationaler Erwartungen', *Konjunkturpolitik*, vol. 27 no. 1.

Wallace, N. (1980) 'The Overlapping Generation Model of Fiat Money', in Kareken and Wallace (eds).

Wasserfallen, W., and H. Kyburz (1985) 'The Behavior of Flexible Exchange Rates in the Short Run - A Systematic Investigation', *Weltwirtschaftliches Archiv*, vol. 121 no. 4.

Webb, D.C. (1981) 'The Net Wealth Effect of Government Bonds When Credit Markets are Imperfect', *Economic Journal*, vol. 91 no. 362.

Wenninger, J. (1988) 'Money Demand - Some Long-Run Properties', *Quarterly Review*, Federal Reserve Bank of New York, vol. 13 no. 1.

White, L.H. (1984) 'Competitive Payments Systems and the Unit of Account', *American Economic Review*, vol. 74 no. 4.

White, L.H. (1986) 'Competitive Payments Systems: Reply', *American Economic Review*, vol. 76 no. 4.

Wicksell, K. (1898) *Geldzins und Güterpreise*, Jena, Gustav Fischer.

Wicksell, K. (1965) *Interest and Prices*, New York, A.M. Kelley. Translation of Wicksell, 1898, first published 1936.

Witzel, R. (1984) 'Overshooting des Wechselkurses, Substituierbarkeit der Finanzaktiva und J-Kurve', *Weltwirtschaftliches Archiv*, vol. 120 no. 3.

Wogin, G. (1980) 'Unemployment and Monetary Policy under Rational Expectations', *Journal of Monetary Economics*, vol. 6 no. 1.

Woo, W.T. (1987) 'Some Evidence of Speculative Bubbles in the Foreign Exchange Markets', *Journal of Money, Credit, and Banking*, vol. 19 no. 4.

World Bank, *Report 1989*.

Yeager, L.B. (1985) 'Deregulation and Monetary Reform', *American Economic Review*, vol. 75 no. 2 (Papers and Proceedings).

Yeager, L.B. (1989) 'A competitive payments system: some objections considered', *Journal of Post Keynesian Economics*, vol. 11 no. 3.

Zervoyianni, A. (1988) 'Exchange Rate Overshooting, Currency Substitution and Monetary Policy', *Manchester School*, vol. 56 no. 31.

Zis, G. (1988) 'Theories of balance of payments and exchange rate determination', in G. Zis *et al.*, *International economics*, Harlow, Longman.

Index

Applied Probability and Statistics (Continued)

JUDGE, HILL, GRIFFITHS, LÜTKEPOHL, and LEE · Introduction to the Theory and Practice of Econometrics, *Second Edition*
KALBFLEISCH and PRENTICE · The Statistical Analysis of Failure Time Data
KASPRZYK, DUNCAN, KALTON, and SINGH · Panel Surveys
KISH · Statistical Design for Research
KISH · Survey Sampling
LAWLESS · Statistical Models and Methods for Lifetime Data
LEBART, MORINEAU, and WARWICK · Multivariate Descriptive Statistical Analysis: Correspondence Analysis and Related Techniques for Large Matrices
LEE · Statistical Methods for Survival Data Analysis, *Second Edition*
LEPAGE and BILLARD · Exploring the Limits of Bootstrap
LEVY and LEMESHOW · Sampling of Populations: Methods and Applications
LINHART and ZUCCHINI · Model Selection
LITTLE and RUBIN · Statistical Analysis with Missing Data
MAGNUS and NEUDECKER · Matrix Differential Calculus with Applications in Statistics and Econometrics
MAINDONALD · Statistical Computation
MALLOWS · Design, Data, and Analysis by Some Friends of Cuthbert Daniel
MANN, SCHAFER, and SINGPURWALLA · Methods for Statistical Analysis of Reliability and Life Data
MASON, GUNST, and HESS · Statistical Design and Analysis of Experiments with Applications to Engineering and Science
McLACHLAN · Discriminant Analysis and Statistical Pattern Recognition
MILLER · Survival Analysis
MONTGOMERY and PECK · Introduction to Linear Regression Analysis, *Second Edition*
NELSON · Accelerated Testing, Statistical Models, Test Plans, and Data Analyses
NELSON · Applied Life Data Analysis
OCHI · Applied Probability and Stochastic Processes in Engineering and Physical Sciences
OSBORNE · Finite Algorithms in Optimization and Data Analysis
PANKRATZ · Forecasting with Dynamic Regression Models
PANKRATZ · Forecasting with Univariate Box-Jenkins Models: Concepts and Cases
RACHEV · Probability Metrics and the Stability of Stochastic Models
RÉNYI · A Diary on Information Theory
RIPLEY · Spatial Statistics
RIPLEY · Stochastic Simulation
ROSS · Introduction to Probability and Statistics for Engineers and Scientists
ROUSSEEUW and LEROY · Robust Regression and Outlier Detection
RUBIN · Multiple Imputation for Nonresponse in Surveys
RYAN · Statistical Methods for Quality Improvement
SCHUSS · Theory and Applications of Stochastic Differential Equations
SCOTT · Multivariate Density Estimation: Theory, Practice, and Visualization
SEARLE · Linear Models
SEARLE · Linear Models for Unbalanced Data
SEARLE · Matrix Algebra Useful for Statistics
SEARLE, CASELLA, and McCULLOCH · Variance Components
SKINNER, HOLT, and SMITH · Analysis of Complex Surveys
STOYAN · Comparison Methods for Queues and Other Stochastic Models
STOYAN, KENDALL, and MECKE · Stochastic Geometry and Its Applications
THOMPSON · Empirical Model Building
THOMPSON · Sampling
TIERNEY · LISP-STAT: An Object-Oriented Environment for Statistical Computing and Dynamic Graphics
TIJMS · Stochastic Modeling and Analysis: A Computational Approach
TITTERINGTON, SMITH, and MAKOV · Statistical Analysis of Finite Mixture Distributions
UPTON and FINGLETON · Spatial Data Analysis by Example, Volume I: Point Pattern and Quantitative Data

Applied Probability and Statistics (Continued)

COCHRAN · Sampling Techniques, *Third Edition*
*COCHRAN and COX · Experimental Designs, *Second Edition*
CONOVER · Practical Nonparametric Statistics, *Second Edition*
CONOVER and IMAN · Introduction to Modern Business Statistics
CORNELL · Experiments with Mixtures, Designs, Models, and the Analysis of Mixture Data, *Second Edition*
COX · A Handbook of Introductory Statistical Methods
*COX · Planning of Experiments
CRESSIE · Statistics for Spatial Data
DANIEL · Applications of Statistics to Industrial Experimentation
DANIEL · Biostatistics: A Foundation for Analysis in the Health Sciences, *Fifth Edition*
DAVID · Order Statistics, *Second Edition*
DEGROOT, FIENBERG, and KADANE · Statistics and the Law
*DEMING · Sample Design in Business Research
DILLON and GOLDSTEIN · Multivariate Analysis: Methods and Applications
DODGE and ROMIG · Sampling Inspection Tables, *Second Edition*
DOWDY and WEARDEN · Statistics for Research, *Second Edition*
DRAPER and SMITH · Applied Regression Analysis, *Second Edition*
DUNN · Basic Statistics: A Primer for the Biomedical Sciences, *Second Edition*
DUNN and CLARK · Applied Statistics: Analysis of Variance and Regression, *Second Edition*
ELANDT-JOHNSON and JOHNSON · Survival Models and Data Analysis
FLEISS · The Design and Analysis of Clinical Experiments
FLEISS · Statistical Methods for Rates and Proportions, *Second Edition*
FLEMING and HARRINGTON · Counting Processes and Survival Analysis
FLURY · Common Principal Components and Related Multivariate Models
GALLANT · Nonlinear Statistical Models
GROSS and HARRIS · Fundamentals of Queueing Theory, *Second Edition*
GROVES · Survey Errors and Survey Costs
GROVES, BIEMER, LYBERG, MASSEY, NICHOLLS, and WAKSBERG Telephone Survey Methodology
HAHN and MEEKER · Statistical Intervals: A Guide for Practitioners
HAND · Discrimination and Classification
HEIBERGER · Computation for the Analysis of Designed Experiments
HELLER · MACSYMA for Statisticians
HOAGLIN, MOSTELLER, and TUKEY · Exploratory Approach to Analysis of Variance
HOAGLIN, MOSTELLER, and TUKEY · Exploring Data Tables, Trends and Shapes
HOAGLIN, MOSTELLER, and TUKEY · Understanding Robust and Exploratory Data Analysis
HOCHBERG and TAMHANE · Multiple Comparison Procedures
HOEL · Elementary Statistics, *Fifth Edition*
HOGG and KLUGMAN · Loss Distributions
HOLLANDER and WOLFE · Nonparametric Statistical Methods
HOSMER and LEMESHOW · Applied Logistic Regression
IMAN and CONOVER · Modern Business Statistics
JACKSON · A User's Guide to Principle Components
JOHN · Statistical Methods in Engineering and Quality Assurance
JOHNSON · Multivariate Statistical Simulation
JOHNSON and KOTZ · Distributions in Statistics
Continuous Univariate Distributions—1
Continuous Univariate Distributions—2
Continuous Multivariate Distributions
JOHNSON, KOTZ, and KEMP · Univariate Discrete Distributions, *Second Edition*
JUDGE, GRIFFITHS, HILL, LÜTKEPOHL, and LEE · The Theory and Practice of Econometrics, *Second Edition*

*Now available in a lower priced paperback edition in the Wiley Classics Library.